302 Page
Negro Song
...first
time I just finished
reading Stephens H
songs ... Book
I sent it to
... Fisher

Page 40
Have township
Counties ... banks

44 Catholic Church
...

162
Rattle snake
... killed
140 young ones
in Belly

Page 171
Chichago
means Pigeon Root

Page 123
Mounds of St Louis
are they still there

144 Indian dress
like Romans so are
... shelter

867 How
Indians die

432 no white
man in area
before

Page 259 — 1800
... of
... in

"In print 70 00 in Europe ..."

Total ...
... in
Saint Martin
44956

Happy Father's Day!
from Mark & Sue
6/17/81
purchased
O'Donoghue Books
Anoka MN

178 Prairie Fire
220 Chief Paoust of All

346
Selkirk Colony
not to good

Page 430
Beaver ... outlaws ... of

A PILGRIMAGE IN AMERICA

Leading to the Discovery of the Sources of the Mississippi and Bloody River; with a Description of the Whole Course of the Former, and of the Ohio

By J. C. BELTRAMI

AMERICANA CLASSICS
QUADRANGLE BOOKS, INC.
Chicago

First edition in English published 1828, London
This edition published 1962 by
Quadrangle Books, Inc. / Chicago

Library of Congress Catalog Card Number 62-13291

MANUFACTURED IN THE UNITED STATES OF AMERICA
BY BOOK CRAFTSMEN ASSOCIATES, INC., NEW YORK

TABLE OF CONTENTS

LETTER X.

Philadelphia, February 28th, 1823.

WHERE shall I begin, my dear Madam? Where I ought to end,—with myself; for you are impatient to hear what is become of me. I know your friendship, and anticipate its wishes.

I am now in America. My hand-writing ought to convince you that I am alive; but, since a very reverend father has made the dead write letters, it is become necessary to explain whether one is still in the land of the living, and particularly when one writes from another world, and has been many times near the gates of eternity.

For a description of our terrible passage, I must trust entirely to my memory; for, during the whole voyage, I was so ill, that neither my stomach nor my head allowed me to write a single line. Besides, being as ignorant of naval affairs as a Tartar, any attempt to describe the nautical occurrences of the voyage would only tire out your patience, and expose my awkwardness and presumption, by a vain parade of hard technical words; it would be only a useless addition to that deluge of *notes, narratives, voyages, adventures, observations, discoveries,* and so forth, with which so many intrepid navigators from Calais to Dover, from Reggio to Messina, from Gibraltar to Ceuta, from one side of the Sound, or of the Dardanelles, to the other, have enriched and inundated the world. I will give you only a slight sketch of what was most remarkable during this passage, although it was protracted to a period of more than three months and a half of suffering; and I shall be the more laconic, because my hand is weak and unfit for writing. Let us return, therefore, to where we should have begun.

At Liverpool, my intention, at first, was to embark for New York, the packets of which are very *comfortable;* but, being informed that the yellow fever had committed considerable ravages there during the summer, and that it still prevailed, I determined to sail for Philadelphia. The persons to whom I was recommended, exerted themselves to secure a comfortable passage for me; but, having been deceived respecting the accommodations of the ship and the character of her captain, they thought no other provisions necessary than wine and liquors. I therefore embarked with confidence;—and miserably was I disappointed.

We left Prince's dock on the 3rd of November, at about five o'clock in the morning. The weather was beautiful, and, as I was told, favourable.

The names of the crew having been called over, it was discovered that the cook had deserted. This beginning was not propitious. A cook is an important personage everywhere; but the resources of his art are particularly desirable, when the contingencies of scarcity of provisions, and other viatic incidents, demand an extra portion of skill and industry.

The steward or servant of the cabin was appointed to fulfil these important functions, and his *portfeuille* was handed over to James, a young American sailor, about twenty years of age, equally insolent and careless; and thus we had two novices, in situations of great difficulty on board ship. The hour of dinner discovered to us that we had neither steward nor cook, and enabled us to form some idea of what we might expect in future. Among other things that threatened us, was uncleanliness, the greatest torment that can be inflicted upon my stomach and senses. The larder and the wardrobe were equally ill-supplied, and dirty; and I was laughed at for asking for implements to wash myself with.

The first day the wind was neither fair nor foul. The second, our passage between the island of Anglesea and the coast of Ireland, was a little opposed by contrary winds; and a storm, which the captain told us was very dangerous on this coast, assailed us on the third, near Cape Clear; from which period I date the beginning of my dreadful sea-sickness. On the seventh the wind subsided; but we made no progress. On the tenth it blew with greater fury than ever, and drove us on the western coast of Ireland. The captain seemed not much delighted, and I was still less so, for the sea tore me to pieces. Fortunately, Killala bay afforded us shelter; but in our endeavours to avoid Scylla, we ran into Charybdis. All this coast is inhabited by a semi-barbarous people, who had risen against the government, because they were starving; and this was precisely the focus of the insurrection of the island. My companions had, however, only the fear of an attack. For my own part, I had not even that; on the contrary, considering the dreadful state of my health and the appalling aspect of everything on board the vessel, and of this sea, (which is always stormy at this season,) I ought to have landed at any risk. I could lose nothing by passing from one set of barbarians to another; I must gain by a change of element, and in every other respect; but my resolution is naturally as inflexible as my destiny. On the thirteenth we continued our voyage.

The sea was still very rough, but the wind was fair for America, and we made some way; this was my only consolation in a state that became daily more terrible. Stretched upon a wretched flock-bed, which the bones of my attenuated body penetrated even to the floor, my only relief was derived from resignation to my fate, and from that courage which, thanks to heaven, does not easily forsake me. My fellow-passengers were Spanish Americans. They were dressed as gentlemen, for which they were indebted to their former profession of piracy. Their manners were in perfect unison with the atrocious character of their countenances, and gave no hope that they possessed a spark of humanity. The appearance of the captain was calculated to alarm a man who was going to visit his country, with a view to admire and to learn free and generous sentiments. The newly appointed cook, a hideous negro, covered with filth from head to foot, had only to show himself to disgust the most intrepid and chivalrous stomach, and to render his absence much more desirable than his presence. Little James was a most extraordinary fellow; a non-descript. At first I called out to him, "Steward!"—"I am not a steward," replied he, "my name is James."—"Well then, James!"—"What do you mean by James? My name is Mr James." "Very well, Mr James, will you . . . . —will you—will you . . . ." "I am not a servant to any body." I then asked the captain who, and where, was the servant. To this question he replied with one of his usual civil looks, and, laughing in my face, turned his back upon me.

By the short sketch I have given you of this delightful company, you may judge of the situation of an unfortunate being, who from complete exhaustion could not even stand. If I left my den I was obliged to drag myself along on my hands and knees; but this excited no pity in these selfish and unfeeling wretches. Nor was my state of animal existence less deplorable than that of my social feelings.

The little fresh meat that remained was become completely putrid, and spoiled the onions, leeks, &c. with which it was cooked. I could not obtain a chicken, because it was first necessary that the whole of this delicious meat should be consumed. I offered, and made presents for good broth, but received only some made from salt meat. I was reduced to the miserable pittance of a few boiled potatoes, with which I had no other sauce than vinegar, for there was no oil.

I had very good wine, both French and Madeira; but these gentlemen did not confine themselves to accepting the offer I voluntarily made of sharing every bottle with them; they had opened, and already emptied a considerable number. Mr James and the cook, thinking probably that I had nothing more to do either with this world or with wine, joined most effectively in the shameful rapacity of the honourable captain and my amiable fellow passengers. I saw this; I might have stopped it; for my mind was not then enfeebled, although my physical strength was utterly exhausted; but I contented myself with heartily despising them all, and suffered them to act as they pleased. Their conduct supplied me with abundant matter for meditation on human life and human nature.

I saw in these wretches a perfect picture of heirs, nephews, *friends* and servants, who surround the death-bed of their fathers, uncles, friends, and masters, like birds of prey, plunder them both before and after their death, and exhaust every expedient for the gratification of their avarice and rapacity. And yet we accumulate, all our lives, at the expense even of justice and humanity—deaf to the groans of the widow, the orphan, and the wretched—and for no other purpose than to feed the profligacy, vices, and voracity of these vultures.

We were now, my dear Madam, ploughing the ocean to the right and left, but without making any progress; the contrary winds had re-assumed the command of our vessel and drove us from our destination. The storms which succeeded left us only just such intervals of calm as allowed us to estimate the different degrees of their violence. The storm which came on during the night of the twenty-sixth was truly terrible.

The waves beat with such force against the ship, that they produced an effect similar to that of the most dreadful earthquakes upon our houses. The shocks were so repeated and violent that they loosened several casks of fresh water which dashed against each other, broke, and inundated the space between the deck and the cabin, occasioned the greatest disorder, drowned almost all the poultry, and spoiled a great part of what still remained of our wretched provisions. I patiently resigned myself to Providence, and repeated—*Fiat voluntas tua.* But my situation brought to my remembrance the saying of a good king, whose name I cannot recollect:

"Purchè il reo non si salvi, il giusto pera."

This king must either have lived before the time of Justinian, or he was unacquainted with his maxim—*Melius est, centum reos absolvere, quàm unum innocentem condemnare;*—but let us return to our delightful voyage.

We proceeded sometimes to the south, sometimes to the north, sometimes to the east, but never to the west, which was our Colchis. Meantime, my sufferings increased. There was nothing but salt meat, and the water, which by the bye was very bad, was measured out to us in a bird-glass. I know not what would have become of me—for my stomach rejected all their dishes, rendered more disgusting by filth—had not a sailor sold me some rice.

Observe, my dear Madam, that American ships are always well provided with rice, which is so abundant with them; but our captain, who had consumed his whole stock during his long stay at Liverpool, where it is much dearer, judged it expedient to defer purchasing any more till his arrival in America. You see therefore that I had embarked with a man who perfectly understood his interest, if not his duty. The difficulty however was to find some charitable person who would undertake to dress it, though

I only wanted to have it boiled in water with a little salt. I could expect no kindness or humanity from my own unfeeling sex; I therefore applied to that which we are not ashamed to oppress and to calumniate in every possible way. There was an Englishwoman on board, who was going to join her husband in America. She offered me her assistance; the more willingly as she had, during her sea-sickness, received relief from my wine, which, as well as my medicine-chest, had been at the service of the whole community. I had now therefore some chance of humane treatment, when I was suddenly seized with a putrid fever.

It is really astonishing that I could resist all these attacks, or support the effects of violent emetics, debilitated as I was by sea-sickness, destitute of every kind of restorative, of all physical or moral aid, and abandoned by all my powers except the energy of my mind.

I know not what that is which is called soul; for as I have already said, I am neither a metaphysician, nor a theologian; but it is unquestionably some divine faculty acting within us, without which it would be impossible for man, by his own unaided strength, to support some of the vicissitudes of life. I was more powerfully than ever impressed with this truth, in the terrible situation in which I found myself in this vessel; and it is principally for the benefit of this moral inference, that I have occupied your attention so long with this recital of grievances. Yes, my dear Countess, man is a mere puppet, acted upon by Providence, against which all human systems and all human powers are vain. How could the extraordinary, the incomprehensible genius of Archimedes, of Galileo, of Descartes, of Newton, operate by the unassisted energy and *free will* of man? They were only machines moved by superior springs; and Providence puts them in motion, more or less, in proportion as it judges them more or less necessary.

At the moment I am writing to you, dear Madam, with a body almost completely restored to its former strength, I feel that my mind is weak, and that I could not now support what I then sustained with so much heroism. I believe that Providence will not again grant me the same firmness, unless it should see fit to place me again in the same dreadful situation. But I forget myself; for although I am writing from Philadelphia, we are still at a great distance from it. The idea of reverting to my subject frightens me, and leads me to indulge in these long digressions: this also will prove to you how much more feeble my mind is now than it was then.

I am sorry to return to my wretched bed. This is perhaps not less painful to you than disgusting to me; but it is the only stage upon which I acted during the whole of my voyage; and the Epopea requires unity of place as well as of action. I hung between life and death till the 11th of December, when I began to revive a little. During the whole of this time, I had eaten nothing but rice, which however my good English nurse had not economized; she and the rest of the passengers had probably little scruple on this head, for she afterwards repeatedly told me that every one on board had completely given me over. I one day saw the captain carefully remove all my effects into his closet, under pretence of protecting them, as he said, "*from the wolves.*" I could not help laughing; and thanking him for this first mark of care so voluntarily bestowed. I just told him that his expectations would be disappointed, and that I should not die yet, in spite of all the sufferings and hardships I had experienced. Indeed I never for a moment thought I should die, so convinced was I that some superior power watched over my existence, as a proof of which, I tell you the following incident.

I was reduced to my last pittance of rice, and no more was to be had. I caused myself to be dragged upon the deck to breathe a little fresh air. I observed a pig with an ear of maize in his mouth. I asked the captain if he would have the goodness to allow me a little of this maize. "What shall I give my pig then?" was his philanthropic reply. The same evening a storm arose. During the night it raged with great fury; the waves washed over the deck; one broke into the sty, which it carried away together with my rival, as an offering to the offended deities of ocean. By priority of demand, I became the rightful heir to his pittance, and this pittance kept me alive till we entered the Delaware. But, to make the hand of Providence more clear in the matter, while a sailor was endeavouring to save the captain's pet from the first wave, a second rolled over him, as if to punish him for his presumption; and, had it not been for the cordage of the mast, he would have shared the fate of the pig. The poor captain was inconsolable; he was very fond of it, and scratched it every day with great tenderness; he declared it was very intelligent. I had some thoughts of recommending myself to his favor, by imitating the courtiers of Madame de Pampadour, who asked her every morning if she and her *Mouflet* had slept well.

The captain himself and all on board now seemed convinced that some superintending deity interposed its protection in my favour; and if I had before obliged them to treat me with some degree of respect, I was from that time regarded with a species of veneration.

It is useless to repeat how often contrary winds drove us, sometimes towards Greenland, and sometimes towards the Azores. One day we were only sixty miles from the latter. I requested the captain to put into one of them that he might give us the opportunity of recruiting our strength, and provide a supply of provisions and fresh water; for that which was in the casks had been so agitated by the storms that it was scarcely drinkable. He gave us a good reason for his refusal, viz. that he was forbidden to deviate from his course, unless on account of injury sustained by the ship, or loss of masts, or from being driven upon a dangerous coast; so that my first lesson in navigation was, that we were not permitted to save ourselves till we were first at the bottom of the seas, or swallowed up by a whale. *Apropos* of whales; I have been often very near realizing the promise I made you, in my last, from Liverpool, for we saw a great number of them towards the coast of Greenland. Here however the great question arises . . . . *Can* one be swallowed by a whale? I think the Inquisition ought to settle this as it did the question of the motion of the earth, which, Galileo would have it, moved round the sun, though Joshua makes the sun turn round the earth.

Naturalists assert that the whale feeds upon

a small marine insect, that its throat is so narrow that it could not swallow a fish so big as a herring, and that it can only swallow its food, having no power of mastication. How then did Jonah find his way down? To accommodate matters with the holy office, the naturalists must adopt some other hypothesis. But let us leave them to settle the question, and continue our voyage.

We had not gone far before we were assailed by another terrible storm: the night of the 26th of December—it was terrific. A chain belonging to the rudder broke. The waves broke into the body of the vessel, swept over it, and so completely drenched it every instant, that everything in our cabin was afloat. One of our pirates was thrown out of bed, and received so severe a bruise in the leg, that he did not recover from it during the whole voyage. All was confusion and tumult. Several resigned themselves to despair; and even the captain confessed, that this was a case which would justify his putting into port: but the Azores were not now within reach. The two pirates wept with all the cowardice of the base and sordid. I told them that, as they had boasted so much of having been sailors, they had better assist the crew; but they were too busy with St Jago de Compostella, and our Lady of Cuba, to attend to worldly affairs. My poor Englishwoman was almost dead with fear; I felt nothing like dying, for having been preserved so long, I had a persuasion that I should not die during this voyage. Everything was in disorder: in short, the captain determined to resign the ship to the winds and waves and let her drift; for, in the latitude and longitude in which we then were, he had nothing to apprehend, either from the rocks or the coast.

We were between the Old and the New World; each seemed to drive us from its shores towards the abyss.

There were but a few inches of timber between me and eternity;—but when our hour is not come, eternity itself must recede;—and thus it did recede from before my eyes.

The following day, although the storm had not subsided, there was the serenest sky I ever beheld. I dragged myself on deck, to enjoy the scene which the sea and the ship, still the sport of the waves, presented. It was indeed truly grand. We were sometimes upon a mountain, then in a plain, and then in an abyss. It was a perfect representation of our country, diversified by the most varied features of nature. Sometimes I saw the beautiful *plateau* of your *Cimerella,* and the illusion which painted you to my imagination was a delightful relief from this terrific picture. But a most extraordinary phenomenon presented itself, both to my eyes and to my mouth. I will make a present of it to the naturalists, to atone for having set them by the ears with the inquisition.

A north-west wind passed with such force over the surface of the waves, that it blew up the water in a kind of fine dust into the air, where it was penetrated by the rays of a most refulgent sun, and fell again in a shower of brilliants, far more beautiful than the golden one which fell on Danaë. So much for the eyes; now for the mouth.

This shower in its descent was changed into fresh water, though there could be no doubt that it was the very identical sea-water which the winds had dispersed in the air, for not the smallest cloud was perceptible in the whole firmament; the weather was perfectly clear, and nothing was seen in the air but the *tourbillons* occasioned by this great conflict between the two elements. This is a fact, my dear Countess, and was recorded by the captain in his log-book. *Au reste,*—as people have believed in showers of *blood, stones,* &c. I think they may very fairly believe in this; such a transformation is not difficult to account for, if it be true that the saline particles are lost at a certain elevation from the earth, as some naturalists pretend. Icarus, or Simon the magician, or some aeronaut, may perhaps have made some experiments on this subject. Learned men and naturalists, who are very happy at conjectures, may extricate this difficulty from the obscurity in which I leave it. I am not versed in natural philosophy; I am a naturalist only in the sense of wishing to *leave nature to herself*, or at most only to aid her operations. I am but the herald at arms, who opens the lists for them, and retires.

January 6th 1823, we passed the southern point of the bank of Newfoundland; we had, therefore, performed two-thirds of our voyage. This, Madam, is the famous bank which has so often been the apple of discord. The Americans, the French, and the English, contended for the exclusive privilege of the fishery, which is very valuable. The riches of this bank are one of the causes of our poverty: its cod, stock-fish, &c. which come and infect our country, lower the price of our produce and cattle, our principal commercial resources: our money thus goes into the pockets of foreigners, and our produce sells for nothing. This also is one of the blessings we owe our governments. But what is most singular is, that orthodox Catholics impoverish true believers to enrich orthodox heretics; for this trade is now monopolized by the English and Americans. Well, my dear Countess, would you believe it? This bank, which has so often poisoned my meals during Lent, refused to give me one of its myriads of fishes when it would have contributed to restore my health. All our efforts to catch any were vain. I must, however, acknowledge that our ship was not better supplied with the necessary implements for fishing than with other articles.

I passed the bank without giving it one *salve*, although it told me that my trials were near their close. These trials were rendered more endurable by my improved fare: the maize held out, and the *bouillie* was my ambrosia. As to nectar, I cannot say much; the water was become more bitter than gall; and unfortunately, the pirates, the captain, Mr James, the cook, with the assistance of the lady and *her mate*, had drained all my bottles of Cognac brandy. The captain one day drank so liberally of it in private, that he was ill for a week of an inflammation in the throat, which nearly killed him: they had fallen foul even of the whole stock of spirituous liquors, elixirs, &c. in my medicine chest. I was sometimes tempted to be angry, but having from the beginning discovered what sort of company I was in, I had always had sufficient self-command to look upon them with an eye of pity and contempt, and sometimes even to laugh at them. I mention these trifling incidents for the pleasure of indulging that unreserved communication which your friendship allows, and to give such hints to our common friends as may induce them, in similar circumstances, to be more cautious than I was in ascertaining the accommodations of the ship, the character of the captain, the company, &c.; that they may avoid the situation in which I was placed. I have described it *en badinant* that I might not wound your sensibility: but it was really dreadful. The stench alone, which, from the dirt and the destitution to which we were compelled to submit, infected everything, even our own persons, was sufficient to kill a man, however enured to all the vicissitudes of life. It is said that we may accustom ourselves to anything, and this I can now attest from experience; but I assure you I often wished myself an oyster, which, according to naturalists, is destitute of the sense of smell.

But we will turn from this disgusting picture, and, whilst advancing with a tolerably favourable wind, direct our attention to our pirates, who were arrayed in battle against Mr James and the captain.

It would be difficult in any monastery to find a greater glutton than this Mr James. Our pirates carefully concealed their dry provisions; and to escape the danger of either having to offer, or being asked for, any, they ate them in secret during the night, or clandestinely in their berths during the day. Mr James, however, found an opportunity of making a skilful and successful attack upon these eatables, in which he was greatly favoured by the dampness and the stench of the room, which obliged them to expose their stores to view. James, moreover, was like the rat in the fable: "I do not want eyes to know where there is anything good,—my nose is sufficient." These gentlemen had perceived his exploits. One day they caught him in the act, and a severe kicking was the consequence. The captain ran to ascertain the cause of the disturbance, and took the part of his servant, or rather that of the offended sovereignty of the American people. The Spanish Americans would have been in a disagreeable situation if the mate had come to the assistance of his Anglo-Americans, for he would have brought the whole crew with him; but, fortunately for them, he was jealous of the captain's attentions to my good Englishwoman, and left him and Mr James to sustain the brunt of the battle. So long as the only weapons employed were fists, I forbore to interfere; but when the Spaniards threatened to terminate the quarrel after their fashion, with knives, I used every means of conciliation. I must observe, that a considerable degree of irritation had for some time prevailed between the belligerent parties: the captain was not pleased to see his adversaries eat their provisions without inviting him to partake of them; and they were equally dissatisfied with his solitary visits to his beer. These ridiculous scenes, together with the undisturbed enjoyment of my *bouillie*, had contributed a little to the recovery of my spirits and strength.

One more storm, my dear Countess; it was the last, and it procured us a supply of food. It came on in the night of the 13th January, 1823, and continued almost the whole of the following day. As our vessel was much damaged, the waves washed over the deck at their pleasure, and sometimes brought with them the inhabitants of ocean; but as they met with no obstruction, they generally returned the way they came. That night however we succeeded in capturing three that were entangled in the cordage, &c. I can give no description of them, for I did not see them till the following day, when they were cut into pieces and salted; but they were of the *cetaceous* genus, which is very extensive. Their oily flesh, under any other circumstances, would have been insupportable; but I thought it pretty good in such a famine; the very idea of anything fresh was sufficient to stimulate the appetite, and give a relish to the food.

The captain was more alarmed by this, than by any former storms, though comparatively slight, for the vessel was in a most shattered condition, and he was apprehensive of being thrown against St George's bank, which was not very distant, and the shoals of which are numerous and dangerous.

The 28th was a beautiful day and brought with it a ray of hope which revived our drooping spirits. Heaven sent us two beneficent messengers, to announce to us that the land, which had so long seemed to recede before us, was at length at hand. But alas! my dear Madam, like the unfortunate son of Idomeneus, they received death from the hands of those whom they came to console, and to congratulate on their arrival at the desired port, and at the termination of their sufferings. They were two of those lovely beings which embellish our forests and enliven our rural walks; which cheer and amuse us in the gloom of solitude and in the splendour of a palace, and divert the mind from its oppressive load of thought and care; which speak the language of harmony and innocent love; which never inspire fear, and whose pleasures, desires, and even little animosities add new attractions to the magnificent picture of nature, and impart unspeakable delight by the sweet emotions they excite. They were two little birds of the continent of North America:—they were devoured. By the bills and feet I found that they were of the *passerine* tribe, and of the species of greenfinches; which in America are redbreasts.

From the arrival of these unfortunate guests, our course was, for a considerable time, tolerably good and undisturbed by storms. Had the sea again visited our cabins, I know not how we should have resisted the cold, which was already most piercing, destitute as we were of fire, or any means of warming ourselves.

At length on the 6th of February, feeble as I was, I climbed up the main-mast and called out "Mountains!" The captain, with a sarcastic smile and his usual civility, replied that the mountains I saw were clouds. I confess I deserved to be laughed at, for the mountains in that part of America are at more than 200 miles from the coast, which was not very near us; but a mountaineer dreams only of mountains, as a fisherman does of nets and hooks.

On the 8th we saw, not mountains but forests, which, from the flatness of the ground, seemed to rise out of the ocean. We also discovered the mouth of the Delaware, between Cape May on the north, and Cape Henlopen on the south; but from contrary winds we were not able to double the latter before the 11th. We had a pilot who steered the vessel from thence, between the dangerous banks of the bay and river, as far as Philadelphia. Thus we arrived at the last act of this tragi-comedy, and the *dénouement* was *assez plaisant*. It was a true Epopea; and, what is better, a Helen was the *causa mali tanti*. You must have understood before now, my dear Countess, that my good Englishwoman had not discouraged the attentions of the mate. To do her justice, however, I must confess that he was an attractive young fellow, and the opportunity was extremely *proximate*. Besides, confined as she had so long been in this terrible prison, subject to every species of privation, and to every temptation that could beset her, it was to be expected that a little gallantry would be the effect of so many powerful causes. I had foreseen that *this* was to be an episode in the drama: but, as she had not purchased a right to occupy a place in the cabin, and as the captain had, in a few days, generously offered it to her, she had not been able to resist the tender declarations with which he also every now and then entertained her. The accursed and almost inseparable companion of love, who spares neither the cottage nor the palace, neither the crew of a ship nor the inmates of a family, took posession of the heart of the mate; and, as she was extremely free in the use of her tongue, and not very delicate as to the sentiments she inspired, she provoked him to strike her. Not being disposed patiently to bear this outrage, she courageously returned his blows, and hence ensued a noisy scuffle, which attracted the attention of the persons in the ship. The captain undertook, as it might be expected, the defence of his Dulcinea more warmly than he had before undertaken that of his Sancho Panza. Thus our champions valiantly entered the field of battle, and as, to the honour of the English, there is no danger of their having recourse to the *stiletto,* I let them take their fill of fighting. As to our pirates, no suffering inflicted on the whole species would have induced them to raise a finger: at last, however, Mr James interfered, and effected a separation in a manner which added much to the interest of the scene. He happened to have his plates in his hand, preparing to lay the cloth. The two gladiators came in contact with him,—the shock, together with the rolling of the ship, caused him to lose the centre of gravity, and laid him prostrate: the awful sound of broken plates was the signal of retreat, and put an end to the battle. Providence, by this last incident, harmonized all around us; for what is the use of plates, without something to eat? They were an insult to our misery. For my own part, I rejoiced at it, and the cause made me laugh.

It is a pity that Calliope turned her back upon me; otherwise I might, *en badinant,* have had a fine opportunity of introducing myself to the notice of the world, by a grand poem, adorned with every diversity of colour; an *epobaterion-propemptico - elegiaco - epicedion - threno - soterico - epithalamico - genethliaco - exegetico - nautico - epic* poem. After this long word, my dear Countess, you must take breath.

Some ill-natured critics might perhaps find fault with my poem for deficiency in great characters and a moral. To a philosopher, however, the heroes of Homer, and most other poets, are little better than my pirates, my captain, mate, Mr James, and my Helen: and, as for a moral, it is probably to be found only in Telemachus.

We are now in the bay of the Delaware; a large basin about twenty-four miles in width and length, which is considered the mouth of this river. At length then we are upon the shores of this great continent, the honour of naming which was snatched from its Genoese discoverer by a Florentine, and which awakens in the heart of an Italian that national pride, which the stranger, not content with oppressing our unhappy land, has always striven to degrade and to stifle. This continent, as well as Europe, Asia, and Africa, will ever recall to the memory the bold enterprizes, the important discoveries, the courage, and the glory of our ancestors.

Cape May, and the countries to the right, as far as the river Hudson, in ascending the bay and the river, belong to New Jersey: Cape Henlopen (formerly Cape St James's) and all the country to the left, as far as the bay of Chesapeake, once belonged to Pennsylvania, but now form the state of Delaware, created since the formation of these colonies, into a confederate and independent republic.

At the bottom of the bay the bed of the river contracts, though still in some places three or four miles in breadth. But the view of the country speaks to the mind only by the ideas and reflections it suggests. The eye sees nothing but a flat country and vast forests, intersected at considerable intervals, by a few scattered farms or hamlets, almost as far as Newcastle, where the country begins to be more populous, more flourishing, and more diversified by plain, hill, and valley.

From Newcastle, a delightful little commercial town belonging also to the state of Delaware, you ascend the river forty-five miles; and there, amid the windings of the Delaware, and, as it were, from the bosom of a majestic forest, emerges that stately city which is considered the largest and most important in all America; and on whose site, before the time of Penn, the savage chased the bear and the panther. Two miles farther, it rises before you in all its majesty and extent, from north to south, commanding this superb river, which is still above a mile in breadth, although more than one hundred and fifty miles from its mouth; and which, with the tide, conveys large three-mast vessels to the very doors of the opulent inhabitants. There we received the visit of the proprietors of the vessel, of the arrival of which they had been informed by signal from Cape Henlopen. They believed she had experienced the fate of many others, which had been lost during the last two months; and although they knew that she was in the river, the floating masses of ice which covered its surface made them very uneasy; so that, in spite of her shattered condition, they thought themselves happy at seeing her at all. And here I must stop one moment to pronounce the parting eulogium on my friend the captain.

I cannot advise the Americans to send him forth as a specimen of the nation, or of the generous sentiments which they so proudly arrogate; if they do, they will stand a chance of being considered as Turks, or perhaps worse. But as a sailor, prepared to battle with every storm, he may justify their boast of the probability that

America will become one of the most formidable maritime powers in the world. I spoke to him very plainly about his barbarian manners; but I willingly forgave him, in consideration of his address and courage in those dreadful storms, when the elements seemed every instant to threaten our destruction; I therefore forgot my indignation, and converted a notice of his private behaviour, which in my wrath I had intended to insert in the newspapers, into an honourable certificate to his public conduct. The only revenge in which I indulged was, to pay him my passage without any discussion or allusion to the shameful violation of his engagements, which he obviously expected; in short, without saying a single word, good or bad; and when he saw this accompanied by his certificate, which certainly he did not expect, he looked extremely mortified. As for the mate, my dear Countess, it is impossible to describe to you his indefatigable activity, his courage, intelligence, and experience, at the early age of twenty-one. He quite captivated me. Is it, therefore, surprising that he should have captivated one of that sex whose hearts are so much more tender and impressible?

For this unhappy woman I feel real and deep compassion: she is in despair at the prospect of meeting her husband in a situation which reveals her fault. Let us drop the curtain on our drama, before we reach the catastrophe of the heroine, which will, I fear, be truly tragical, or behold the miseries which the pirates, who have already sailed for Cuba, are preparing to inflict.

Thus then, my dear Madam, the 21st instant, after three months and a half of suffering and vicissitudes, ordinary and extraordinary, brings us to the end of this voyage; which, although three thousand five hundred miles, is generally performed in thirty or forty days. Happy shall I be if I am permitted to tell you the end of my future wanderings. I wish this letter may find the elements more propitious than I did, and that it may convey to you, without delay, the expression of my Transatlantic friendship.

LETTER XI.

Pittsburg, March 31*st* 1823.

I WRITE to you from a place, my dear Madam, which only fifty years ago even the colonists of America regarded as the end of the civilized world; in which white men and red men hunted each other by turns like wild beasts; a place where I am opposite to you on the other side of a branch of the Apalachian mountains, the highest in North America, as you are opposite to me on the other side of a branch of the Apennines, some of the highest in Europe. In short, Madam, we are pretty nearly foot to foot, if the world be really a ball. I do not like this. I had much rather be face to face; and am tempted to go over to the party of the reverend father inquisitor, who, in his zeal for burning, wanted to burn the antipodes;—perhaps for the same reason.

Formerly a man who had wandered hither

would have been given up for lost; now that there is no such thing as *travelling*, now that what used to be a journey is a *promenade*, I seem only to have come a few steps since my last letter, and here I am in one of the most flourishing countries in the world: it is so, because the earth is still under the dominion of nature, and but little reclaimed by art; and it is one of the most civilized, precisely because not over-civilized. After all, since the happy invention of letter-writing, distance, my dear Countess, is rather imaginary than real. But we must go back to show you Philadelphia, and to teach you the road hither.

I hope you are not going to question me as yet about people, manners, sects, &c. &c. for you must be sensible that, in forty days, I cannot be prepared with very satisfactory answers. If ever I return to these parts I will endeavour to satisfy your curiosity; but, for the present, we must content ourselves with rambling about a little, and must only pause long enough to look back upon a few historical facts, that we may know where we are; and to observe *en passant* the most striking and interesting objects of nature and art, so that we may just be able to say, "I have been there!" until the time shall come when I can tell you at length the result of all my researches and reflexions into the character and institutions of the people.

Let us begin with Pennsylvania,—if it be but to know the derivation of its name.

This state forms a part of those immense regions, the coasts of which were discovered in the reign of Elizabeth, by the celebrated Italian navigator, Sebastian Cabotto, who was also the first to set on foot a commercial intercourse between Russia and England. These regions now comprise South Labrador, Lower Canada, Nova Scotia, and all the eastern states of the Union.

He planted a colony, first in the island which he called Terra Nuova, a name which it still retains; afterwards in that part of the continent called the Carolinas; and lastly, in that which he himself christened Virginia, in honour of the Virgin Queen, in whose behalf all these discoveries were made.

This latter colony was the only one which prospered at the time, and all these countries were then dependencies of Virginia; so that a little colony possessed an extent of territory greater than the whole of Europe. What was afterwards called Pennsylvania belonged therefore originally to Virginia.

Hudson afterwards ascended the river which bears his name, and discovered the country through which it flows, afterwards called New York. He thought himself proprietor of it—perhaps under the auspices and sanction of Alexander VI's bull,—and ceded it all to the Dutch, together with much unexplored country, part of which was the district now forming the states of New Jersey, Pennsylvania, and Delaware; which the Dutch called New Belgium.

James I, and Virginia on his behalf, protested against this sale: the peace of Breda revoked it, and it reverted to the English. A great part of the land was afterwards granted to the heir of Penn, an English admiral, in payment of sums due to him from the government, and from him it was called Pennsylvania, or Penn's forests; for at that time it was all forest, inhabited only by savages and wild beasts.

The history of Penn and of Pennsylvania, is intimately connected with that of the Quakers. It is the history of a true patriarch, and a good legislator; of the gentle and humane manners of the best ages of the world; of the true morality of the Gospel. I think therefore you will not be displeased if I give you a slight sketch of it. You might otherwise think I passed with insensibility and indifference over a country which is perhaps the only true theatre of that golden age, which everybody talks of, though nobody knows when or where to place its existence.

Quakerism, if we are to believe its votaries, is

as old as Christianity. They go so far as to say that Jesus Christ was the first Quaker, and that they do but tread in his footsteps. Thence they trace their austere morals, their simple and patriarchal manners, their hospitality, their humility, their truly Christian charity, their aversion to all the pleasures of worldly vanity, to pomp, luxury, and intemperance; their horror for war; (and not from fear of death, which they, living *in justitia et equitate*, have perhaps less reason to dread than any other persons, but from genuine humanity and philanthropy;) thence that harmony, that true brotherhood, which reigns among them, and which ought to serve as an example and model to those who pretend to excel in the Christian virtues, and who demand that all the rest of the world should take them as models only *because* they demand it.

The Quakers say that they do not baptize, because Jesus Christ never baptized as we do; that they should be disciples of John and not of Christ if they did:—that John himself said that another would come who would baptize by fire; and that Christ did baptize his apostles in the tabernacle by the fire of the Holy Spirit;—that they believe themselves baptized by this same spirit, and inspired with what they ought to say and to do, *rectum et divinum*, on earth; that Jesus Christ never made obeisances with his hat, nor required others to make them to him;—that he never used any other appellative than the second person singular;—and that they do not find in the Bible, or in any other sacred book, the titles of our terrestrial divinities,—*majesty*, *highness*, *eminence*, *excellence*, *grace*, *reverence*, &c. &c. They assert that after the death of our divine master, his principles became corrupted, but that there were always some few good Quakers dispersed about the world who kept alive the sacred fire; until Fox arose in 1642, and kindled it into fresh brightness and vigour in England. It was precisely the period at which three or four hostile sects tore Great Britain with civil wars, as cruel as they were fanatical, which gave birth to the most tolerant, the most humane of all which have sprung from Christianity—the sect of the Quakers.

The young and ardent Penn, though educated in the orthodox principles of the University of Oxford, was warmed by this sacred flame, and became one of the most zealous proselytes of the new apostle of England. His eloquence made many converts among the men, and his beauty and sweet expression still more among the women. His father's interest and money were often employed to rescue him from prison and from persecution. He even quarrelled with his father, who was of the orthodox faith, but their mutual affection re-united them; at length, being left sole heir of his father's property, which was considerable, and absolute proprietor of an immense territory in America, he turned his back on persecutions and persecutors, and came hither with Fox and a great number of his followers to plant the standard of his faith, and of the generous and humane principles which characterized it.

Here then, my dear Madam, you have a Quaker turned sovereign;—invested with the right of making laws, of establishing a government, of granting lands, of levying taxes, &c. The use which Penn made of this right, places him in the rank of the greatest benefactors of his race. He converted the whole of the vast province which had been granted to his father, and which, as I have already told you, he called Pennsylvania, into one great theatre of beneficence, industry, and of the purest morality.

After he had rendered this country a secure asylum for himself and his brethren, he turned his attention to the means of providing for their future wants, without molestation to the Swedish and Dutch settlers, who already cultivated a part of it, and who readily submitted to a ruler as just as he was benevolent.

He granted a thousand acres of land to any man who applied for it (for twenty pounds, and a small yearly rent); he gave fifty acres to every young man and young woman, who had been engaged for some time, and had completed their term of service; and the same quantity to every married couple, who had no means of paying for it. An equitable treaty protected the colonists against the incursions of the Indians, and wise laws secured them in the enjoyment of their liberty and property. He decreed that every man who acknowledged the existence of a God, might be admitted a citizen, and that every Christian was eligible to every office of state; that every one was at liberty to invoke the Great Being in the manner most satisfactory to his own conscience; that no one was compelled to furnish contributions or tithes for the building of temples. In order to deserve the most perfect protection the colony could afford, it was only necessary to take an oath of obedience to the crown, and fidelity to the lord proprietor. The Quakers, who never mingle the Deity in human affairs, and consequently do not take oaths, merely promise by a *yes* or a *no*, and their simple affirmation is more sacred and inviolable than the pretended religious *formulæ* of many other Christians, who perjure themselves upon the Gospels.

Lastly, Penn resolved that no tax should be imposed, or law enacted, without the consent of all the inhabitants of the colony, whose age and sex rendered them fit to vote, and reserved no other power to himself than that of watching over the security and happiness of his province.

He divided it into counties, in each of which he established a court, where justice was to be administered gratis; justices of the peace, arbitrators, &c.; in order, as far as possible, to banish or to prevent chicanery and litigation. Such, in a word, were his justice and generosity, that, not thinking his right to the possession of these lands established by the cession of England alone, he treated with the Indians for theirs, and purchased it on equitable terms, and by the common consent of all the contracting parties. So just was his conduct in this treaty, that the name of Penn is still held in the greatest reverence among the Indians; and, when they have any treaty to conclude with the present American nation, they always invoke the same spirit of loyalty and sanctity which dictated that of Penn with their ancestors.

You may readily imagine, my dear Madam, that everybody would be eager to live under the protection of such a government and such a legislator; equal, perhaps superior, to any whom antiquity can boast:—a legislator, who founded all his institutions on the solemn guarantees of property and liberty, and of the most extensive toleration. Pennsylvania accordingly was soon the resort of numerous European and American families, who brought with them industry, arts, manufactures, and commerce; and rendered it the most flourishing colony in the world. It is now one of the most important states of the Union.

The diversity of nations, religions, and languages, might have given cause to apprehend that jealousy, and those hostile feelings which are frequently the ruin of ancient establishments and the great obstacle to the formation of new ones; but, such was the wisdom of the legislator, that the utmost concord and harmony prevailed. Every individual readily contributed his own labours in *the Lord's vineyard,* to ensure the well-being, physical and moral, of the great family.

As all enjoyed an unrestrained and equal freedom, no man envied the liberty of another. Though the Quakers were the most numerous of the various sects assembled round the banner of toleration, though the legislator was himself a Quaker, they enjoyed no other precedency or supremacy over others than what they obtained by the excellence of their example and the practice of all the Christian virtues. If there was not unity of opinion, there was perfect co-operation in beneficence; and even where there was not the common bond of Christianity, that of humanity was sufficient to check the spirit of fanaticism, persecution, and intolerance. Such, in short, were their union, their mutual sentiments of philanthropy, that they took or received the name of the Philadelphi.

It was necessary to build some great and permanent monument, as a lasting record of the foundation of this holy colony, and accordingly, Penn planned and built its capital, Philadelphia. During the war of independence, it was the capital of the whole Union, and is now that of the state of Pennsylvania; that is to say, it is the centre of the most important business and commerce and institutions of the state; but Harrisburg is the true capital. Harrisburg is more central, and American wisdom supplies the deficiency of commerce by the resources necessarily arising from the seat of the magistracy and the bustle of a metropolitan city.

I shall not detain you long at Philadelphia or anywhere else, for, to reach this place (Pittsburg) in the short time that has elapsed, it is clear that we must not stay long, nor observe minutely. For the present, then, we will content ourselves with a superficial glance at what falls in our way in the country through which we pass, and with noting its origin and progress.

Philadelphia is built in the form of a parallelogram, lying north and south, in a peninsula formed by the Delaware and the Schulkyll, which meet five miles lower down, where a fort, built by the Union, commands both these rivers. Having told you how recently it has emerged from its surrounding forests, you will learn with surprise that it already contains 115,000 inhabitants. Ask the countries under the sway of intolerance, whether population encreases thus with them?

It contains large squares, which are laid out like those of England with grass-plats and trees; almost everything about them is English. If one could sleep through the whole passage, and wake in the United States, one might believe oneself still in England, at least so far as externals go. The houses are English. The Americans have constructed some large buildings, to be more *à l'Anglaise,* and have completed the resemblance by similar architectural extravagances. Like the English, they will insist on knowing everything of themselves, without being in the slightest degree indebted to foreigners. This sort of conceit is not very favourable to their architecture, though exceedingly so to their patriotism: they would however do wisely to keep to the simple. If they *will* ascend to the heights of Pantheons, Parthenons, Capitols, &c. they must learn, and they must go and study in those countries where the art is understood, or get foreigners to come and teach them what they do not know.

There is a university which enjoys some reputation; there is a philosophical society for the encouragement of science and letters; a museum of natural history; a public library bequeathed to the town by the celebrated Franklin; hospitals, which are not, at present, very well managed, except that of Pennsylvania, in which the patients pay for attendance. In this hospital, West has left his country a splendid memorial of his talents; his picture of Christ Healing the Sick is certainly one of the *chef d'œuvres* of modern art.

There are many handsome churches for various modes of worship. The Catholic church of St Mary has lately been the scene of great scandal. The congregation actually came to open blows about a priest who was the choice of the people, but rejected by the bishop and his partisans; this is the way in which our holy religion is everywhere honoured and recommended by the conduct of its professors.

The institutions for public education are very numerous. They build as many schools as churches, and manufactures and arts have already made astonishing progress.

I have reserved the markets as a *bonne bouche,*

for they are really beautiful, and the quantity and excellence of the provisions, and game of every description, is a novel and striking sight to a stranger. The great building on the Schulkyll, containing the engines for raising all the water for the use of the town, is a grand work and deserves a volume to itself: it is therefore out of the reach of a man who flies along like the stage coaches of England, or of the steam boats of America. The season was moreover very unfavourable to any examination of a work of this kind, for all the water was frozen, and one walked upon the Schulkyll and Delaware just as securely as in the Tuilleries. If we had arrived a week later, I should have ascended the Delaware in a carriage or on horseback. Your curiosity about Philadelphia is not satisfied, I know;—so much the better. You will be the more glad to return.

Let us set out for Washington, and travel with all expedition, that we may reach it before the dissolution of Congress.

At the distance of a mile from Philadelphia we cross the Schulkyll by a magnificent wooden bridge of bold and wonderful construction.

At Chester, fifteen miles from Philadelphia, is a fine manufactory of cloth, established by a Frenchman, and worked by the Chester river. But of these you have seen enough in France.

We crossed the Susquehana on the ice. It is a great river, sixty-six miles from Philadelphia. Its western sources are in the Appalachian, and its northern in the Chenectady mountains. It flows into the Chesapeake.

You want to stop a moment at Baltimore. Well, one moment;—but take care we do not forget ourselves, for it is a delightful town;—I prefer it, on every account, greatly to Philadelphia. It might easily seduce us into a long stay.

This province was also part of Virginia. Charles I. gave lord Baltimore all the land lying between the Potowmac, which was its boundary on the side of Virginia, and the Susquehana, which divided, and still divides it from Pennsylvania, on the other. Lord Baltimore called it Maryland, in honour of Queen Mary, and built a town, which he also called Mary, or St Mary. He was a Catholic, and converted this territory into a refuge for Catholics; but by a fatality, which seems to attend Catholicism, that colonies founded under its auspices never prosper in this world, (perhaps because the prosperity of the faithful is reserved until their final migration to another), division and discord found their way among the inhabitants; the town, instead of encreasing, shrunk to a miserable village; the colonists were poor and lazy; busied in nothing but attempts to convert the savages to a religion which they prophaned and dishonoured, instead of recommending it by evangelical morality, union, and courage. Such, in short, was the state of the colony, that the lord found himself compelled to get an act approved by the general assembly, by which every man who was a Christian was admitted to an enjoyment of all the advantages common to the ancient colonists, and of perfect indulgence and toleration for his political and religious opinions. This act attracted a great number of families of different creeds. The colony prospered, the city encreased, and the Indians retired at the sight of these new auxiliaries, whose orderly habits, good morals, and firm measures of defence, awed them into respect and submission.

But, my dear Countess, you must not fall into the mistake of thinking that the city of Baltimore, though thriving, was really a city. Any place was then called a city which was the seat of a colonial establishment. Fifty years ago it did not perhaps contain a hundred houses; it now contains one hundred thousand inhabitants, and is one of the most flourishing towns in the union. It commands the northern side of the great bay of Chesapeake, more than two hundred miles from the sea, and is surrounded by beautiful hills and magnificent country-houses. It is the most important town of Maryland, though Anapolis is the capital; and is the *entrepôt* and the seat of a considerable commerce with all parts of the world.

It has been called Baltimore ever since it became part of the union. The Catholic church alone, which has a bishop, has retained the name of St Mary's.

The town is pretty and cheerful in all parts. The streets and houses are perfectly brilliant with neatness; the churches are handsome, and some magnificent; the exchange, surmounted by a large tent-shaped cupola, is a large and rich building. The column erected to the memory of Washington is perhaps the most gigantic existing, but it is very ill placed; and the ascent to the gallery round the capital is by an internal staircase, without the least air-hole; so that you are almost dead before you reach the top, from the foulness of the air. A colossal statue of Washington is to be placed, I know not when, on a plinth upon the capital.

In a pretty little square, surrounded by the handsomest houses in the town, public and private, is another monument, in commemoration of the *battle* of North Point, fought five miles to the south-east of Baltimore in the last war between the English and Americans. It cannot be to commemorate the *victory*, for certainly this was not the best scene of their valour or their glory. With fifteen or sixteen thousand men, who had the choice of their ground, and time for preparation, it surely could not be very difficult to take five or six thousand English, whom general Ross's imprudence had delivered into their hands. This imprudence, however, cost only his life; for the Americans suffered nearly the whole of his little army to escape, and to re-embark nearly as easily as they landed. When I was shewing you the monument at the Seven Mountains on the Rhine, I remarked that nothing blinds princes so effectually as flattery; here we find it has the same effect on republics.

Baltimore has a great number of philanthropical institutions, and of places of public instruction: it is a very interesting town in every respect; and, if I were to live in the United States, I had rather live at Baltimore than at Philadelphia. The latter has many noble recollections and associations, but apparently the inhabitants are contented with this stock, for it does not seem to me that they are in the way to add to it. Philadelphia is not the place to go to for amiable or courteous manners; and in the higher classes I thought I perceived symptoms of an illiberal and spiteful ambition. Let us go on to Washington.

The road from Baltimore to Washington has nothing interesting. Washington has not long been to be found in the map of America. It stands on the northern shore of the Potowmac. It arose, together with the prosperity of the

United States, after the termination of the war of independence, under the auspices of the great citizen whose name it bears. The ground on which it stands belonged to Maryland. This state consented to give it for the site of the capital of the whole union. Virginia also granted a portion on the southern bank, and thus was formed the district of Columbia, that is to say, a certain circumference round the city, which serves as a sort of *appanage* or anti-chamber to the queen-city of America. Perhaps I am using this epithet rather rashly; but the influence she exercises on this new world, already so astonishingly mature, seems to justify me even at this moment, and time will justify me yet more fully. There are some things in which rashness is more shewn in rejecting too much than in believing too much.

The Capitol is a large building, in a situation worthy of a name of such awful grandeur. It commands the whole city, which, like all infant cities whose origin is to be found in political causes alone, and whose growth is not hastened and directed by commerce, still consists of scattered sections. From its western balcony you look down the whole of the High street, which begins at the foot of this building, and, crossing the city for nearly two miles, terminates at another elevation, upon which, directly fronting the Capitol, stands the president's house. This edifice (the Capitol) is vast, and might have been rendered grand, if the Bostonian architect had not preferred the new to the regular;—if he had not thought extravagancies more striking than the rules of art, harmony too monotonous, and fantastic embellishments grand and magnificent. Such probably were the tastes that induced him to place on the outside the grand staircase leading to the dome which rises majestically in the centre of the eastern façade. So grand an edifice, and one bearing so stately a name, ought to have had a majestic entrance, where carriages might have set down the members of congress at the foot of a grand interior staircase, then crossed a court and passed out on the other side. The architect probably thought this too aristocratical an indulgence, and accordingly he makes them alight democratically in the rain.

The great dome is handsome, but would be more so if it were not so dark in the inside. On either side of it is a large hall, one for the lower chamber, or representatives, the other for the upper, or senators. The first is a magnificent room, in the form of a crescent, and a *foramen*, after the manner of the ancients, lights it from the top of the ceiling; but thick columns, perfectly idle and useless, and galleries of too great depth, round the whole concave part, impede and absorb the voice, so that it is extremely difficult to hear in it. The statue of Liberty, which presides in this truly august congress, is placed in a most singular situation. She is reposing on the cornice which runs quite round the hall above the great pillars. You see her, but you cannot distinguish her. The statue itself was only a model which the Italian artist, whom they sent for on purpose, presented for approbation; but the honourable gentlemen apparently thought it so beautiful, that they contented themselves with the plaster, so that the poor artist is still waiting, and probably will long remain so, for the order to execute it in marble. And indeed a statue of marble on a cornice would have a most threatening appearance, and might endanger the head of the speaker who sits directly under it.

The hall of the senate is much smaller and more modest, but it is also handsome. The supreme court, which has cognizance of all the law affairs of the union, holds its sittings there, in a room which is well-contrived, if not magnificent. There is even a little closet in which the attorney-general keeps his breakfast, which I saw him eat in very good earnest and without the slightest constraint, in full court and in the midst of the audience. The library, which is still without books, is a fine room: all the rest has rather the air of a monastery than a palace.

The English, as you know, made a descent

upon Washington in the last war, and burnt this national monument of a rebellious people; a Vandalism which certainly is not one of the brightest pages of the history of England. It has arisen, therefore, under a new form from its ruins. It might have been rebuilt better; but it must always be regarded as a grand structure,—the earnest of a transatlantic Rome. To aid this allusion, the Americans have given the name of Tiber to a little muddy stream which creeps humbly at its foot, and soon hides its obscurity and its shame in the Potowmac.

I guess your thoughts, dear lady; you want to know what these representatives and senators are about. But this is not an affair for a passing spectator to meddle with. All I can tell you is, that they assemble there to defend and maintain, valorously and powerfully, the rights and liberties of their constituents; the independence, honour, and glory of their country, against all assailants. You think I may at least tell you with what sort of air these gentlemen sit in their arm chairs. To form any idea of the moral habits which influence their manners is very difficult for a rambler; mere external appearance will hardly perhaps satisfy your question. But I can tell you just what I saw, and how it struck me. They do not sit with such perfect nonchalance as the gentlemen of St Stephen's Chapel:

they have to do with a people more jealous, more suspicious, more vigilant, and this keeps them a little in order; nor are elections bought so easily as in England: nevertheless one sees that they have an extreme mind to ape them if they dared. Perhaps they will succeed when they are richer, and the people more docile and more habituated to regard them as *demi-sovereigns*.

This is no place, too, to enter into a disquisition on the details of the government, much as I know you desire to hear all you can on that interesting subject. Its fundamental basis you doubtless know; I will give you such a slight idea of its composition as I have been able to form for myself.

The twenty-four states which compose the union have, by a perfectly new political system, the sovereignty of this vast empire divided among themselves; at the same time concentrating the general government in the neutral city of Washington, which belongs to all and to none; and in which the Americans meet yearly, as the Amphictyonic council met at Delphi; whilst, like the members of the Achæan league, each state has its particular government. You must understand me as well as you can; for the present I cannot explain myself better.

I must say a word about the President, were it only to have the pleasure of telling you the strange way in which I entered his apartment. I went to the door of the President's house,—I found it open, and walked in; I turned in vain on every side to find some one of whom to enquire for him; there was nobody. Nearly opposite the entrance of the vestibule I saw a door open;—I advanced, crossed a room, asked at another door whether I might go in;—nobody answered. I asked again and again, like a Swiss; —at last an old man, in leather-breeches, top-boots, and spurs, with a riding-whip in his hand, came up to me: "Is the president at home?" said I; "can I have the honour of seeing him?" "You do see him," replied he, "I am the president, at your service." I found that I was still the mountaineer who comes gaping down to the low-lands full of admiration and awe for everything superior and venerable; I could not utter a word. But his kind courtesy soon relieved me from the embarrassment into which I was thrown by his unexpected presence: I gave him my letter of recommendation. He received and talked to me with the greatest kindness, and our conversation would perhaps have been a long one, had not a senator, wrapped in a great boat cloak, and very muddy, come in loaded with papers, and interrupted it. His manners were as coarse as those of the president were polite. I went out by the same way as I had gone in, and quitted this illustrious chief magistrate with an impression of the deepest respect and veneration.

What a difference, my dear Madam, between his noble manners and the disgusting *morgue* of a miserable French diplomatist, to whom I was afterwards ashamed to have presented a letter of introduction! What a difference between the frank and liberal tone of conversation of the one, and the pitiful inquisitiveness of the other! You know, doubtless, that the present president is James Monroe. We must quit Washington; but it is impossible to do so without being struck with a sort of amazement and admiration, and filled with a crowd of secret and busy thoughts which it is difficult to define.

The principal interest of the road from Washington to Pittsburg arises from the reflection, that all these fields, these villages and towns, have just arisen, as it were, out of nothing, and that they are all the seat of the greatest prosperity and the most perfect and solid liberty. The sight of poverty would here be considered a phenomenon; competence and comfort are universal.

The country is diversified by forests, *prairies*, tilled fields, plains, hills, vallies, mountains, rivers, and torrents, so that there is no room for monotony, and the eye is continually solicited by boundless variety. It passes rapidly from the gloomy to the gay, from the lovely to the terrific, and *vice versâ*. It is one continuous gallery of the finest pictures from the hand of Nature.

The most considerable town on the road is Frederick's-town in Maryland, forty-five miles from Washington. It already contains four thousand inhabitants, and is a delightful little town. Here I was compelled to halt. We were packed like red herrings, in a bad stage-coach, full of Kentuckians, whom it is really impossible to endure. It is a pity that a people so brave, industrious, and active, should be so coarse and insolent: one can and must esteem them, but it is a difficult matter to like them. As this is the season of their annual migration from east to west, and consequently all the stages swarm with them, I hired a kind of waggon and went to Chambersburg in Pennsylvania, on the road from Philadelphia to Pittsburg. It is a much larger town than Frederick's-town. Here begins the eastern ascent of the Apalachian mountains, which are neither so high nor so horrible as some geographers represent them. On this road they divide into three distinct ridges, from north to south.

The line of the great road, which crosses them up to this point, is well chosen, but the road itself is detestable, as are almost all American roads; indeed any reasonable man must see that some time must elapse before an easy circulation can be opened through this mighty body. The descent of the western side of the mountains is worse than that on the east, which also was to be expected; it is farther from the centre of civilization, and nearer to the region where things are yet in *statu quo*. However, one finds good inns everywhere; and with their fine horses, which for strength and fire perhaps surpass the English, the stages do get along.

I was surprised to find so little snow at this season on mountains which make so much noise in the world, and in a country where the cold is more intense at a latitude of 40° than it is at 50° in Europe. This cold is the very thing which brings my ramble to a close;—and closed it is.

What,—without a word of the American women? Indeed, my dear Countess, they deserve that I should bespeak your esteem for them, though in so short a time I do not pretend to appreciate all their merits.

They are generally pretty—at least their countenances are extremely interesting to me; they are agreeable without forwardness, modest without affectation, well-informed without pedantry; and are excellent housewives. In all respects, they are very superior to the men.

You are astonished, are you not, dear Madam, that an European should come to America, pass very often by Joseph Buonaparte's door, and not say a word about him.

It is my system never to mention individuals if I can say no good; you know, besides, that the name of Buonaparte died—as it was born—with Napoleon; unless indeed it should revive in his son.

Au revoir, my dear Countess—a little farther—but where I know not.

P. S. Continue, if you please, to send your letters through Baring, Brothers, and Co. London.

LETTER XII.

Confluence of the Ohio and Mississippi,
April 20th, 1823.

I HAVE made another very long and beautiful excursion, my dear Countess, since I wrote to you from Pittsburg. How much do I wish that I possessed the pencil of Claude or the pen of Delille, to place so enchanting a picture before your eyes; or that I were gifted with the sagacity of Anacharsis and the wisdom of Mentor; I could then select and appreciate whatever is calculated to arrest the attention of the present, or excite the hopes of future generations, in the country through which I have passed.

I must entreat you to receive with indulgence the communications of a man, whose mind so often wanders back to those scenes whither the love of country and of home are continually recalling him; where the admiration of the most extraordinary virtue, the consolations of the noblest friendship, so long and so delightfully occupied him; and whose eyes would fain rest only upon what are most difficult to describe,—objects which interest his heart. But let us return to Pittsburg.

Pittsburg, before the war of independence, was only a small port, called by the name of *du Quêsne,* when these wilds belonged to the French; and by that of *Pitt,* when the English took possession of it under the ministry of that man whom Mr Nicoll, one of his coadjutors in parliament, has described better than fame did. This fort was at that time one of the bulwarks which defended the western frontier of the European colonies. At that time, the savages or aborigines inhabited all the vast regions which now constitute the states of Ohio, Indiana, Illinois, Mississippi, Kentucky, Tennessee, Alabama, and a great part of those of Louisiana, Georgia, New York, Pennsylvania, and Virginia. Pittsburg is now a city, containing about twelve thousand inhabitants.

The rapidity with which the human species has multiplied in these countries is astonishing; it seems as if death had lost his empire in this country; but now it is rich and flourishing, and physicians are flocking hither in abundance.

It would be difficult to find a situation so far inland, and at the same time so favourable to internal and external commerce.

Pittsburg belongs to the state of Pennsylvania, and is situated at the foot of the western slope of the Apalachian or Alleghany mountains, which, from Canada to the gulph of Mexico, from N.N.E. to S.S.W., divide the United States into Eastern and Western. Here, the Alleghany and Monongahela rivers unite, and, losing their respective names, take that of Ohio, which, in the Algonquine or aboriginal language, signifies "beautiful river." The former, which flows from the north, affords a safe navigation as far as Presqu'isle, where, by means of a very short land carriage, there is a communication with lake Erie. The latter also conveys large boats along a course of about two hundred miles, to within a short distance from its sources towards the S. E. in the Apalachian mountains.

Pittsburg is already in a flourishing state; it has a number of manufactories all in great activity, and moved by steam. So powerful is the mechanism employed in the manufacture of nails, that, with my watch in my hand, I have seen more than three hundred made in a minute with the aid of one man; and in the iron-foundry, the metal is reduced perhaps in still less time, from its primitive state to that of a polished bar of any dimensions or size. In countries where it will soon be attempted, as in former times, to make the sun move and the earth stand still, the inventors of these machines would be considered as sorcerers, and exposed to the cruel punishment inflicted upon our celebrated Galileo. Pittsburg is the little Birmingham of the United States.

This city receives goods from the Atlantic by way of New York, Philadelphia, and Baltimore, and sends them to the western states by the Ohio, the Muskingum, the Kentucky, the Tennessee, the Cumberland, the Mississippi, the Missouri, the Illinois, &c.; and to the countries situated upon the gulf of Mexico, by the canal of New Orleans, lying upon the Mississippi, at a short distance from its mouths; and receives the produce of all the countries washed by these great rivers, as well as that of the West Indies.

The steam-boats and other vessels by which they are conveyed, cross these vast countries of the new world in every direction. The former are fitted up with every possible accommodation, and a tolerable degree of neatness. The passengers are provided with plain but plentiful breakfasts and dinners; with suppers, which are rendered less heavy by tea; with beds, to which the noise of the water and the machinery imparts a soporific virtue not to be found elsewhere; and there is a numerous company, which is almost always enlivened by some original character.

I embarked in one of these steam-boats on the morning of the 1st of April; and I had arrived at some distance from Pittsburg, before I perceived that the weather was serene, and the sky brilliantly illuminated with the rays of the ancient God of the land; for the coal-smoke, the only incense which the manufacturing and heretical inhabitants offer to their two divinities, Avarice and Industry, enshrouds the sun by day and the stars by night. But for this thick cloud, the prospect, at the point where these two great rivers meet, surrounded by hills, intersected by vallies, and losing itself in the romantic distance, would have been much more picturesque and surprising.

The appearance of the two bridges by which the city communicates with the opposite banks of the two rivers, was quite enchanting, aided as it was by the effect of the mist. The bridges are built entirely of wood, resting upon stone pillars, and are *chefs-d'œuvre* of their kind. The timber-work is admirably united, and supports, as by magic, the flat arches, which, although held together by the sole effect of pressure, are of a considerable span. They are beautiful proofs of the progress of mechanism among the Americans. It appears, that they build much better bridges than Parthenons and Capitols.

Each of these bridges has a *trottoir* on both sides, where foot-passengers cannot be incommoded by the horses or carriages, for which there are separate entrances; they are like spacious galleries which afford a shelter from the wind and rain. That over the Monongahela is about half a mile long; that over the Alleghany somewhat less. They are both lighted by glazed windows at equal distances; the lattices with which they are adorned add to their beauty, and when the sun raises the vapour from the water to the top of the pillars, it gives them the appearance of floating palaces.

The bridges belong to a company of speculators, whom the toll, though high, will probably never repay for the sums they have expended upon them; for the numerous facilities which so many navigable rivers afford to commerce and to travellers, and the bad state of the roads, are great obstacles to the interests and profits of the constructors of bridges.

You would be astonished, my dear Countess, in a country where everything seems rapidly advancing towards civilization, to find roads which seem to belong to a state of savage wildness. Nor do I believe they will be improved whilst the influence of the several states in the general government continues to be so unwisely distributed; that is to say, whilst the number of the representatives in congress is in proportion to the population of each state, by which means the four or five most populous have a preponderance over all the others. This great Union is consequently always disunited when legislating on a matter which, like high-ways, is more beneficial to one state than to another. This must indeed be the case, unless the measure happen to interest the three states of Virginia, Pennsylvania and New York, which can always command a majority over the twenty-one others. Generally speaking, they are unanimous only in one point, that is, the jealousy with which they watch each other.

If this jealousy never transgressed the bounds of moderation, it might perhaps contribute to the safety of the republic: but, as the western states manifest on all occasions a violent opposition to those of the east, and as the federalists or aristocrats are often at open variance with the popular or democratical party, rivalry may be strengthened into hatred, and may become fatal to the Union and advantageous to their common enemy, who has his eye upon them, and, I believe, leaves no means untried to foment divisions among the leaders of the different parties. All parties are alike to the cabinet of St James's, provided they promote discord and anarchy, which its machiavelism has made the strong-hold of the political existence of England, and to which it is, in a manner, obliged to condemn every nation that gives it cause for jealousy or alarm.

Almost immediately after we had passed this great confluence, we saw a delightful little island, in which a clump of lofty tufted trees seems to offer its leafy homage to the majesty of the newly-formed river.

Eight miles farther, another island, named from its extent Long Island, divides it in the middle. The pretty little houses and cottages scattered over it form a delightful landscape, which was softened into tender tints by the smoke curling amid the trees.

Neither time nor my pen would suffice to describe to you all the impressions which the different aspects of this magnificent river produce upon the mind; and a detailed description of the immense tract of country through which it flows would fatigue your magination, which I wish to keep unsated I shall therefore only give you a sketch of the principal places it washes, and of the most considerable rivers that flow into it; after which, I will take a rapid survey of the whole valley it embellishes in its course.

As the direction of the Ohio, from Pittsburg to its mouth, is nearly from E.N.E. to W.S.W., to avoid confusion and ambiguity, (notwithstanding its frequent deviations from this line,) we will call the right bank the northern, and the left the southern, whenever we have occasion to distinguish them.

The vast state of Pennsylvania extends upon these two banks forty-one miles southward to Grape Island, and continues forty-four northward to Little Beaver Creek, which separates it on one side from the state of Virginia, on the other from that of Ohio.

We arrived in the evening at Weeling, on the southern bank, as by enchantment. Although ninety-one miles from Pittsburg, I was unconscious of the distance, so much were my eyes and my imagination occupied and delighted by the charms of this river.

Weeling is the great rival of Pittsburg, as Virginia, to which it belongs, is of Pennsylvania. Its situation is very favourable. Almost all the inhabitants of the west, going eastward, come to this place to take the stage-coach, which arrives three times a week, and sets out again regularly for Washington, Maryland, Virginia, Pennsylvania, &c. But it has by no means all the advantages of Pittsburg, whence the trade of the Delta, of the Monangahela and of the Alleghany, extends to all points, and where the abundance and cheapness of coals greatly facilitate manufactures.

Marietta, eighty-four miles lower than Weeling, on the northern bank, has not been long built; nevertheless it is the chief town of the county of Washington, in the state of the Ohio. In 1800 this place contained only a few families; it is now adorned with beautiful public and private buildings. General Putnam, the father of the colony, is still living. Education is promoted by an academy erected for that purpose, and a pretty good library is open to the citizens. It has a printing press which is never idle; for in the United States, the public papers are as much read in small villages as in great towns,—in the cottage as in the palace. A Presbyterian church, although large, is scarcely sufficient to contain the population, which now amounts to 2,000 persons, and increases prodigiously every year with the growth of the city. Its situation is most delightful, and the Muskingum, which falls into the Ohio, gives it the advantage of an extensive inland navigation. By a very short land journey from near the source of the Muskingum, you reach the river Cuyahoga, which runs into lake Erie.

The current of the Muskingum is so gentle that, when the Ohio is swollen, its waters are driven back to a considerable distance. This occasioned a curious incident. A flat boat, laden with provisions for New Orleans, had arrived near the confluence of the Muskingum and the Ohio. The latter having swelled prodigiously during the night, turned the current of the Muskingum back towards its source. From the darkness of the night, the boat followed the same direction. The day after, a thick fog, which concealed the banks of the river, concurred with the carelessness of the boatman to favour the mistake which continued the whole of the second night; but the following day, the fog having dispersed sufficiently to render the boat visible from shore, they were hailed with the usual questions,—whence they came,—where they were going,—and what their boat was laden with? They then made the discovery that, instead of going to New Orleans, they had been carried up the Muskingum.

General Putnam is the patriarch of the colony of Marietta. He is a venerable old man, and has a claim to honourable mention in the interesting, and hitherto entirely neglected history of these western parts of the United States. An humble individual like myself can only pay him the tribute of a few words expressive of the respect with which he filled me. He has watched the growth of this country from the time when no sounds were heard but the roaring of wild beasts, the croaking of the raven, or the death-song of the savages against whom he fought. He has seen the trees of these forests fall under the axe of the cultivator, and their places supplied by the alternate succession of log-houses, then of cottages, and lastly of the beautiful houses which now adorn the surrounding scenery. He has beheld the whole country inundated by an extraordinary rise of the Ohio and the Muskingum; all the cattle, and many men, drowned; and watched the desolation, disease, and death, consequent upon such an event. He has witnessed all the horrors of the vindictive incursions of the savages, and seen the exhaustless fertility and natural advantages of the soil triumph over the ravages of fire and sword. In this place he witnessed the construction of the first steam-boat that traversed these vast regions, and from this spot he himself has sent vessels to the gulf of Mexico, a distance of more than 2,000 miles. He has survived all the vicissitudes of an infant colony; and in this peaceful seclusion he awaits the termination of that mortal career, in which he has distinguished himself as one of the great men of the revolution, and as the most skilful and enterprising of settlers. He is simple and unostentatious in his manners; he has acted upon Cato's precept—*Melius est esse quam videri*.

The situation of Belpré upon the north bank, and in the same country, is very agreeably in unison with its name. It was given to it by some Frenchmen, who, after fighting for American independence, settled in this place to enjoy the fruits of their valour in peace. When one considers how much the French have achieved for the liberty of others,—that they sacrificed their good king to the vain phantom of their own,—and that they are now forging chains for Spain and Portugal, and perhaps for themselves, with the same alacrity with which they offered hecatombs to the terrorism of the *sans-culottes*,—one is filled with a thousand mingled and contending feelings.

The island of Blennerhasset claims the attention of the traveller from its length, which is three miles, from its enchanting beauty, and from the recollection of the unhappy catastrophe to which it owes its name.

An Irish gentleman, flying from the horrors with which the rebellion of 1801 filled his country, took refuge in America, and settled in this island with all his family. Rich, and an admirer of the beautiful, he converted it into a perfect Tivoli. In December 1810, a terrible fire buried his only daughter under the ruins of the beautiful house which he had built. He immediately quitted this abode of sorrow, and the island now retains no other memorial of his splendid residence than the name of the unfortunate girl who perished in it: with her, perished everything. What a wound must this cruel loss have inflicted upon the feelings of the wretched parent! Having afterwards engaged in a conspiracy, the object of which was to break up the Great Union, he was obliged to quit America.

The *Great Kenhawa* is the first great river that flows into the Ohio from the south. It descends from the western Apalachians of north Carolina, and is navigable to a considerable distance from its mouth.

Gallipolis, also founded by Frenchmen, who fled at the approach of the first terrors of the revolution to the state of Ohio, is now the chief town of a county, although it was not in existence before 1790: but the most astonishing place is Burlington, which, though built only five years ago, is the metropolis of the county of Lawrence and the seat of a court of justice.

The only remarkable circumstance in the little river Sandy is, that it fixes the boundaries of the state of Virginia and that of Kentucky upon the southern bank, at about 300 miles from Pittsburg.

Portsmouth, upon the northern bank in the

state of Ohio, is situated at the confluence of Scioto, a considerable river, and navigable to the interior of the state.

Maysville, or Limestone, upon the southern bank, is one of the most flourishing towns in the state of Kentucky. I walked about its environs, and the varied prospects and enchanting scenes which every instant presented themselves so occupied my mind and invited my steps, that the steam-boat, after having waited for me a long time, sailed without me. Fortunately a raft passed, by means of which I overtook it at Cincinnati, where it stopped to unload goods and take in others. I passed the whole night in rowing, to protect myself from the frost.

The infancy of Cincinnati promises much. Although Columbia is the capital of the state of Ohio, Cincinnati is its largest and most commercial town; it is inferior only to Pittsburg in riches and manufactures, but is much prettier and more agreeable. It is conspicuous from its situation on three *plateaux*, which rise gradually from the bank of the Ohio; it is enclosed by hills on the north, and the Ohio washes it in a semicircle on the south. It is our own Genoa in miniature, and its environs are equally embellished with beautiful villas. Its steam-boats navigate the Ohio and the Mississippi. Activity and industry are everywhere obvious. An academy and museum shew the love of the inhabitants for science and literature; and five hundred scholars whom I saw at the school, conducted upon the system of mutual instruction, proved the wide diffusion of education. I was surprised to see the girls mixed *pèle mèle* with boys. Notwithstanding the respect due to the morals of the Americans, one cannot help fearing that opportunity will prevail over the most austere principles. There may be the most primitive simplicity and purity, but nature speaks a still more seducing language than the corruptions of society. I have been told that it owes its illustrious name to Mr Wergenton, who first settled there towards the end of the last century, and whose virtue gave him a just claim to the surname of Cincinnatus. I am inclined to believe the name of so illustrious and so republican a Roman may have contributed, among a people just emerging into republicanism, to attract a number of persons and thus to render it so soon flourishing. It has a population of about 14,000, the greater part emigrants from New England. It is about 450 miles from Pittsburg.

The river Miami, which descends from the north, separates the state of Ohio from that of Indiana. It is navigable far up the country, and communicates with other rivers which considerably extend the navigation into the interior of the two states. It is four hundred and seventy miles from Pittsburg, and nearly midway of the course of the Ohio.

I cannot help detaining you an instant, my dear Countess, at the small village of *Rising Sun,* situated upon a little eminence. Its brilliant beauty and picturesque situation perfectly justify its name. It is in the state of Indiana, upon the northern shore of the Ohio.

It is impossible to pass Vevay without travelling back in thought to Europe, and to that wondrous work in which the great citizen of Geneva, whilst he unfolds the weaknesses of the human heart, shews how completely virtue triumphs over them; in which he proves that love may be as pure and irreproachable as it is ardent and elevated; in which human nature is painted under an aspect at once extraordinary and natural, and the heroine is the model of the wife, the mother, and the friend. This little town, although in the bosom of America, is, like the *Pays de Vaud,* inhabited by Swiss who are very successful agriculturists. It is situated upon the northern bank, and in the state of Indiana, five hundred and fourteen miles from Pittsburg. These Swiss cultivate the vine: they are the only settlers who have hitherto had any success in this branch of agriculture.

We are now arrived at one of the greatest tributaries of the Ohio—the river Kentucky. It descends to the south from a branch of the Apalachian mountains, which forms a kind of chersonese towards the west, and separates the state of Kentucky on the north from that of Alabama on the south. This branch is called the Cumberland Mountains. The river Kentucky crosses the state to which it has given its name, and falls into the Ohio, at about five hundred and twenty-five miles from Pittsburg; between Port Williams on the right, and Prestonville on the left. It is daily productive of new advantages to these two infant towns, as well as to the country in the interior, by the facility with which it enables them to exchange their surplus produce for foreign commodities.

At five hundred and eighty miles from Pittsburg, you arrive at what are called *the Falls,* i. e. the cascades of the Ohio.

I make it a rule never to ask questions beforehand about any great exhibitions either of art or nature, that I may secure to my curiosity the gratification of a surprise either more agreeable or more intense; and that my eyes and my judgment may be under the influence of no other impressions than their own. But here my expectations, raised by the idea of the fall of so large a volume of water, were grievously disappointed;

and my only astonishment was, that there was nothing to be astonished at.

These falls are nothing more than an inclined plane of only twenty-two feet in the space of two miles; which in fact produces no other effect than that of rendering the current more rapid. I observed, however, a phenomenon which appears extraordinary.

I thought that the velocity impressed upon such a volume of water by this descent, must have given it an irresistible force, and have accelerated the current to a considerable distance; but this was not the fact; the river, at the bottom of this inclined plane, immediately resumes, as if by magic, its level and its ordinary rapidity, without the least reflux. We, my dear Countess, who are only inquisitive observers, must leave the solution of this problem to the learned.

These rapids, besides the check which they might oppose to the progress of an invading army, have been extremely beneficial in giving birth to two commercial *entrepôts* for goods: one where they begin, the other where they terminate. They are the two flourishing towns, Louisville, where all vessels coming down, and Shipping-port, where those going up the Ohio, stop. They are both on the southern bank. When, however, the waters are high, the rapids may be ascended without danger.

Other small towns and villages have sprung up on the opposite bank, and form similar *entre-pôts* for the state of Indiana. In my opinion, a canal, which has been projected, between Shipping-port and Louisville, would be in many respects very disadvantageous.

Louisville is the principal key to the commerce of the state of Kentucky. If Pittsburg be the Tyre, and Cincinnati the Carthage of the Ohio, Louisville is its Syracuse.

A short time before the beginning of this century, it was only a small fort of observation, built by general Clark, who was the terror of the Indians. He was one of the first who drove back these savage tribes to the north and west; or rather, one of the first who invaded and usurped their lands. This town contains already more than 8000 inhabitants. What renders the population more astonishing is, that a great number of the inhabitants yearly fall a sacrifice to the pestilential exhalations of the surrounding marshes, as well as to the contradictory systems of the swarm of medical men by whom it is infested. On first entering the city, I inferred, from the bills which these gentlemen post up in every corner of the streets, that the country must be a dangerous one; just as the traveller who had long wandered in deserts and among barbarous nations, perceived that he was got back to civilized lands by the appearance of a man hanging on a gibbet in the square of the first city he came to. Such however is the thirst for gold, that it daily attracts new victims, who die off in regular succession.

Shipping-port is not more healthy than Louisville and is much smaller; for the speculators of this place prefer living upon the right bank of the river in the pretty little towns of Clarksburg, Albany, and Jefferson, the elevation of which above the river affords them delightful views and salubrious air; to which may be added, that there are only two gentlemen of the faculty,—that their theories are in complete unison,—and consequently do not compel them to try experiments upon their patients.

If I were to advert to every object that struck my eye or touched my heart, language would not furnish me with a sufficient variety of expressions, and you would be doomed to tedious repetitions. I shall, therefore, pass by those scenes which offer nothing more interesting than what we have already seen; and after having pointed out to you the Wabash, which descends from the north and separates the state of Indiana from that of Illinois, eight hundred and twenty-five miles from Pittsburg; and on the south, the Green river, the Tennessee, and the Cumberland, four large rivers, important for their navigation;

we will stop at the little place called Wilkinson-ville, to talk a few minutes on a matter which its name suggests, and which deserves a place in the history—whenever there is one—of the United States.

This town had its origin in a little fort built against the Red men by general Wilkinson, who, after having been the Marcellus, wished to become the Cæsar of his country. He distinguished himself by his courage in all the wars, both against the English and the Indians; but, like the conqueror of the Gauls, has been accused of conspiring against the liberty of his country.

He was commander in chief of all these western regions, at the time colonel Burr, under pretence of commercial speculations, was lurking about the country, and holding secret meetings, which, as I have been informed, had very little to do with commerce. Colonel Burr, you must observe, had been vice-president, and, being extremely ambitious, could ill brook the necessity of yielding his pretensions to the presidency, to his illustrious competitor Thomas Jefferson.

A correspondence long kept up between Wilkinson and Burr excited suspicion; I know not how well founded. They were accused of a conspiracy against the government, for the purpose of separating the eastern from the western states;

and were even suspected of some secret intelligence with the cabinet of St James's. But, after a long trial and interminable debates, they were both acquitted; Wilkinson by a court-martial, Burr by a court of justice; but neither by public opinion. It is lamentable that two men of distinguished talents, who had done good service to their country and the cause of liberty, should have incurred the stigma of such an accusation.

We have not made much progress, my dear Madam, and we are still stopping at a place which, although it contains only two cats and a chimney, is called *America*. It is an embryo *entrepôt* of Lower Illinois: the steam-boat touched there to take in flour, of which this state already grows a quantity much beyond its consumption. I availed myself of this opportunity to ramble a little in the woods, the attractions of which I can never resist. These primeval forests are extremely inviting to a man born in the midst of the gardens of the beautiful but over-cultivated Hesperia. One of the passengers of the steam-boat accompanied me; and we returned with a stock of laughter which lasted us and the company for a long time. I send you your portion of it.

I was behind a large oak watching a squirrel, when suddenly my companion called out,

"*A deer!*" I asked where? He replied, "Upon a tree." Wishing to return the jest, I desired him to get some bird-lime and catch it, like a beccafigo; but seeing that he actually believed what he wished *me* to believe, I suspected there was some strange blunder; I therefore approached it:—it was a panther! I cannot tell which became the paler of the two, but certainly the face of my American friend was not blooming. Our guns were loaded with small-shot, so that to fire would only have been to irritate her. We were perfectly agreed as to the propriety of not disturbing her, since she was so obliging as not to stir. We retired, and, borne upon the wings of fear, with the sun for our compass, we soon reached our steam-boat, though we had plunged into a very thick, pathless forest.

We immediately returned to the spot, accompanied by some huntsmen of the village, and better armed; but the animal was gone.

When we first saw her she was carelessly lying upon the junction of two large arms of one of those venerable maples which still abound in these regions. There are a great many panthers in these immense forests: they remain thus motionless upon the trees that they may more easily fall upon the squirrels which abound there, and which are their favourite food.

They are very different from those of Africa

and Asia; at a distance their skin resembles that of a deer:—but a deer grazing upon a tree! I leave you to judge, my dear Countess, whether this, with the bird-lime, and our surprise, were not sufficient to make us laugh. I cannot help laughing still, when I think of the whole scene.

A vast wooden house, which performs the functions of an inn, built upon stakes driven into the water, marks the place called *the Mouth;* that is to say, the mouth of the Ohio, where it joins the Mississippi. The current of these two rivers is, as it were, paralyzed for about twenty miles above their confluence, which seems to shew that the volume of the Ohio is as powerful at this place as that of the Mississippi.

This junction is one of the grandest spectacles of nature; and the theories of gravitation and pressure, of attraction and repulsion, of inclination and equilibrium,—in short, all that concerns the general laws of the motion of fluids,—here offer a vast field of battle to the learned in hydraulics, hydrometrics, hydrostatics, hydrodynamics, and a whole dictionary of such hard words. I give place to them; for all this is worse than Greek to me; and whilst the *savans* are fighting, I will return to Pittsburg to give you a slight sketch of the Tempè of this great Peneus of the United States.

The valley of the Ohio appears to be only the

bed which it has formed for itself by the gradual wearing away of the land by its waters. From Pittsburg to its mouth, it winds between small hills, which are almost always of equal height, and the tops of which are generally on a level with the immense plain which it penetrates and divides; for all that vast tract inclosed by the Apalachian and Rocky Mountains, from east to west, is nearly a flat, intersected with small hills, which seem to have the same character and the same origin as those which inclose the valley of the Ohio; and it is the general level of this region, joined to their small degree of elevation, which facilitates the navigation of the many considerable rivers intersecting it in every direction. Another circumstance concurs to support the opinion which I have before advanced; I mean the great number of islands in this river. I think I counted about sixty.

The banks have the varied aspect of a country which has been but a few years opened to the eye of man; where art and civilization have produced but slight changes in the picture, which it still exhibits of its primitive state; and the reflections and feelings arising from it heighten the charms with which it delights the eye and the imagination. The places which bear traces of the hand of man form the most striking contrast with those in which nature is still uncultivated. The most smiling towns and villages are often separated by an interval of gloomy solitude. Fields and meadows of extraordinary luxuriance and beauty are intersected by gloomy woods and impenetrable forests; the log-houses and cottages, the farms and hamlets, scattered here and there, diffuse over the scene a variety so interesting, that it is impossible for the coldest heart to be insensible to it.

Few rivers, I think, afford such diversity of pleasing objects as the Ohio. The most lively fancy and the most profound meditation find perpetual food and exercise, and one may be in turn a poet, a political economist, and a philosopher, and always a wondering admirer. Thirty years ago all this extent of country washed by the Ohio, which has been only recently formed into states and incorporated with the union, was inhabited only by ferocious beasts, or by people still more ferocious; especially the part comprehended in the states of Illinois, Indiana, and Ohio.

It was the property and the abode of the Sawanoes, Miamis, Piankiciawoes, Wayaoes, Kaskasias, Delawares, and Illinois; nations which have been partly annihilated and partly incorporated with the Owatawas, the Sawkis, the Foxes, &c. The river Alleghany was inhabited by the Senekis, a part of whom have merged in the Six Nations; and Kentucky itself, when Boon first penetrated thither with a company of Virginia huntsmen, in 1770, was marked by no track, no path, except those which had been made by the savages, the buffaloes, wolves, bears, and panthers. It was in Kentucky, after the forests were felled and the bosom of the earth laid open, that were found those gigantic monsters which excite the wonder of an observer in the museums of Philadelphia, Baltimore, and Cincinnati. They extremely resemble the elephant, and modern naturalists have given them the name of Mammoth.

Lexington, one of the principal towns of the state, and the one which those who believe in the possibility of a political separation already designate as the capital of all the western states, was then the centre of those savage nations, a part of whom have been driven back, and now inhabit the river Osage which flows into the Missouri three hundred miles above its mouth. The first civilized men who descended the Ohio from Fort Pitt, so late as 1773, were doctor Wood and Simon Kenton, according to a manuscript which I saw at Pittsburg.

These countries afterwards became the scene of those atrocious wars which the Americans had to sustain against these savage nations; and notwithstanding the peace concluded with them in 1806, they were not able entirely to expel them till after that of 1814 with England; and even then it was by purchasing their claim or right of property on these lands; but principally by establishing military posts and forts upon lakes Michigan, Huron, Erie, and Ontario; upon the rivers Mississippi, Missouri, Illinois, Wabash, Miami, Arkansas, &c. A lady at Louisville herself told me, that in 1809 her three sons were butchered before her eyes by these barbarians, and the fourth, whom she held in her arms, threatened with the same fate.

You will no doubt conjecture, my dear Madam, that these reiterated incursions on the part of the Indians, were not quite unconnected with the influence of the cabinet of St James's; but you will find it difficult to conceive the truly machiavelian devices by which this cabinet endeavoured to keep up the hatred and cruel hostilities of the savages against the Americans, whom it cannot yet accustom itself to consider in any other light than that of colonists and rebellious subjects.

All the treaties which the Americans concluded with the savages, either for restoring peace or for fixing the boundaries of the respective territories, were commented upon by the English; they, of course always found something which they could turn against the Americans, upon which the savages immediately violated their treaties, and renewed their devastations.

It is one of the fundamental principles of all cabinets,—and *à fortiori* of that of St James's,—that every nation must have a religion; not that ministers and kings wish their people to go to heaven, which, I believe, they consider as exclusively their property as the earth; but because a people without religion cannot be worked upon by fanaticism or superstition; two ingredients necessary in their political *recipes*, and without which they could not bend them to their wishes. The cabinet of St James's therefore sought and found means to give a religion, no matter how transitory, to these savages. But it was indispensable that the mobile—like that of the heaven of ancient astronomers, which encircled and put in motion the other heavens—should be sufficiently powerful to give impulse to this new Congrevian machine. The cabinet of St James's is never at a loss; it therefore immediately created, *ipso facto*, a prophet, with the same facility as it restored the Jesuits; and naturally found him in the man of the greatest ability, and the most powerful connections of his tribe;—in the brother of the famous Thecumsen, the most valiant and formidable of all the Indian chiefs. By the pretended credulity of some hired believers, he was first represented as inspired. He was then made to preach that the Great *Manitou,* or spirit, had commanded him to collect all the tribes into one single family of concord and fraternity, and to march against the Americans who were plotting their total destruction, as well as that of their *Manitous.* He was afterwards made to raise a standard, in which all their superstitious emblems were blended; for in such a case, every nation, every sect, has its *cross.* More than 3000 savages, with all the ardour of fanatics, flocked to this new "oriflamme," and fire and sword soon laid waste the American territory. General Harrison marched with superior forces against these crusaders, and, like another Saladin, defeated them; but never was a battle between savage and civilized people more obstinately or more bravely contested than that of the 6th Nov. 1811, at the confluence of the Tippacanoe and the Wabash. The prophet encouraged his warriors to battle by displaying his standard and his *Manitous;* but as, in his character of high priest, it became him to act with discretion, he carefully kept himself at a great distance from danger, upon a little eminence, whilst his brother fought like a lion at the head of his savages. At last he prudently fled with those who were able to make their escape, and left the field of battle covered with his faithful believers and with their arms and baggage, which were of English manufactory.

Before the attack, he assured his heroes,—by the inspiration, I suppose, of the *Manitou* of Westminster,—that those who might happen to perish in the battle, were expected at dinner with the great spirit; for there are paradises of every kind, and for every people.

The savage of New Mexico, from ignorance, promises one to his horse, when he aids him in the commission of his crimes, and extricates him from danger; but it is to serve the ends of a crooked and selfish policy, that we prostitute this sacred name by promising the rewards of virtue to every villain.

But to come to the *dénouement*. The Americans, although almost always conquerors, have suffered much from these cruel wars, during which their *English half-brothers* compelled them by tyrannical maritime prohibitions, to sustain another struggle, which terminated only in 1814, at the treaty of Ghent. It was also at that time, that, taking advantage of the situation to which the Indians were reduced, they threatened to abandon them to the vengeance of the Americans, which they represented as terrible; and by this stratagem easily drew them over to their side. They were thus all enlisted under the British standard, with the pompous title of the allies of his Britannic Majesty George III. Tecumseh received a brevet of general in the service, and was decorated, together with other chiefs, with a medal in which the king was represented on one side as a hero, and on the other as extending the hand of friendship and fraternity.

These details, my dear Madam, though perhaps too long for a letter on the Ohio, are necessary preliminaries to heighten the surprise with which you will learn the actual prosperity of these countries, notwithstanding the recent date of their civilization and the evils which desolated their infancy.

Kentucky, which is the Eden of the United States, possesses the necessaries of life in abundance, exports largely its surplus produce, and contains about 600,000 inhabitants. They are industrious, enterprising, and brave; but, as I have before observed, they are insupportable from their insolence and coarseness. They are sometimes amusing, but always exceed all bounds of decent manners.

The inhabitants of the state of Ohio are more numerous, although they were not incorporated with the Union before 1803. The rapidity with which the population has increased is a sufficient proof of the abundant means of subsistence;

for in 1790 it had only 3000 inhabitants, and in 1800 the number did not exceed 43,000; while they are now calculated at 700,000. This is perfectly unparalleled in the history of colonization, or of the most flourishing nations. Never did any country, at its first rise into political existence, advance with such gigantic strides. Its progress will be more and more astonishing; for it is inhabited by a people more addicted than any other to the pursuits of agriculture. You recollect the opinions I have already expressed in one of my letters on England, on the superiority of agriculture to manufactures as a permanent source of national wealth and happiness.

The state of Indiana, whose very name suggests the idea of a new creation, was not admitted to the federation before 1810, and now contains a population of more than 150,000 souls. You have seen at Shippingport that its cities and villages are worthy of a civilized country. You must observe that a colony or province cannot be admitted as a member of the great union, as a state, until it has 30,000 inhabitants.

The state of Illinois did not form part of the Union till 1818: it has more than 60,000 inhabitants. It is distinguished for its industry and its agriculture. Its capital, called Vandalia, is a memorial of the state of barbarism from which it has so lately emerged. In short, my dear Countess, in your course along this river, you see pretty houses and smiling towns springing in all directions from the depth of primeval woods and the gloom of solitude, just as the superb Venice and the formidable Holland sprung from the bosom of the deep.

It appears incredible, that a country possessing a soil enriched with vegetable juices which have been accumulating ever since the creation of the world, and a climate whose just proportion of heat and cold promises to render it an exhaustless source of the riches of Ceres, Flora, Pomona, and even of Bacchus, (for the vine, which grows here as in its native soil, seems to invite the hand of man to cultivate it);—a country, where the prodigious number of navigable rivers raises the value of labour, and facilitates exportation and importation over such an immense extent;—a country which, in spite of its vast quantity of water, enjoys, by a singular exception, a salubrious climate (of which its population is an incontestable proof);—could remain concealed from mankind during a period of more than fifty centuries. But Providence had, perhaps, reserved it for times of public calamity, that it might afford an asylum and a consolation to the victims of despotism and tyranny. It is in fact inhabited by a great number of European emigrants. This is one of the cases which would tempt one to believe that everything is foreseen and predisposed by fate, if there were not dogmas which we are bound to respect, and which teach that everything depends upon the will of man, and that this will is free even when he is fettered by the chains of slavery.

But permit me, my dear Countess, to say one word concerning the other emigrants, who contribute in so extraordinary a manner to the prosperity of this New World.

These are the Yankees: a few words will make you acquainted with their origin and character.

The north-eastern states,—New York, Connecticut, Rhode Island, Massachussets, Vermont, &c. are very populous, and consist entirely of free people. Their inhabitants already think they have not room enough, though in Europe each state would form a kingdom; or they perhaps think it not sufficiently fertile; so that when a young man arrives at a certain age and is able by his own strength and intelligence, which are early matured, to provide for himself, his father says to him, "*Go, my son, and make money.*" If the son ask, "*How?*" he only repeats, "*Go, and make money.*" The only patrimony he gives him is an axe, a pick, a cord, and a bridle. You will understand by these symbolical implements, that he must fell forests with his axe, and open the ground necessary to his subsistence with his pickaxe; that the cord and bridle signify that he must provide himself with a cow and a horse; and that he must seek all these requisites wherever fortune may direct his steps. Every year, accordingly, multitudes of Yankees survey, from the tops of the Alleghanies, these immense regions of the west, which they consider as a common patrimony; and each descends into the plain to provide himself with the necessaries suggested by his father's advice and gifts. The first thing he does, after building a house of trunks of trees, is to marry; for a wife is not less indispensable to him than a horse and a cow. The human animal, unfettered by the fear of wanting bread, is as prolific as the soil. In a few years, the spot which only swarmed with insects, swarms with children; the log-house becomes a hamlet, a village, a town, the capital of a province; and states are formed, as by enchantment, from an axe, a pickaxe, a cord, a bridle, a man, and a woman. The creation of a new world, and the history of Adam and Eve, are continually renewed here; here, more than in any other country, the prodigies of nature are manifest; here, the created comes forth visibly from the hand of the Creator. But it appears that man can never escape the scourges which afflict humanity! Herds of doctors and lawyers follow these industrious people, and chicanery and death have already established their empire there. Unfortunately there is no Chinese wall to prevent the incursions of these terrible Tartars.

The Yankees were so called, I believe, from the name of the savages who inhabited the east at the time of the conquest. They are a people as laborious as the Swiss; as frugal and economical as the Tyrolese and the inhabitants of the Lucchese mountains; as cunning and industrious as the Genoese; as droll as the Gascons; as cold and proud as the English; and as selfish and avaricious as those men of all nations who banish themselves from their country to *make money*.

The same phenomenon, which I remarked to you in my letter on the Rhine, has attracted my observations during the whole course of the Ohio. Here, as in the former river, the water loses itself. The Alleghany and the Monongahela are, I believe, about as large as the Tiber. The Kentucky, the Cumberland, and the Tennessee, are much larger. The Kenhawa, the Muskingum, the Scioto, the Miamy, the Green River, and the Wabash, are but little smaller; it receives the waters of more than sixty other tributary rivers, and yet it nowhere presents that enormous volume of water, which it would be reasonable to expect from the influx of so many streams. I am of opinion that subterranean falls and swallows carry off a great part of it. May not the extraordinary *paralysation* of its current at the rapids of Shippingport be an indication that this is the fact?

There are other characteristic features which, in my opinion, are striking proofs that its bed was much more extensive.

In those places where rocks overhang the banks of the river, there are horizontal abrasions which run in a parallel direction, and at the same elevation, on both sides. They are caused by the violence of the current, or more probably by the breaking up of the ice. The soil of the valley is alluvial, whilst that of the heights which border it is diluvial. Lastly, the sands at the back and on both sides of Louisville bear obvious traces that they once formed a branch of the river, and that consequently the elevated ground upon which the city is built, was an island. I firmly believe that the greater part of the waters which fill the great basins called oceans, flow invisibly to the eye of man, and penetrate through the bosom of the earth; which is, perhaps, the still unknown cause of their saltness.

Kant, in his sublime Physical Geography, declares that he found this saltness greater in some seas than in others. This circumstance seems to indicate that the waters pass through strata more or less salt, and confirms my opinion.

We are now got back to the log-house, where I am expecting a steam-boat for New Orleans. I am informed that there is one in sight. I must be at my post when it arrives: farewell, therefore, dear Madam.

LETTER XIII.

St Louis, May 1st, 1823.

In my last, I left you at the confluence of the Ohio and the Mississippi, where I was waiting for a steam-boat. It arrived, and gave my excursion a direction quite contrary to that which seemed determined. At last, my dear Countess, you will assent to the justice of my profession of ignorance of the future; a profession, however, which has no influence either on my conduct or my principles, unless to render me more cautious in declaring my plans; though some persons have very unjustly represented it as fatalism.

All my letters of recommendation and of credit,—the company with whom I had associated,—the *United States* steam-boat, which was soon to return,—in short everything seemed to concur to lead me to New Orleans, to the mouths of the Mississippi, where I was expected on my way to Mexico. Well, my dear Countess, I am now on my way towards its sources.

The steam-boat which arrived, was the *Calhoun;* it was bound for this place. General Clark, the worthy brother of him I mentioned in my last, and major Tagliaware, were among the passengers. I learned that they had often been among the Indians, having been sent by government on some mission into their territory. This was sufficient to induce me to besiege them with questions respecting that people. The descriptions I had read of their extraordinary character had, from infancy, excited both my astonishment and my incredulity; what these gentlemen had the goodness to communicate justified both, and re-awakened a curiosity which I had always intended to gratify before my departure from America: never could a better opportunity arise, nor could anything, I thought, be more interesting to a foreigner; I therefore determined to accompany them.

But before I take you up this river,—the Queen of North America,—we must ascertain clearly where we are; for things, you know, like men, sometimes change their names, when they change their masters. You have not forgotten what became of Napoleonville, swallowed up by the Restoration;—Last year at Paris I inquired for several days for a gentleman with whom I was formerly intimately acquainted, under the name of Mr L . . . . but in vain; the Restoration had changed him into the Comte de la G . . ; and the same Restoration has given our poor departed kingdom of Italy as many names as masters.

We have now, my dear Madam, entered the country which was discovered under the reign of the Mazarins and Louvois,—the Montespans and the Maintenons,—and to which flattery gave the name of Louisiana, in honour of a king who was great only in the panegyrics of his courtiers, and the verses of his pensioners; and whose *bon-mots*, which have been so puffed, and which were so often made for him, afford but poor atonement for the evils he inflicted. A part of this country, to the east of the Mississippi, was ceded with Canada to the English by the treaty of Fontainbleau, in 1762, after that unhappy war in which Louis XV lost New France in America, and ruined Old France in Europe. It was one of the hot-beds of that revolution from which the mother country has so long suffered and has yet to suffer.

The western part, with New Orleans, was

ceded to Spain by a secret treaty, in 1763; as an indemnification for the great sacrifices she had made to France by her co-operation, agreeably to the family compact of 1761.

The war of independence, in which the United States triumphed over the English, and which ended with the peace of 1783, transferred that part of Louisiana which had been yielded to the latter by the French, into the hands of the Americans.

In 1801, Napoleon acquired all the territory belonging to Spain; that is, Lower Louisiana and New Orleans.

As the great preparations he had made to carry these important projects into execution were stopped, in the ports of Holland, by the war which immediately succeeded the peace of Amiens,—a peace, which the English concluded for no other purpose than to gain time, —he sold all the rights he had obtained there to the United States, in 1803, by a treaty of cession. The latter are thus become the exclusive masters of the whole course of this river, and consequently of all Louisiana.

This was the most important of all acquisitions to the United States; for a foreign nation, possessing the mouths of the Mississippi, might ruin all these western and northern countries by a blockade. The name of Louisiana is now confined to the small state of which New Orleans is the capital; the rest of this immense province has been divided into states and territories.

The French gave the name of Louisiana to the whole tract of country extending from the sources to the mouths of the Mississippi, from north to south; and from the Alleghanys to the mountains of New Mexico, from east to west. Profiting by the bull, so celebrated for its justice, which Alexander VI had granted to the Spaniards, they appropriated, by right of discovery, all the countries which were then, or might subsequently be discovered, and even re-baptised the Mississippi under the name of the river St Louis. The ancients would have placed this mighty river among their gods, and its aboriginal name would have been inscribed in the celestial hierarchy.

The Americans, heretics as they are, and rebels to the authority of the popes, have recently done nearly the same thing with respect to the countries which extend from the sources of the Colombia to its mouths in the Pacific Ocean; for what is expedient seems easily reconciled to every system of religion, or of policy.

By this great accession, much superior in extent to that which the English colonies possessed before the war of independence, you may form an idea of the vast territory over which the United States possess dominion in the manner I mentioned to you when at Washington. You may also judge of the immense losses France has sustained since 1763. Now, my dear Countess, we may pursue our journey with more certainty.

We set out, on the 21st of April, from the mouth of the Ohio;—from that fairy land which, like the island of Calypso, enchants by the beauty of its inhabitants; happily, however, there is no need of the wisdom of Mentor, to induce one to leave it: their *bills* are quite sufficient. On quitting it, the grand and terrific scenery which surrounded us was truly magical, imposing, and novel. The waters, extremely increased by a flood, covered the piles of this singular building, and formed an ocean around it; the rain fell in torrents, so that, in the midst of the deepest silence and solitude, it was easy to fancy a new deluge and a new ark. Seated, as if entranced, on the deck of the steam-boat, you may more easily conceive than I can describe, the thoughts awakened within me by this extraordinary scene.

Bird's Island leads the way, and prepares the eyes and the mind for the impressive views, delightful emotions, and heart-stirring wonder with which the majesty of this river affects them, at varied intervals throughout the whole space I have hitherto traversed.

The Two Sisters and Dog-tooth Islands, differing in form, come next in succession, and insensibly lead you to English Island, remarkable as the first place where the English formed a small settlement on this river, in 1765, to establish a claim to it by right of possession. This settlement was almost entirely destroyed by the savages, who liked and still like the French for their manners, and detest every conqueror that has succeeded them.

Cape La Croix, a picturesque promontory at about forty miles from the confluence, rises upon the western bank; and, at a short distance on the same side, Cape Girardeau is not less interesting. These two places were named by the first Frenchmen who saw them in 1674. They had been sent by M. de Frontenac, governor of Canada, who had learnt from the savages, *that a great river flowed from the north, and went neither towards the place where the Great Spirit rises, nor towards that where he disappears.* The little town just formed at Cape Girardeau, is entirely the offspring of the United States. It is a thriving place, and has more than doubled its population in the course of a few years. This is one of the salutary effects of religious and political toleration. It contains many foreigners, and the despotism of Europe will supply it with a still greater number.

You know, Madam, that I am no friend to republics, which often end in *sans-culottism* and factions,—the greatest scourges of society and of the prosperity of nations. Of the two kinds of despotism, the republican and monarchical, the latter is the less dangerous; it is more easy to subdue the passions of one, than of many. The violent acts of republican despotism are generally more atrocious and cruel, because they are the effects and the causes of a greater aggregate of private passions and private interests. In republics, the tyranny scarcely ever perishes with the tyrants, and their demagogues are generally worse than the most profligate of kings. Of this truth, history furnishes convincing proof; and the thirty tyrants of Greece, the triumvirs of Rome, the Cordeliers, Jacobins, Girondins, and Marseillois of France, sanction the belief that their succession is more uninterrupted. Besides, the people of Turkey and Morocco, who know under what despotism they are doomed to live, sometimes succeed in protecting themselves, if not entirely, at least partially, against its cruelty and oppression; whilst the Greeks, the Romans, and the French, who fancied themselves free, were blinded to their danger, and neglected the means of defending themselves against the Lysanders and Callibiuses, the Syllas and Mariuses, the Marc Antonys and Octaviuses, the Pétions, the Brissots, the Dantons, and the Robespierres.

Some men seem to think they can plant republics in all directions as easily as carrots. I like republics when there are no obstacles to their establishment; but in Europe, I think, they are not likely to be productive of any good. It is indisputable that when men become kings they generally become wicked; and it is equally so that it would be difficult now-a-days to find a Leonidas, an Agesilaus, a Marcus Aurelius, a Trajan, an Alfred, or a Henry IV. It must, however, be admitted that the government best adapted to the actual state of Europe is a constitutional monarchy, in which the liberty of the press, the balance of the three powers, and consequently an opposition, which is to empires what light is to darkness, form one combined, harmonious system.

As to republics, we are too old and decrepid. *Bis pueri, in infantiâ et in senectute.* In the first case, though we do not walk firmly, our physical and moral faculties are free to unfold themselves, unfettered by long-established prejudices; in the second, we walk with crutches, which, like the vices of inveterate habit, shew at once feebleness and decline. Republics are, therefore, adapted only to a new people, who still retain some traces of patriarchal and domestic government; who are strangers to the tumultuous conflicts of passion, to luxury, and to the *prestige* of titles, dignities and privileges; whose necks have never bent under the yoke of theocracy and superstition;

> Et où l'air de la cour, et son souffle infecté
> N'altéra de leur cœur l'austère pureté.

The history both of ancient and modern times confirms my opinion: a republic would be fatal even to England; it would alarm the prejudices, the habits, the privileges, and the aristocratical spirit, which are so firmly rooted in the country; it would convert the whole kingdom into one scene of anarchy, and would eventually substitute slavery for that rational liberty which alone is durable, and in which she now so justly glories. It appears to me, therefore, that the inhabitants of the United States are at present the only people who can live under the order of things which they so happily enjoy, the duration of which must depend upon their own conduct and wisdom.

But if I detest the anarchy of republics, I must yet wish that monarchs were more virtuous, just, and consistent; more disposed to recollect that their subjects are men like themselves, and to admit that *plus vident oculi quâm oculus*. I was at Rome, when our celebrated abbé Maï discovered upon some ancient *palimpsesta*, the fragments *De Republicâ* of Cicero. The words which attracted my attention, in this sublime work, were "*Optimam puto esse rempublicam, quæ ex tribus ordinibus constituta est; regali, equestri, et populari.*" What I value in this form of government is, that, while it provides for the happiness of the people, it secures that of the sovereign, accurately defines his duties, and thus tends to keep his mind in that tranquil state which has the most beneficial influence on his subjects. A king under the guidance of these three oracles, which are rendered almost infallible by the check they exercise on each other, is invested, as Fenelon says, with absolute power to do good, but is powerless to do evil. The laws confide a nation to him,—the most precious of all deposits,—on condition that he become the father of his subjects. An inspired voice seems to address him in these words: "Favourite of heaven, to whom the sons of men, thy equals, have entrusted sovereign power,—to whom they have assigned the office of their leader,—consider less the splendour of the rank, than the importance of the deposit. The purple is thy garment, and the throne thy seat; the crown of majesty decks thy brow; the sceptre of power adorns thy hand; but from these thou derivest no other lustre than in as far as they are emblems of thy high services to the state."

A prince (said some one whose name I cannot recollect) who aspires to despotic power, aspires to die of *ennui*. If you wish, in any kingdom whatever, to find the most miserable man in it, go straight to the sovereign,—above all if he be absolute. It is an admirable piece of calculation, to be sure, to render so many persons discontented and unhappy, only to live surrounded by suspicion, fear, and hatred; feelings not less dangerous to the happiness of the state, than to the security of the throne.

Still preaching, my dear Countess, and what is worse, preaching like St John in the wilderness; but a desire for the public good, and for some degree of individual tranquillity, speaks as eloquently in forests and steam-boats, as in great cities and parliaments.

The town of St Geneviève, at about sixty miles from the east, and also upon the western bank, bears the same appearance of *aisance* and population we have already remarked, and suggests the same reflections and the same conjectures.

The policy of Castlereagh in giving a triumvirate to Europe, has, I think, sealed one of the greatest faults of the cabinet of St James's; for while he inflicted this cruel wound on the rights and liberties of the people of the several European powers, he not only put formidable weapons into the hands of their despots, but, by encouraging, or rather forcing emigration, opened to the United States, the great rivals of England, an exhaustless source of population, industry, talents, opulence, and physical and moral strength.

Between Cape Girardeau and St Geneviève is the afflux of the river Kaskaskia, which descends from the east and gives its name to a village five miles from its mouth. This was one of the first establishments formed by the French in the valley of the Mississippi. Almost immediately after the English made themselves masters of it in 1763, it began to decline from its prosperity. The settlers, who hated their new masters, abandoned it, and joined the Spanish settlements on the opposite bank.

Fort Chartres, which the French built at a great expense, on the eastern bank, and which the Americans abandoned as useless, is now of no value but as a subject for a picture of romantic ruins.

Groups of islands scattered here and there, frequently formed most delightful views; they seemed embedded in liquid fire, as the golden rays of the sun were reflected in the water.

At one hundred and forty-five miles from Ohio, a lovely distance—rendered still more lovely by the softening shades of aerial perspective—opens upon you, as by enchantment, for five miles, to the village of Herculaneum, which, in its turn, delights you with the most beautifully varied landscape. If it were crowned too by a Vesuvius, it would be as interesting, and more picturesque than that Herculaneum whose venerable ruins lie hidden under Portici and Resina. Towers built upon the rock, by which it is irregularly encircled, while they enhance its natural beauties, excite an interest and surprise by the use to which they are applied.

From the tops of these towers, which project from the perpendicular rock, is thrown melted lead, that cools in its descent through the air, becomes round, and falls in a shower of pearls, or, in other words, of shot. The large or small holes of the iron sieve through which the boiling metal is poured, regulate the sizes required. A lead mine gave birth to this village, which daily increases in extent and prosperity.

At a short distance from Herculaneum the steam-boat stopped at a little cottage, built with trunks of trees, placed horizontally one upon another, the interstices being filled with a cement of earth, intermixed with straw. It consisted of a ground floor only, and its roof was formed of pieces of wood cleft with a wedge.

I saw a lady come out, very well dressed, and followed by a negress carrying a child wrapped up in very fine linen; she was going by the steam-boat. I thought I was dreaming one of the tales of the *Noyer de Benevento*, when informed that this hut was her habitation.

I immediately jumped on shore, and asked for a glass of spring water; this gave me an opportunity of entering the only door it had, and which made me bow very low. The interior and exterior presented as striking a contrast as that of a lady and a cottage. Her husband, to whom the house belonged, had a small farm, out of which he had to provide for the maintenance of a mother, a sister, and two children of his own.

The luxury in this log-house astonished me; and reminded me of what I had observed in the eastern states: it also led me to reflect, that the decline of this nation might be as sudden as its rise, were not the natural resources of the country so unbounded that its improvement keeps pace with the encreasing wants of the people.

At one hundred and fifty miles from the Ohio is the river Marimak, which descends from the west, and leads to some lead-mines, enriching the banks to a considerable extent in the interior.

On the morning of the 24th, pretty country houses, on the tops of smiling hills, commanding the river—lands cleared for cultivation, interspersed with woods and forests, and the distant view of a number of houses, shewed that we were approaching the principal town of Upper Louisiana, which we reached at eight o'clock in the morning. It is about one hundred and seventy miles from the mouth of the Ohio.

Houses with Chinese projecting roofs, that cover the galleries round each story, and which are rather pretty, though in a whimsical style of architecture, prove that St Louis was a town of some importance even under the Spaniards; but new streets, a new market-place, large stores, busy manufactures, gay gardens, all of recent date, shew that it is greatly encreased since it belonged to a government under whose auspices, merit is the sole distinction; which asks no more than is necessary for the supply of the real and known exigencies of the state, and whose executive is vigilantly watched by a senate, a congress, and by the jealousy of a suspicious and distrustful people.

It is true that there are many abuses in the United States, particularly in the provinces remote from the capital. This is more especially true with relation to the administration of justice, to the appalling number and chicanery of the lawyers, and to the laws which afford security and encouragement to the frequently impudent frauds of merchants. It is true that individuals are not always the representatives of those liberal principles that form the basis of the government; but it is indisputable that their constitution bears the stamp of wisdom and of magnanimity, that it affords the people ample security for person and property, and for their privileges as citizens; and even to foreigners, not only a safe asylum, but a new country, with the free exercise of their religion, talents, and industry, and a perfect independence.

A slight historical sketch will show that it was the restless desire for change, and thirst for gold, which first prostrated these regions, and that perseverance and enlightened principles have now rendered them flourishing settlements.

Father Marguette was the first person sent by the governor of Canada, in 1673, to explore the Mississippi. From lake Michigan, he entered Green Bay on the west, ascended Fox's river, that communicates by a short land passage with the Owisconsin, which he coasted until its confluence with the Mississippi, and descended the latter river as far as the mouth of the Missouri. But as he did not find what he sought,—that is to say, gold and silver mines,—and as he had then neither time nor means for attempting the conversion of the savages, he abandoned his mission, and returned to Quebec without having accomplished any of the projects of the speculators of that place.

Some time after, De la Salle, who was more greedy perhaps of glory than of money, voluntarily undertook to examine this country more accurately. He crossed lakes Ontario and Erie, traversed a desart, and came out at the southern extremity of lake Michigan; he descended the Illinois, but finding nothing answerable to his hopes, he stopped midway in his course, at the point where that river swells into a lake; built a little fort, the name of which *(Crève-Cœur)* was probably but too expressive of the result of his expedition, and soon returned to Canada.

The chevalier Tonti, to whom De la Salle had left the command of this little settlement, was soon weary of enduring all that its name imported, and followed him; while father Hannepin, whom he had sent up the Mississippi, was not long absent from his neophytes at Quebec, whither he brought home no better treasures to the expecting and disappointed governor, than the hope of winning Indian souls to the Catholic religion and to Paradise.

In a subsequent expedition, the French gave the name of *Pain-court* to the spot where St Louis now stands, and that of *Vides-Poches* to a little village five miles from hence, which still bears that name. These names, like that of *Crève-Cœur*, were not very encouraging; and accordingly their settlements had fallen almost to nothing, towards the middle of the last century.

The taking of them by the Spaniards—resisted by the settlers, who did not choose to have any masters but the French—was so marked by perfidy and cruelty, that the name of O'Reilly is never uttered by the people without the epithet, *the cruel;* and they were henceforth subject to the most unbridled licentiousness and the most arbitrary despotism. It is therefore only since they possess a constitution founded on respect for popular rights, and for the general welfare of society, that they have begun to prosper; appearances now promise them ample indemnification for their past calamities.

When we see so many benefits flow from a free government, our surprise is equal to our disgust at the efforts made by sovereigns to strengthen their power by arbitrary principles. A free government invites, encourages, animates; a despotic one enfeebles, degrades, paralyzes. The former attaches people to their country, where they can live tranquilly, surrounded by the objects of their dearest affections; the latter forces them into exile, or embitters their lives by fear, or compels them to live in dreary celibacy rather than furnish new subjects for slavery. The former affords security and content to all; the latter renders even kings insecure, and makes them and the flatterers, the courtiers and the ministers who delude them, a prey to continual alarm; their lives are beset by agitations and dangers; their minds are tormented by remorse,—that terrific chastisement of heaven, which no human power can avert;—the public wait eagerly for their death, to load their memory with louder execration and deeper infamy: while the monarch who spontaneously and sincerely grants a constitution to his subjects, consonant with the claims of reason and of justice, reaps the first and best fruits of the happiness it bestows, both in the benedictions of his people, in the delightful sight of the benefits he has conferred, in the tranquillity which attends every hour of his life, and in the hope that history will immortalize his name; a hope so animating and so ennobling, that Plato took it as the foundation of his system of future rewards.

Thus, as I have told you, the king of Bavaria and the grand duke of Baden can walk through the streets, market places, and public walks of their dominions, without any guard but the testimony of their own consciences, and the love of their subjects. In such a manner, with such principles, under the guardianship of public veneration, and at peace with heaven and earth, it is indeed worth while to bear the burthen of royalty.

All these vast western regions have been much neglected in the history of America: indeed a new one is greatly wanted; for the most recent is obsolete: the country is continually changing its aspect, and furnishing new materials. Few Europeans take such a ramble twice in their lives, and the last comer always knows more of the country than any of his predecessors; who could not see what did not yet exist. This induces me to depart a little from my plan of describing only what I see, and to detain your attention and my pen a little more on these regions.

St Louis, after Napoleon ceded it to the United States, became the residence of the governor, and the metropolis of those vast regions constituting the territory of the Missouri.

Since a part of this territory has been erected into a state, St Louis is only the seat of a district court of justice. St Charles's, on the Missouri, is the capital, and is already a small town, though it was but a little village two years ago (1821) the time at which the state was received as a member of the federate body under the name of the *State of Missouri*. The *territory*, which still exists, is governed by a separate administration, appointed by the executive of the general government of the union.

The trade of St Louis is prodigiously encreased. The merchandize which it furnishes to the traders with the Indians of the north and west, in exchange for their furs, which are almost all sent hither,—the provisions with which it supplies all the garrisons and new settlements over the whole extent of this vast country,—are sources of great profit, as well as of constant employment for all classes. The beneficial effects of its prosperity are widely felt. From New York, Philadelphia, and Baltimore, it receives all the products of Europe or Asia, while New Orleans furnishes it with all that it requires from the West Indies and South America.

The savages, instigated by the great enemies of America, have committed extensive ravages here at various times; but now, with a population of more than seven thousand souls, and defended by several distant forts, built on the principal rivers which flow through their tribes, it has little to fear from their tomahawks.

St Louis has likewise its antiquities. There is no proof that the ancients had any knowledge of the existence of America. Plato's Atlantis appears to me only a dream or allegorical fable; and those who have imagined allusions to America in Aristotle, Diodorus, Theopompus, Seneca, &c., did not perhaps consider that with vessels like those of the Phœnicians, Greeks, and Romans, it was impossible to perform so long and difficult a voyage; particularly without the guidance of the mariner's compass, which was not known till the beginning of the fourteenth century. We are likewise completely at a loss as to whence and how this continent (or island) was peopled; and all the contradictory conjectures of different writers have but shed additional darkness on the subject. It is however certain, that Columbus, Cortez, Pizarro, Verazani, (a Florentine, who first led the French into America,) and Cabot, or Gaboto, all found traces of ancient civilization. To the times when this civilization existed, I think myself warranted in referring the elevations or mounds, in the neighbourhood of St Louis and elsewhere, evidently the work of art, and which attracted my attention, and excited my surprise.

The ancients paid greater honours to their gods than we do; and also to the manes of their heroes or their kindred. Persepolis and Palmira in Asia, Memphis and Thebes in Africa, Rome and Athens in Europe, still bear witness to this by their magnificent ruins, while history gives concurrent testimony to the same fact. The mounds of St Louis appear to me to prove the same in favour of the aborigines of America. Some of them are parallelograms, like the Parthenon and the Basilica at Pæstum; others circular, like the ancient temples of the sun; others are pyramidal, or in the form of the sarcophagi of the Egyptians, Greeks, and Romans. One of them is particularly worthy of mention: it is of an oblong form; its circumference at its base is about three hundred feet, it is sixty feet high, and its summit is a plateau, also oblong, five feet wide and forty-five feet long. A stage of triangular form, which rises to the height of seven or eight feet, embraces the whole eastern side of its base. This is exactly like the altar which the Persians consecrated to their god Mithra; and the great altar of the Olympic Games, and others in Elis were simply mounds of earth.

The gods of ancient idolaters were probably only beneficent heroes, who were first the objects of their gratitude, and gradually of their adoration. The simple heap of earth which covered their remains would thus become an altar; and such perhaps was the origin of these Indian monuments.

From the top of this great sanctuary, the eye commands a delightful and extensive prospect over land and water.

As the population of St Louis is an assemblage of various nations, society is less cold and formal than in purely American towns. The evening before last I was at a very brilliant ball, where the ladies were so pretty, and so well dressed, that they made me forget I was on the threshold of savage life.

I saw some of the Indians land yesterday from their canoes; I was surprised at their grotesque appearance; for being a little given to pyrrhonism, I had always doubted the accounts I had read of them. However, my dear Madam, I hope soon to see them more closely, and to observe the workings of their minds and the habits of their lives, and I shall then be able to judge better of them than by books; for writers often follow the fashion of an artist I once saw at Rome: he was painting a valley of St Bernard, which he had never seen, and without a sketch.

Here, as in the cities of the east, all sorts of religions are permitted. America is a perfect Babel in this respect; it exceeds even England; and the emulation among all these different sects will be still more advantageous to industry and to morals than in that country, from their perfect equality in the eye of the law. The government affords equal protection to all, and recognizes no dominant faith. It has reserved to itself only the right of punishing any who might dare to raise the standard of intolerance.

The Catholics are the most numerous at St Louis ; but their priests here, as everywhere else, bring shame and contempt on Catholicism. They arrogate a spiritual jurisdiction over balls, polite amusements, &c., and pry into family secrets ; then they sow discord among some, disgust others with their interference, and thus scatter schism and scandal in all directions: instead of gaining proselytes, they make apostates. It appears that even here they are resolved to justify the often-repeated accusation, that bishops and Jesuits are the fittest instruments for the oppression and degradation of mankind. It is to be hoped, however, that more enlightened clergy will arise, and will see the danger of defiling religion, and irritating the people; and, like St Chrysostom, Massillon, and other fathers of the church, will denounce the vices of *Tartuffes* and the ambition and tyranny of princes.

Adieu, my dear Countess.

LETTER XIV.

Fort St Anthony, at the confluence of rivers
St Peter and Mississippi,
May 24th, 1823.

One comes to America, my dear Countess, to see a new world; but it is only here, in these desarts, that it is to be found in all the extension of the term.

A river of vast extent, of a majesty which it is difficult to conceive; a country presenting extraordinary features at every step; a race of men entirely different from those of Europe; afford abundance of new and important subjects for philosophical meditation, gratify the curiosity with the most agreeable surprise, and divert the afflicted mind from the subject of its regrets. I have felt every impression which so novel a scene is capable of producing; but it opens a field of reflection and conjecture beyond the extent of my limited understanding, and accessible only to minds of the highest attainments in knowledge.

I will, however, tell you, my dear Madam, what I have seen and felt: you will sympathise in it all.

On the 2nd inst. I set out with major Tagliawar from St Louis, where general Clark, who resides there, remained. Our antiquaries will, I think, this time be satisfied with me. I recommended to his special protection the savage antiquities by which he is surrounded; one of which, a presumptuous hand has already profaned. As an additional gratification, I will tell them that these are by some persons believed to be the military posts of the Indians; but erroneously, for elevations completely exposed, like these, are in direct opposition to their whole system of warfare.

Our passage to this place forms, I think, an epoch in the history of navigation. It was an enterprise of the boldest, of the most extraordinary nature; and probably unparalleled. Never before did a *steam-boat* ascend a river twenty-two thousand miles above its mouth. The vessel which conveyed us was the *Virginia*, one hundred and eighteen feet long, and twenty-two wide, drawing six feet water, and of two thousand tons burthen.

The name of captain Perston deserves to be proclaimed by one of the hundred mouths of Fame. He is justly entitled to the admiration of mankind, to the gratitude of his fellow-citizens, and of his government.

To add to the novelty, the *Great Eagle*, a chief of a tribe of the Saukis, was of our party. General Clark, with whom he had come to hold a conference, persuaded him, with much difficulty, to consign his canoe to some other savages, and join our company. The first thing he did, when we were some distance from shore, was to take off the uniform which had been given him by the general, as a present from the *Great Father*, (the name used by the savages to designate the president of the United States.) He shewed great satisfaction at finding himself once more in *statu quo* of our first parents. The youngest of his two children had not even a fig-leaf, or bit of cloth round the loins, whilst we were shivering with cold, though wrapped in our winter flannel and great coats.

At six miles from St Louis, the current of the Mississippi becomes very rapid. We were approaching the mouth of the Missouri, which is only eighteen miles from that town; and, notwithstanding the power of our steam-boat, we did not come in sight of this river before eight o'clock the following morning.

An island, which obstructs the flow of this mass of water at the very point where it falls into the Mississippi, protects the boats which pass behind it, and breaks the pressure of its enormous volume: but for this precaution provided by nature, it would perhaps be dangerous to pass when the river is full.

Notwithstanding the travels of Messrs Lewis and Clark, (the general Clark just mentioned) and the subsequent accounts of Messrs Brakenridge and Bradbury, the sources of the Missouri are still unknown: it appears certain, however, that its course, from its confluence up to the highest known point, is almost as long as that of the Mississippi, and perhaps the liquid volume of each is equally powerful at their junction. The Missouri should therefore, I think, have retained its name as far as that part where the Mississippi loses its own in the Gulf of Mexico; its course would then have been about four thousand five hundred miles. But a great part of the Mississippi was known when the Missouri was undiscovered; and all the rivers of Louisiana flowing into it, as into a central basin, had already been declared its tributaries. History and geography had already settled its name, so that there was no appeal. But perhaps it has juster claims to its sovereignty. If I can survey the whole of its course, I will endeavour, as far as my attention and knowledge permit, to fill up this chasm in history and geography.

If, however, the Missouri must resign its preeminence to the Mississippi, no one will dispute its supremacy over all the tributary rivers in the world.

The afflux of the Illinois, which is also a very considerable river, is twenty-one miles higher, towards the east. At about two hundred miles above its mouth, Mr La Salle built the fort *Crève-Cœur*. This name appears not to have been more propitious in the estimation of the Americans than in that of the French, for they soon abandoned and demolished the fort. The Illinois took its name from the savage nation that dwelt upon its banks; a nation which, like that of the Missouris, has ceased to exist, or has merged in others. The eastern bank of the Mississippi, opposite the village called the *Portage des Sioux*, leading from the Illinois to the Missouri, rises in abrupt rocks, hewn by nature into perpendicular pillars. They are so like the substructures of the palaces of Pompey and Domitian in the Villa Barberini upon Lake Albano, as to be a perfect illusion. I almost imagined I was there.

This excursion, my dear Madam, is nearly as long as that on the Ohio. It is much more fertile in incidents, and in scenes but slightly known even in America. This may sometimes retard our progress, but I will confine myself to what is most essential or most singular; to the most interesting points, and to the distances most necessary to be known; lest my letter should be converted into a volume, and your patience into martyrdom.

Clarksville and Louisiana are two pretty rising villages; the latter is a hundred and twelve miles from St Louis.

From the top of a pretty hill which overlooks it, the eye rests on nothing but immense and impenetrable woods, the only asylum we have henceforth to expect; for, with the exception of the forts established upon the Mississippi, and a small village called the *Prairie du Chien,* this is the last vestige of civilization towards the north.

The morning of the 6th presented to our view one of those great natural features which mark many districts on the north-west of North America, and especially in Upper Mississippi;—the *Prairie aux Liards,*—one hundred and eighty miles from St Louis.

The United States and Canada, with all their immense dependencies, exhibit one continued forest, the largest perhaps in the world; interrupted only by vast glades inlaid with villages, market-towns, cities, fields, ponds, and intersected in every direction by rivers. Eighteen parts out of twenty, perhaps, still remain in a wild, uncultivated state; of these the forests of the Mississippi are a continuation.

In the midst of these impenetrable masses of trees which cover the face of the earth, and whose birth, life and death are exclusively in the hand of nature, one meets with extensive and beautiful tracts of meadow land, destitute not only of trees, but even of shrubs or bushes; or they sometimes exhibit the still more remarkable appearance of groves and clumps of trees, disposed with so much art and symmetry, that, but for the death-like silence which pervades this vast solitude, it would be impossible not to think that they had been placed there by the hand of man. It is evident too that the grass in these places has never fallen under any scythe but that of Time. This, my dear Countess, is a phenomenon which bewildered my eyes and my imagination.

On the 9th, whilst the steam-boat was taking in wood, I wandered into a forest which bounded one of these beautiful caprices of nature. The varied forms and tints which this contrast imparted to the landscape, whilst they continually arrested my steps, insensibly led me on; and a flock of wild turkeys, which eluded my pursuit, induced me to go so far that I was unable to regain the place where the steam-boat had stopped. In this dilemma my compass was my guide; but what was my suprise at finding the vessel gone! A bend of the Mississippi concealed every signal I could make; and the discharges of my gun resounded vainly in the forest, and under the canopy of heaven. At last I betook myself to my last resource—my legs; but the speed of Atalanta would have been useless among the brushwood and the ruins of *pre-adamite* trees, scattered around like the ancient monuments of Egypt, Greece, and Rome: all my efforts would have been vain, but fortunately, the steam-boat ran a-ground on a sand-bank. At this moment my companions made the discovery that I was missing. The canoe which was dispatched to meet me arrived just in time, for I was so completely out of breath that I must have given up the pursuit. It seemed as if the moment of my appearance had been appointed as that of her extrication; for I had scarcely arrived when she was a-float. If I had been as ready to believe in divine interpositions as some good people, I should certainly not have let slip this opportunity of proclaiming a miracle in favour of a Catholic over a number of heretics, who seemed plotting his destruction.

You are a little angry, dear Lady, with the captain of the steam-boat; but I must, in some measure, take his part. The Americans have a sort of evasive "Yes," very convenient for settling doubts or shuffling off troublesome enquiries; and with a *yes* of this kind he had been made to believe that I was on board. But be this as it may, it is a good lesson for those who, like me, are not punctual when they travel by a public conveyance. Fortune, too, seemed willing to compensate me for any little ill-humour I might have felt at a mark of indifference which certainly seemed *un peu sauvage*. A scene was preparing which afforded me abundant cause for laughter. The Great Eagle, vexed and angry that the pilot had not taken his advice respecting the choice of the channel, jumped into the river and swam to the western bank, whence he spoke to his children; and disdaining to remain any longer in the steam-boat, returned home, that is to say, into the forest. This was the first incident that gave me an insight into the character of these people. The following day we found him surrounded by his tribe at Fort Edward, where he had arrived before us. They had formed a temporary encampment and were exchanging furs with the traders of the South-west Company.

Scarcely were we within sight of the encampment, when the children of the Great Eagle plunged into the river and swam to their den with all the eagerness of wild beasts escaping from a *ménagerie* into their native forests. The Great Eagle came on board to take his bow, quiver, and gun; and although he was exasperated against the people of the boat, he put out his hand to me as a mark of friendship, and as a proof that I had no share in the resentment which he felt for the others. I availed myself of this favourable moment to ask him for a scalp suspended by the hair to the handle of his tomahawk. It was the pericranium of a chief of the Sioux, whom he had killed with his own hand the preceding year. Savages have no control over the impulse of the moment; and as the Great Eagle was now as much softened as he had been the day before irritated, he could not refuse my request. This scalp is as honourable a trophy to an Indian, as a horse's tail is to a Turk, a Tartar, or a Chinese.

Fort Edward is built upon a promontory on the eastern bank of the Mississippi; its situation, which is very pleasant, commands a great extent of the river and the surrounding country, as well as the mouth of the river Le Moine which descends from the west and is navigable for three hundred miles into the interior. The banks of this river are inhabited by the Yawohas, a savage people, who have been almost entirely destroyed by the Sioux.

Fort Edward is two hundred and twelve miles from St Louis; it is on the boundary of the two states of Illinois and Missouri.

It will be necessary, before we proceed, to endeavour to form some notion of the geographical and statistical divisions of the countries we are preparing to visit. Without this preliminary information we should often be quite at sea.

The American government, after having incorporated the whole of Louisiana with the Union, divided into Territories all those countries not sufficiently populous to be formed into States. The whole extent of country beyond Fort Edward, on the east of the Mississippi as far as its sources, belongs to the territory of Michigan, which also comprises all the regions along the western banks of lakes Erie, St Clair, Huron and Superior. All the country beyond the fort just mentioned, on the west of the Mississippi as far as its sources, and even still farther, which belonged to the territory of the Missouri before it was formed into a state, is now distinguished only under the name of *Savage Lands;* for throughout their whole extent there are no other traces of civilization than a few scattered huts belonging to traders, who are themselves the descendants of savages. Arkansau and Florida form two other territories. Each territory is entirely subject to the general government of the United States, at Washington; that is to say, it is under its immediate jurisdiction, and receives from it a governor, judges, and receivers of taxes, as a country still in the infancy of civilization. A territory has the right of sending only one representative to the national congress, who has no vote but in discussions concerning his own territory.

As all these territories are chiefly inhabited by savage tribes, the government has had the wisdom to organize in each of them an *intendancy* and *subintendancies,* whose business it is to watch over and protect these people; to prevent abuses on the part of those who are authorized to trade with them, and to oppose the usurpation of that right by foreigners.

This measure was particularly necessary, because the English North-west company had already extended its establishments very far into the territory of the United States, which enabled the cabinet of St James's to excite and direct, as opportunity offered, the passions of the savages against the United States.

The governors of the different territories are, *ex officio,* the *intendants* of the Indians within their jurisdiction, and general Clark is the *intendant* of all the Indian tribes lying upon the Missouri and Mississippi above St Louis.

After this brief sketch of what is most essential we might more advantageously pursue our excursion; but it will not be amiss to stop an instant longer for the purpose of taking a transient view of these Indians,—the first we meet with towards the north.

The Saukis, half a century ago, were one of the most numerous and powerful Indian nations. The famous Pontiac, the bravest and most formidable savage ever known, was their principal chief. Next to the Montezumas, and the Incas, no one among the aborigines of America has an equal claim to historical celebrity, yet his name is nowhere recorded. He was the implacable enemy of the English, who in vain exerted every effort to bring him over to their interests. He continually harassed them in their conquests of those countries from the French, to whom he showed the most devoted and unshaken attachment.

With a cunning, courage, and ferocity more than savage, he repeatedly massacred their garrisons in several forts, and particularly in those of Détroit on Lake St Clair, and Michilimakinak on lake Huron. At the moment when with unconquerable hatred he was meditating other acts of hostility, he was assassinated by an Ottawais, an emissary in the pay of the English.

His tragical end was the signal for an atrocious war between his nation, who determined to avenge him, and the Ottawais, the Winebegos, and the Potomawais,—savage nations which still exist in small numbers upon lakes Michigan, Erie, Huron, and in the countries east of the Mississippi,—who formed a coalition against them in favour of the English. The greater part of the Saukis were destroyed: their number now scarcely amounts to 4,800.

I visited their camp: their flying tents or huts, which are their only houses, are covered with mats or skins. The Canadians, who may be considered as the classical nomenclators of these countries, call them lodges. They are elliptical. Each of them generally contains a family, sometimes two, with or without their relations; they sleep in a circle upon skins, mats, or dried grass. The fire is made in the centre, as among the ancients, who gave the name of *imagines fumosæ* to the pictures and statues placed in the room containing the fire, from their being blackened by the smoke. In the Indian huts the smoke passes through the round opening in the centre of the roof, the *foramina vel oculi*, by which the light was admitted into the temples and houses of the Romans.

A copper or tin boiler which they get in exchange from the traders, often supported only by a wooden fork stuck in the ground, pieces of wood hollowed into spoons, bits of the bark of trees formed into plates and dishes, the horns of buffalos or other animals cut into cups, constitute the whole of their *batterie de cuisine,* their plate, and their table service. A stake supplies the place of a spit, their fingers serve for forks, the earth for a table, and a skin or the beautiful carpet of nature for their table-cloth.

They all sit indiscriminately around the food with which Providence and their guns supply them. Neither kings, ministers, nor courtiers are treated with any distinction.

In this perfect republic, equality is not less the privilege of animals than men. The dogs, although *illegitimate* and descended from wolves, are seated at the same table with the savages, and at the same *divan;* they partake of the same dishes and sleep on the same beds. I have seen young bears and otters treated as a part of the community.

The faces of the Saukis, although exhibiting features characteristic of their savage state, are not disagreeable; and they are rather well made than otherwise. Their size and structure, which are of the middle kind, indicate neither peculiar strength nor weakness. Their heads are rather small; that part called by French anatomists *voute orbitaire,* has in general no hair except a small tuft upon the pineal gland, like that of the Turks; this gives the forehead an appearance of great elevation. Their eyes are small, and their eye-brows thin; the cornea approaches rather to yellow, the pupil to red; they are the link between those of the Orang-outang and ours. Their ears are sufficiently large to bear all the jewels, &c. with which they are adorned: two foxes' tails dangled from those of the Great Eagle. I have seen others to which were hung bells, heads of birds and dozens of buckles, which penetrated the whole cartilaginous part from top to bottom. Their noses are large and flat, like those of the nations of eastern Asia; their nostrils are pierced and ornamented like their ears. The maxillary bones, *or pommettes,* are very prominent. The under jaw extends outwards on both sides. Their mouths are rather large, their teeth close set, and of the finest enamel; their lips a little inverted. Their necks are regularly formed: they have large bellies and narrow chests, so that their bodies are generally larger below than above. Their feet and hands are well proportioned;

their arms are slender: this may be attributed to want of exercise, which checks the development of the muscles; the only part of the body which savages inure to fatigue is the legs, which are therefore more robust than the rest of their frame. Their complexion is copper-coloured, whence they call themselves the *red people,* as a distinction both from whites and blacks. Except the tuft in the head, which we have already remarked, they have no hair on any part of the body. Books, which deal greatly in the marvellous, convert this into an extraordinary phenomenon; but the fact is that, from a superstition common to all savages, they pluck it out, and as they begin at an early age and use the most persevering means for its extirpation, nothing is left but a soft down.

You know that many of our drivers and coachmen believe that the manes of their horses are haunted by devils who make their nests in them, and that they employ conjurations to drive them away: the Indians, who have the same creed on this point and have neither saints nor *holy water* wherewith to exorcise them, prevent the effect by tearing up the cause by the roots. The Greeks and Romans had similar superstitions, and the Egyptian kings, like others, carefully infused them into the minds of the people the better to enslave them.

You would be astonished, my dear Madam, at the striking coïncidences between the character and habits of the Indians and those of the ancient and modern people of the old world, though their country was entirely unknown to the former, and very imperfectly to the latter.

Notwithstanding the continuance of the cold weather, the men had nothing but a single covering of wool or skin, which serves them by day and by night. They throw it about them with extraordinary grace and dexterity, as the Romans did their *pallium*. Their coverings for the feet and legs, which they call *mokasins*, are made of the skin of the roe-buck, buffalo, or elk, and are precisely like the *perones*, *cothurni*, *mulei* and *calcei* of the Greeks and Romans; but in summer they generally go barefoot. In winter they wear a kind of skin or cloth gaiters, like those of the Cimbri in the time of Marius, which they call *mytas*. They wear a covering round the loins; all the rest of the body, even the head, is naked, whether it rains, hails, or freezes, or the earth is parched with the burning heat of the dog-days.

Their offensive weapons are the bow, the arrow, the pike, the lance, as among the ancients; the axe, the club, the dagger, as among the combatants of the middle ages; the *casse-tête*, the tomahawk, as used by the Tartars of Tamerlane; and the gun used by modern nations.

The shield is their only defensive weapon. It is precisely like that of the early Romans, of leather, round like the *clypeus*, or oval like the *scutum*; but the most singular instance of resemblance is that they paint it as the Romans did, and, like them, trace the origin of their armorial bearings from it; they have already begun to paint upon their tents and elsewhere,—as we do upon the doors or walls of our mansions, —those glorious hieroglyphics formerly painted only upon shields. I have one in my possession which is ornamented with plumes, and bears the head of the *Manitou* or peculiar god of the hero from whom I received it. It is the head of a wild duck, by means of which he expected perhaps to petrify his enemies, as Perseus did with the head of Medusa.

The ephod, from the Hebrew word *aphael*, which signifies to *dress*, was a kind of short tunic with large sleeves. It was first confined to the Jewish high priest, who could not perform his sacerdotal functions without it; and was afterwards in a manner profaned by David, who had the presumption to wear it; after him it was irreverently worn by the whole family of Gideon; and when this nation addicted itself to idolatry, it became a part of the fashionable dress of every woman of rank. It passed from Asia to Greece, thence to Rome, and lastly to these savage countries; for the species of short tunic with large sleeves which comes down to the girdle of the female Saukis, is precisely like the *ephod:* plates of white metal, fixed upon the part which covers the breast, seem an imitation of the *fibulæ* of the ancients. By their roundness they appear to be an emblem of the sun, which the Peruvians also wore upon their breasts.

A petticoat, fitting close to the body, descends to the bottom of the knees, and their legs are covered with a kind of gaiters, resembling those of the ancient Scythian women. The covering for the feet and legs is distinguished from that of the men only by its elegance: in summer, however, their feet and legs are always uncovered. During the period of youth their forms are attractive, but these flowers soon fade: the evening succeeds to the morning without the interval of noon; for these poor women are the porters, the beasts of burden of the men, who, they say, would lose all dignity and become as vile, abject, and despicable, as the whites, if they condescended to submit to any other occupations than those of hunting and war. There is no slavery more abject than that of the Indian women. They are looked upon with such contempt, that the greatest insult to an Indian is to say to him "Go, you are a *squaw* (a woman.)" It frequently happens that these victims of the instinctive tyranny of man have such a horror of the fate of their sex, that they destroy their daughters at their birth, to save them from the wretched, miserable life which awaits them.

They have very luxuriant hair which they tie into what some people call *catogans*, like the carters and *poissards* of the south of France. Their heads, like those of the men, are uncovered, and, like them, they wear a covering for the body, consisting of a piece of coarse blue or red cloth. This is a recent fashion.

The men and women daub their faces with red, yellow, white, or blue. When they are in mourning they paint the whole face, and even the body, black, during a year; the second year they paint only half; and, at last, merely streak themselves with it in various patterns. Both men and women wear ornaments on the neck and arms: some wear what we call *margaritines*, that is to say, small glass beads, or composition trinkets, which the traders sell them in exchange; others, the teeth or claws of wild beasts:—here, you will admit, is something of every age—the most antique, the ancient, the middle ages, the modern, and the very modern.

Enoch tells us that, before the deluge, the angel Azaliel taught young women the art of painting their persons. Isaiah alludes to the same fact in respect to those of Sion; the Greek and Roman women borrowed it from the Asiatics, and Juvenal represents the effeminate priests of Athens as painted with white and red. Ambrose exclaims loudly against the vanity of this custom; the famous monk Hildebrand, (Gregory VII,) imputes this vice with many others to the women of his time, the more highly to exalt the virtues of Matilda, who gave him pretty substantial proofs of her gratitude. Before the time of Peter the Great, the Muscovites striped their faces with all sorts of colours: even in our time, this is practised by many of the nations of Asia; and our ladies, and even our *dandies*, seldom blow their noses without leaving some of their complexion upon their handkerchiefs. It is not a little singular that antimony is an ingredient in the most ancient *rouge*, as well as of that which the Indians regard as the paint *de grand parade*.

That the female savages should wear necklaces, like the Greeks and Romans, is not extraordinary, for they are worn everywhere; but what does surprise one is, that like the women of antiquity they offer them to the departed spirits of their relations, of which I have been an eye-witness.

The custom of wearing necklaces, prevalent among the men, reminds us of that of the Egyptians; it is still more singular, that their bracelets are precisely like the *armillæ* of the Romans, and that they wear them on the upper part of the arm, as they did.

I saw one of these tribes break up their tents to go in quest of a new domicile, or forest. In half an hour everything was ready for their departure.

The lustres, wardrobe, sideboard, equipage, plate, kitchen utensils, &c. occupied the centre of the canoe; the house, that is to say, the mats and skins for the tent, served to cover them; the children, the dogs, the bears, &c. were placed opposite; the men on either side; and the women, at the two extremities, exercised the functions of pilots and sailors: sometimes, however, the men row too.

Their vessel is the hollowed trunk of a tree, and the oars resemble those of our ancestors,— such as artists put into the hands of painted or sculptured deities of rivers. The ease with which they manage these *liburnicæ* is astonishing; and considering how narrow they are, how unsteady on the water, and how heavily they are laden, it is surprising that they so seldom upset.

On the evening of the 6th we set out from

Fort Edward, where we were treated by the officers with much politeness; we soon returned, however, for the steam-boat, being too heavily laden, was unable to make a very difficult and dangerous passage at a place called the Middle of the Rapids of the Moine, nine miles above the Fort. By great good luck we escaped from a rock which might have dashed our steam-boat to pieces; it was only slightly damaged.

On the 7th, while the steam-boat was getting ready, I made a little shooting excursion. I killed a monstrous serpent, almost entirely black, spotted with yellow; it is called by the Indians *piacoiba* (i. e. terrible animal.) They dread it more than the rattle-snake, though its bite is not so dangerous, because it glides silently and insidiously among the briars and grass, and its attacks are unexpected; whereas, the other gives notice of its approach by the sound of that substance with which nature has providentially furnished its tail, that man may have time to escape its pursuit. I have preserved its skin, because I do not recollect to have seen one like it in the museums I have visited, either in this world or our own.

The Indians, at the sight of my prize, welcomed me as if I had been a beneficent *Manitou*. Their nakedness and their wandering life render *wamenduska* (reptiles) objects of great terror to them, and yet no one dares kill them, for they believe that they are malevolent spirits, who would visit their families and camps with every kind of misfortune if they attempted to destroy them.

The next day we ascended, though not without difficulty, these rapids, which continue for the space of twenty-one miles, when we saw another encampment of Saukis upon the eastern bank.

Nine miles higher, on the western bank, are the ruins of the old Fort Madison.

The president of that name had established an *entrepôt* of the most necessary articles for the Indians, to be exchanged for their peltry. The object of the government was not speculation, but, by its example, to fix reasonable prices among the traders; for, in the United States, everybody traffics *except* the government. Fearing, however, the effect of any restraint on the trade of private individuals, it has withdrawn its factories and agents, and left the field open to the South West Company, which has been joined by a rival company, and now monopolizes the commerce of almost the whole savage region of the valleys of the Mississippi and the Missouri. Its two principal centres of operations are St Louis and Michilimakinac, on lake Huron.

At a short distance from this fort, on the same side, is the river of the *Bête Puante,* and farther on, that of the Yahowas, so called from the name of the savage tribes which inhabited its banks. It is ninety-seven miles from Fort Edward, and three hundred from St Louis.

The fields were beginning to resume their verdure; the meadows, groves, and forests were reviving at the return of spring. Never had I seen nature more beautiful, more majestic, than in this vast domain of silence and solitude. Never did the warbling of the birds so expressively declare the renewal of their innocent loves. Every object was as new to my imagination as to my eye.

All around me breathed that melancholy, which, by turns sweet and bitter, exercises so powerful an influence over minds endowed with sensibility. How ardently, how often, did I long to be alone!

Wooded islands, disposed in beautiful order by the hand of nature, continually varied the picture: the course of the river, which had become calm and smooth, reflected the dazzling rays of the sun like glass; smiling hills formed a delightful contrast with the immense prairies, which are like oceans, and the monotony of which is relieved by isolated clusters of thick and massy trees. These enchanting scenes lasted from the river Yahowa till we reached a place which presents a distant and exquisitely blended view of what is called Rocky Island, three hundred and seventy-two miles from St Louis, and one hundred and sixty from Fort Edward. Fort Armstrong, at this spot, is constructed upon a *plateau*, at an elevation of about fifty feet above the level of the river, and rewards the spectator who ascends it with the most magical variety of scenery. It takes its name from Mr Armstrong, who was secretary at war at the time of its construction.

The eastern bank at the mouth of Rocky River was lined with an encampment of Indians, called Foxes. Their features, dress, weapons, customs, and language, are similar to those of the Saukis, whose allies they are, in peace and war. On the western shore of the Mississippi, a semicircular hill, clothed with trees and underwood, encloses a fertile spot carefully cultivated by the garrison, and formed into fields and kitchen gardens. The fort saluted us on our arrival with four discharges of cannon, and the Indians paid us the same compliment with their muskets. The echo, which repeated them a thousand times, was most striking from its contrast with the deep repose of these deserts.

We arrived on the 10th, about noon. After dinner I visited the Saukis, three miles to the east, on the north bank of the Rocky River. Here they had formed their most extensive encampment, the only one they constantly inhabit during the summer months.

In this village, if I may call it so, I witnessed, for the first time, the dexterity with which the Indians handle their bows. Children, nine or ten years of age, hit a small piece of money of six sous, which I had fixed up for them to aim at, at a distance of twenty-five paces,—often at the second trial. At last I was obliged to remove it to thirty-five, or they would soon have exhausted the little purse I had filled for this visit. The chiefs offered us a slight refreshment; it consisted of bear's flesh dried in the smoke, which I thought more delicious than our hams, and of roots, resembling chicory, but less bitter and very highly flavoured: they call them *pokinota*.

They had completed their toilet, so that their faces exhibited every variety of colour. Some, by the hieroglyphics painted on their bodies, reminded me of the mysteries of the ancient Egyptian priests. Those who favoured us with the dance called the *Medicine Dance*, or *Wakaw Watà*, had their bodies covered with them.

As the only people the Indians ever heard of are the French, English, Spaniards, and Americans, and as their conception of the world is confined to those nations, the Saukis were much astonished when I told them that I did not belong to any one of them. I made them believe that I came from the moon: their astonishment was then converted into veneration; for they adore this planet as a beneficent deity, whose rays enable them to hunt, fish, and travel, during the night. Whatever is useful seems to be an object of worship in every part of the world.

This *medicine dance* is the offspring of political knavery and superstitious folly and credulity. It has some analogy with the mysteries of Eleusis, and with others which turn the brains of some of the moderns. The initiated are enclosed within a parallelogram, formed by a small barricade covered with skins: the profane may witness the ceremony, but at a distance.

As I wished to know the whole secret, I determined to try the result of a clandestine entrance; accordingly, I glided into the enclosure, but was turned out, although a son or inhabitant of the moon. A sort of president, whose head is adorned with plumes and with the horns of a buffalo, the points of which are turned inwards like those on the mitre of Aaron and Melchisedeck, takes his station, surrounded by a band of musicians, east of the enclosure. At the west, two warriors, armed with bows and arrows, guard the entrance. A master of the ceremonies, with a club in his hand, stands in the centre, and receives the orders of the president. The elect, male and female, (for some were of the latter sex,) are seated on the north and south, according to his or her seniority or respective rank.

An orator, (for there must be one everywhere,) placed at some distance on the left of the president, every now and then raised his eyebrows, as if under the influence of celestial inspiration, and shewed by every movement of his agitated body his impatience to speak,—perhaps to hear the delightful sound of *bravo* or *encore*. As they have no written language, there is no secretary; this is a great defect: in any other country, a session without a *procès verbal* would be absolutely null and void.

I cannot tell what the president said in his opening speech, for nobody could understand him, not even, I think, his neophytes; but the orator, who almost immediately addressed the assembly, must unquestionably have spoken well, for he equalled in eloquent emphasis the greatest orators of Greece or Rome. The vehemence and animation of the oratory of savages excite astonishment, when contrasted with their taciturnity and apathy in the common transactions of life. Sometimes the inspiration is so powerful, that they tremble in every limb, like the Shakers. I could neither understand nor guess the meaning of his speech; but I conclude that with these superstitious people, as with many others, fanaticism holds the place of reason, and blindness, of belief.

On a signal given by the president, the musicians then played upon their horns and drums; the latter, beaten with a stick covered with leather, produce a very touching sound; but the *neniæ* and *ululatus* to which they beat time, were torturing to the ears, and truly terrific.

At this beautiful music, the president, the door-keepers, the orator, the male and female elect, form a circle; and the master of the ceremonies, from the centre, directs the necessary formalities. Each carries in his right hand the skin of an otter, beaver, or some other favourite animal, made in the form of a bag, open at the two ends; and at the moment the president raises his in the air, the *great ceremony* begins.

The president, making frightful contortions, and fervently stammering out a few ejaculatory prayers, first blows into one end of his bag, the other end of which is turned towards his right-hand neighbour. At this instant, the latter suddenly falls to the ground; no matter in what direction, or whether he break his neck or not, for he is considered dead.

He is only restored to life by degrees, and in

proportion as his exorcist—the same person by whose influence he fell—pronounces some expiatory formulæ, which operate upon him like galvanism: the resuscitated person is then completely purified *ab omni maculâ*. Although he retains the same body, the bag and the ceremony have given him a new soul: a doctrine quite contrary to that of the *metempsichosis*, which transfuses an old soul into a new body; it is also opposed to the creed of the savages of several nations, who seem to hold the Pythagorean hypothesis about death.

If I may presume to give my opinion on this farce, I think the *medicine dance* is only a spiritual medicine, given in this transitory life to prepare the soul for a more successful aspiration to a celestial and eternal one.

The president and his neighbours, and the other persons of the mystic chain, become successively active and passive, until the president himself falls, dies, and is restored to life in his turn; he then closes the dance by declaring that *la séance est levée*.

I expected that my philharmonical friends and the master of the ceremonies would have acted the same part; but either they have some other mode of purification, or they purify themselves by sympathy, like bodies attracted by the force of electricity.

Would that I were a painter! But then perhaps my observations would have been superficial. Let people say what they please, Pangloss is a great man; everything is certainly for the best. There is only one exception . . . . with that you are acquainted, my dear Countess.

In the midst of this laughable scene, I suffered much from not being allowed to laugh. My interpreter, who saw what I endured from the violence I did to my inclination, intimated to me that its indulgence might condemn me to an *auto da fè*. One of the actors threw himself into such violent contortions, that he tore his face; perhaps to serve as a *procès verbal* (in default of secretary) of the session, till a renewal of the ceremonies.

I have been told that no one can obtain admission into this fraternity without the requisite qualities, of which that of a fortunate dreamer is the most meritorious. Our lottery gamblers, and dealers in political systems, might become successful candidates.

I have also been told that those who propose themselves for admission make large offerings, and that they are sometimes obliged to give all they possess to the order. Religious systems are to be found at all times, and in all places; but it appears that the salvation of the soul must be paid for under all;—in modern as well as in ancient times, in the new world and in the old, among savage and among civilized nations. I was told, and I believe it, that in this camp, and in others where they are stationary during part of the year, there are houses in which young girls are appointed to watch over a fire which burns in the centre; like the Roman and Peruvian vestals, the guardians of the Prytaneum at Athens, and the Guebres. It appears that they consecrate it to the sun, or consider it as the emblem of that life-giving luminary.

A bag of such miraculous properties as the *medicine bag*, deserved all my attention; I therefore exerted every effort to obtain one. Vain, however, would have been the veneration I expressed for the prodigies it performed, had I not made a present of good whiskey both to the person who gave it me, and to the high-priest, as a bribe for his sanction. This was the first convincing proof I saw of the resistless, and, as you will soon perceive, fatal allurement of spirituous liquors to the savages.

The next day we quitted Rocky Island, where the gentlemen of the garrison were as polite to us as those of Fort Edward.

The rapids above this island, which is three miles in length from north to south, are stronger and extend farther than those of the Moine; and had not Providence come to our aid and swelled the waters of the river for two days, the steam-boat would perhaps have remained nailed to the rock upon which it had already struck.

Whilst the captain allowed some repose to the crew, who were exhausted with fatigue, I paid a visit to the forests as usual. It was generally thought that I should turn savage, and the captain, as you have seen, had done his best to convert it into a reality: but this time I acted with more precaution.

Chance almost immediately threw a rattle-snake in my way. At first it fled from me; it then stopped, and was in the act of looking at me, when I shot it through the head. I have preserved its skin. It is almost five feet in length, and has six rows of rattles, which indicate its age by the same number of years. Although the head is crushed, the organization of the mouth is still visible: it inflicts the mortal wound with a tooth, which it uses as a cat does its claws. It dips it in the poison by passing it, at the moment it bites, across the vesicle which contains the liquid.

At the distance of six miles from the rapids, we met with another tribe of Foxes encamped on the western bank. Higher up, after passing the rivers *la Pomme* and *la Garde*, which run westward, we saw a place called the Death's-heads; a field of battle where the Foxes defeated the Kikassias, whose heads they fixed upon poles as trophies of their victory. We stopped at the entrance of the river *la Fièvre*, a name in perfect conformity with the effect of the bad air which prevails there. It flows from the east, and is navigable for about one hundred miles.

At seven miles from its mouth the Indians formerly collected lead, which they found in abundance scattered over the surface of the earth. They converted it to no other use than that of making bullets, as they wanted them. The government, which never loses sight of its interests when opportunity offers, purchased, or rather obliged the Foxes to sell, these lands, consisting of fifteen square miles; it has thus secured to itself the rich mines, which it has granted out to adventurers, who pay the tenth of the net produce of the lead. It has established an agent there to watch over its rights.

A whole family from the interior of Kentucky have come to establish themselves at a distance of thirteen or fourteen hundred miles from their home. They were in the steam-boat, with their arms and baggage, cats and dogs, hens and turkeys; the children too had their own stock. The facility, the indifference with which the Americans undertake distant and difficult emigrations, are perfectly amazing. Their spirit of speculation would carry them to the infernal regions, if another Sybil led the way with a golden bough.

A cross-road soon brought me to the mines. The rocks are almost one mass of lead, and the ore produces from seventy-five to eighty per cent. The site is a perfect Thebais. I congratulated this good family upon the prosperity they seemed to anticipate; and I wished Mrs R . . . . much more success in her intended biblical missions among the savages than she had met with in the steam-boat. A young man had turned into utter ridicule both her and her attempt to convert him. She was one of those good women who devote themselves to God when they have lost all hope of pleasing men, and whose fervour, like that of almost all bigots, is mysticism. I must detain you one instant longer at these mines, to describe to you, as I heard it, one of the most remarkable phenomena of nature.

A rattle-snake was killed there with a hundred and forty young ones in its belly, several of which contained other young ones. Major Anderson, agent of the mines and a man of unimpeachable veracity, told me this as a positive fact, of which he had been an eye-witness. I was also informed by some of the traders that this was not the first instance of the kind.

Twelve miles higher, upon the western bank of the Mississippi, are other lead mines, called the mines of Dubuques.

A Canadian of that name was the friend of a tribe of the Foxes, who have a kind of village here. In 1788, these Indians granted him permission to work the mines. His establishment flourished; but the fatal sisters cut the thread of his days and of his fortune.

He had no children. The attachment of the Indians was confined to him; and, to get rid as soon as possible of the importunities of those who wanted to succeed him, they burnt his furnaces, warehouses, and dwelling-house; and by this energetic measure, expressed the determination of the red people to have no other whites among them than such as they liked.

The relations and creditors of Dubuques appealed to the congress of the United States to secure to themselves the adjudication of the property of these mines. It is said, that their claim was founded upon a treaty of cession or acquisition between Dubuques and the Indians; that this treaty had been sanctioned by an act of the baron de Carondelet, the Spanish governor of Louisiana, west of the Mississippi,—and that general Harrison had confirmed it when he took possession of it for the United States, in 1804: but the congress decided in favour of the Indians.

What belongs to the Indians does, in fact, belong to the United States; and it is not usual to give judgment against our own interests. Augustus refused to decide in a case in which he would have been both party and judge, and lost his cause. So liberal a government as the United States should have imitated his example.

The Indians still keep exclusive possession of these mines, and with such jealousy, that I was obliged to have recourse to the all-powerful whiskey to obtain permission to see them.

They melt the lead into holes which they dig in the rock, to reduce it into pigs. They exchange it with the traders for articles of the greatest necessity; but they carry it themselves to the other side of the river, which they will not suffer them to pass. Notwithstanding these precautions, the mines are so valuable, and the Americans so enterprising, that I much question whether the Indians will long retain possession of them.

Dubuques reposes, with royal state, in a leaden chest contained in a mausoleum of wood, which the Indians erected to him upon the summit of a small hill that overlooks their camps and commands the river.

This man was become their idol, because he possessed, or pretended to possess, an antidote to the bite of the rattle-snake. Nothing but artifice and delusion can render the red people friendly to the whites; for, both from instinct, and from feelings transmitted from father to son, they cordially despise and hate them.

A very respectable gentleman, a friend of Dubuques, attempted to persuade me that this juggler was in the habit of taking rattle-snakes into his hands, and that by speaking to them authoritatively, in a language which they *understood,* he could tame them and render them as gentle as doves. I merely observed that I believed what he asserted, because he said he had seen it; but that if I saw it with my own eyes I should not believe it.

These people, proud as they are of their independence, are so inclined to superstition (the inseparable companion of implicit subjection) that they would become the most abject slaves, if they were civilized after the fashion of the Jesuits. In fact, these reverend fathers had rendered the Indians of la Plata so subservient to their will, that they induced them to revolt against *legitimacy*. Whenever this mystical body of men present themselves to my thoughts, even in these wild regions, I cannot help lamenting the blindness and false policy which are endeavouring to re-establish their domination over the world.

To form a correct opinion of what has been,

it would be sufficient to recollect what all the potentates of Christendom, and an enlightened pope, unanimously declared against them; and what had been said at an earlier period by Urban VIII, when, in 1630, he suppressed the scandalous order of the Jesuitesses: but the knowledge that the Loyolists were the mortal enemies of all other religious bodies, only because they were more religious than themselves, and opposed the universal despotism which it was their policy to organize over consciences and over empires;—this knowledge might surely convince the most obstinate and fanatical persons of the nature and purpose of the zeal which influences these gentlemen.

I neither am, nor can be, the personal enemy of the Jesuits; for I was not in being when they were expelled from the whole Catholic world; but as I am the friend of public tranquillity and of religion, I cannot be theirs. While they professed poverty and humility and called themselves the *company of Jesus*, they insinuated themselves into courts, and encouraged every vice that prevailed in them; perhaps for the very purpose of bringing them into contempt, and thus promoting the accomplishment of their ambitious views; they have been one of the grand causes of every revolution which has convulsed society, and have vitally wounded religion by the scandal they have occasioned, and by their efforts to secure to themselves the monopoly both of commerce and of faith.

"The morality of Jesus Christ," says a holy father of the church, "is pure and severe, but simple and popular; it is not propounded as a deep and exclusive science: he reduces it to maxims, adapts it to the comprehension of the most ignorant, and confirms it by his example. Mild and condescending, indulgent, merciful, charitable, the friend of the poor and the oppressed; he affects neither the pomp of eloquence, nor the rigour of asceticism; neither austere manners, nor a reserved, mysterious deportment. He promises peace and happiness to those who will practise his precepts, but he does not pretend to compel them. The faith he requires is rational and free; he has no object but the glory of God, his father, the sanctification of man, the salvation and the final happiness of the world. He is poor and humble, and his kingdom is not of this world." Let any one decide how far the morality of the Jesuits accords with this.

It is urged that they are necessary to the world, in its present state of corruption. It was not, however, by the ministry of obstinate, intolerant, ambitious men, that Jesus Christ undertook to reform mankind: the choice of his apostles shews the contrary. Such men, where-ever they have any influence over kings or nations, are calculated only to plunge the world still more deeply into disorder and misery; and which accounts for the English re-establishing the Jesuits on the continent.

My pen was struck motionless during about forty miles; nor amidst the variety of objects that every moment solicited my attention and excited my astonishment, could I determine where to fix my choice: at length a place which might very appropriately be called *Longue Vue,* decided me at once. Twelve small isolated mountains present themselves in defile, and project one behind another, like side-scenes. They are intersected by small valleys; each has its rivulet, which divides it, and reflects from its limpid streams the beauty of the trees by which its banks are adorned. These hills exhibit a mixture of the gloomy and the gay, while those which appear at the back of the scene are veiled with magical effect in the transparent mist of the horizon. On the eastern bank a verdant meadow rises with gentle slope to a distant prospect, formed and bounded by a small chain of abrupt mountains. Little islands, studded with clumps of trees, among which the steamboat was winding its course, appeared like the most enchanting gardens. It would be difficult anywhere to find a picture in which the pleasing and the romantic predominate with such delightful alternation, and such perfect harmony. One would think that it had been designed by art aided by the resources of nature, or by nature aided by the devices of art.

A little above the river Turkey, which flows from the west, and is navigable to a considerable distance inland, is an old village which the Foxes have deserted. Here terminates the pretended territorial jurisdiction of these savages; I say pretended, for savages hunt wherever they find no obstacle; which is sometimes the cause of, or at least the pretext for, the bloody wars by which they are continually destroying each other.

The true name of these savages is Outhagamis. That of Foxes (Renards) is a nick-name, given them by the first Frenchmen who discovered these countries: it was probably significant of their resemblance to these animals; and indeed they are no blockheads. Their number is much diminished. It scarcely amounts to more than sixteen hundred, who, like the Saukis, are distributed into four tribes.

The Owisconsin is a large river, which flows from the east. At three hundred miles from its mouth it communicates, by means of a *portage*, with the Foxes' river, which falls into Green bay, in lake Michigan. This river is therefore the principal channel of the fur trade carried on by all these savage countries, by way of Michilimakinak and the lakes, with Canada and New York; of which the village of the Prairie du Chien, at the distance of six miles higher on the same eastern bank, is a considerable *entrepôt*.

After passing through a space of about six hundred and seventy miles of desert, this village comes upon one as by enchantment, and the contrast is the more striking as it bespeaks a certain degree of civilization; French is the prevailing language, and strangers are well received. It takes its name from an Indian family whom the first Frenchmen met there, called *Kigigad*, or dog, for almost all the savages are distinguished by the name of some animal, which is often their peculiar *Manitou*.

The Americans ought to regard this village as one of the most interesting scenes of the last war against the English. This is the only place where the Anglo-savage army observed the terms of a capitulation during that war.

The American garrison, which general Clark had placed there in a wretched wooden fort, named fort Crawford, in order to neutralize as much as possible the influence and intrigues by which the English emissaries in these forests endeavoured to encrease the number of the *allies of*

Great Britain, after having opposed an heroic resistance, was forced to surrender, but on honourable conditions. Of these, the principal was intended to prevent the massacres so often perpetrated by the savages, their *commilitones,* upon defenceless prisoners who confided in the faith and sanctity of treaties.

The English colonel who commanded the expedition kept his promise, although acting under the famous general ******* who saw with the utmost indifference the tomahawk and knife of these barbarians daily reeking with American blood. I wish I knew the name of this respectable officer, that I might hold it up to public admiration.

Cikago, Pigeon-roost, French town, forts Milden and Meigs, were the scenes of cruelty which would make you shudder. The heart of captain Wells was roasted and eaten; the whole body of a surgeon was served up as a banquet to a numerous party of guests; nor could even the innocent children whom nature held concealed in the bosoms of their mothers, escape the relentless fury of these cannibals. Such was the horrible scene of massacre and slaughter, that Thecumseh, the general of king George, and the brother of the great prophet whom I mentioned to you upon the Ohio, felt himself more than once compelled to exclaim, "Stop!

in the name of the Great Spirit, our brothers are sufficiently avenged."

Not only did this barbarian savage show himself less cruel than *******, but at the battle of the Thames, where general Harrison triumphed over this sanguinary army, he died the death of a hero, while ******* fled like a coward, abandoning both the Indians and his own soldiers to the fury of that vengeance, the whole weight of which ought to have fallen upon himself. His horse, the interpreter of his conscience, saved him from that ignominious end, which ought to have served as a warning to all monsters who trample under foot the laws of nations and the claims of humanity.

I am convinced that the people of England have never known these horrors, or they would have held them up to public execration. They will perhaps thank me for the information.

The *Prairie du Chien* is the rendezvous of a number of Indians who come there in autumn to lay in winter provisions, and in spring to settle with their creditors, who receive skins in payment. They are much more punctual than the whites would be if they had no other guide than the law of nature, nor any other argument than their bow and arrow, their knife and gun.

I also saw there some of the Winebegos, who are distinguished from all the other Indians by their gloomy and ferocious countenances. They are regarded as the most malignant, and in fact they were most intimately connected with *******. Their chief, Mai-Pock, paid his court to him by always appearing before him with a necklace composed of the ears, noses, and scalps of Americans. I saw him, but refused to shake hands with him; an expression of contempt the most severe and humiliating an Indian can receive. He it was who regaled his friends with human flesh.

It is supposed that this nation came from the northern parts of Mexico; and, indeed, they speak a language peculiar to themselves, and are the only friends of the Sioux, who seem also to have emigrated from Mexico. They roam and hunt towards the sources of Rocky River, upon the Owisconsin, Fox River, Green Bay, and upon lake Michigan. They are divided into seven tribes, who disperse their small summer encampments upon these rivers. Their number is about sixteen hundred. The first Frenchmen that arrived among them called them *Puans*, from the disagreeable odour that exhales from their bodies.

I met there some of the Menomenis, whom the French distinguish by the name of *Folle Avoine*; because, with more prudence than most other savages, they collect in summer a quantity of wild oats, which grow in great abundance upon lake Hinlin, the Kakalin, and the river La Cross, where they hunt and often pitch their tents, which much resemble those of the Saukis, Foxes, and Winebegos. They have nearly the same habits and customs, but are considered more industrious and less barbarous. In the last war, they repeatedly refused to join the standards of the English. They replied to the emissaries who endeavoured to persuade them to enlist, "What have the Americans done to us, that we should go and plunge our tomahawks into their bosoms?" This is a savage lesson to civilized people. Their number does not exceed twelve hundred.

I cannot take leave of the *Prairie du Chien* without mentioning the many civilities I received from Mr Roulet, an agent, and one of the principals of the South West Company.

The Americans generally consider the Canadians as ignorant. Whether this be true, I know not; but I do know that I invariably found them very polite and obliging, even among the lower classes.

Heretics always think they know more than Catholics. I am not skilled in controversy: as to religious tenets, therefore, I shall merely observe that, as the sects which have abjured Catholicism are still without a common centre of union, and are continually wandering from error to error, in pursuit of that true *credo* which they never find, the inference seems to be that they know much less than we. But, in point of learning, it would be easy to prove, from the history of science and literature, that the Catholics were as well informed before the existence of an heretical church, as they are now, and that even since that period they have continued to furnish a large contingent to the literary world.

When ministers, faithless to the laws of the divine legislator, and princes, rebellious to God and the people who confide the sceptre to them, that they may govern *in justitiâ et equitate*, conceal, or disfigure the heavenly maxims of the Gospel, in order to render ignorance subservient to their political views, they are the only persons against whom the voice of censure should be raised: but respect is due to the professor of the most august of all religions.

Nine miles above the Prairie, at a spot where the savages pay their adorations to a rock which they annually paint with red and yellow, the Mississippi presents scenes of peculiar novelty.

The hills disappear, the number of islands increases, the waters divide into various branches, and the bed of the river in some places extends to a breadth of nearly three miles, which is greater by one half than at St Louis; and, what is very remarkable, its depth is not diminished;

for from the Prairie to Fort St Peter we ran a-ground only once, whereas, from St Louis to the Prairie, it occurred four times. This is an additional proof of the correctness of my observations, in our first excursion, respecting the waters of the Ohio. Of three parts of the fluid which compose the ocean, two certainly filter through subterranean passages.

We arrived very late on the 16th, but though it was night—*vi si vedea.* I am going to introduce you to a spectacle, my dear Madam, which, I assure you, I had not dreamt of in my wandering anticipations.

The vigorous fertility of these countries imparts such strength to the vegetation of the grass and brushwood with which they are overspread, that they obstruct the march of the Indians, and in spite of every precaution produce a rustling which awakens the wild beasts in their coverts.

The Indians, who are not easily stopped by difficulties, set fire once a year to the brushwood, so that the surface of all the vast regions they traverse is successively consumed by the flames.

It was perfectly dark, and we were at the mouth of the river Yahowa,—the second of that name, which, like the first, descends from the west,—when we saw at a great distance all the combined images of the infernal regions in full perfection. I was on the point of exclaiming, with Michael Angelo, "*How terrible! but yet how beautiful!*"

The venerable trees of these eternal forests were on fire, which had communicated to the grass and brushwood, and these had been borne by a violent north-west wind to the adjacent plains and valleys. The flames towering above the tops of the hills and mountains, where the wind raged with most violence, gave them the appearance of volcanoes, at the moment of their most terrific eruptions; and the fire winding in its descent through places covered with grass, exhibited an exact resemblance of the undulating lava of Vesuvius or Ætna. Ceres was perhaps seeking a new Proserpina:—we had one in the steam-boat, but certainly no one had the least intention of carrying her off. This fire accompanied us with some variations for fifteen miles. The great conflagration which was one of the causes that accelerated the fall of *l'Homme des siècles* might be more terrific, but it would convey only a very faint conception of the sublime and awful appearance of this. I have no doubt the devil himself was jealous of it; and the moon blushed at her powerless attempts to shine.

A good old woman in our *Bucentaur*, who appeared to me the image of our poor Venice, really believed that the day of judgment was come. Showers of large sparks, which fell upon us, excited terror in some, and laughter in others. I do not believe that I shall ever again witness such astonishing contrasts of light and darkness, of the pathetic and the comic, the formidable and the amusing, the wonderful and the grotesque.

But to repeat the burden of Pangloss—"*tout est pour le mieux:*"—these conflagrations destroy a number of serpents and other reptiles, which would otherwise infest the whole earth; for I have been told that they, like fishes, cross the sea without compass or pilot: and you may judge of their fecundity by the serpent of major Anderson.

As we had travelled almost all night by the light of this superb torch, the steam-boat was tired, and ran a-ground in the morning upon a sand bank by way of resting itself. The place is called *l'Embarras*, from a river of that name which runs towards the west. Here we may apply, *conveniunt rebus nomina sæpe suis.*

During the night we passed before the mouths of the rivers *la Mauvaise Hache, la Treille, et de Racoon,* which descend from the east.

Six miles above the river *aux Racines,* at the west, on the same side, is a place called by the Indians *Casse-Fusils.* It alludes to a very remarkable event in the history of these people.

The first time that guns were given to the savages by the English, much jealousy was excited among those who did not receive them. It happened that a small party provided with those weapons, was attacked by another more numerous who had none, and had all their muskets broken. It is one hundred and eighteen miles from the Prairie.

From this spot a chain of mountains, whose romantic character reminds one of the valley of the Rhine, between Bingen and Coblentz, leads to the *Mountain which dips into the water*. This place would exhaust all my powers of expression if I had not seen Longue Vue. Amid a number of delightful little islands, encircled by the river, rises a mountain of a conical form equally isolated. You climb amid cedars and cypresses, strikingly contrasted with the rocks which intersect them, and from the summit you command a view of valleys, prairies, and distances in which the eye loses itself. From this point I saw both the last and the first rays of a splendid sun gild the lovely picture. The western bank presents another illusion to the eye. Mountains, ruggedly broken into abrupt rocks, which appear cut perpendicularly into towers, steeples, cottages, &c., appear precisely like towns and villages.

A little higher on the same side, is a large prairie,

called *la Prairie aux Ailes,* at which begins the tract inhabited by the Sioux. The Great Wabiscihouwa, who is regarded as the Ulysses of the whole nation, has pitched his summer camp there. It is also the commencement of major Tagliawar's jurisdiction. The Indian tribes whom we have already seen are under the inspection of two other agents of the government, established at Rocky Island, and at the *Prairie du Chien.*

The Sioux are the most numerous and powerful of all the savage nations of North America. It appears, indeed, from their language, that they are not natives of the country, but have established themselves in it by conquest: and, indeed, they are to the Aborigines what the Greeks were in Asia, the Romans in Greece, the Goths in Italy, and the English in the East Indies.

To obtain any accurate knowledge of these regions, or of their inhabitants, one must see and examine them oneself; for though a great deal has been written about the new world,—often either from mere distant guesses, or for the sake of making a book,—it seems that we are still in uncertainty or in ignorance as to the most important facts concerning it. But as my researches have hitherto been impeded by jealousy, I have not yet been able to prosecute them far. I shall therefore defer telling you about the Sioux till a future letter, when I may perhaps have succeeded by time and perseverance in taming or lulling to sleep my Arguses. Meanwhile let us continue our ramble.

The Great Wabiscihouwa came on board the steam-boat with his suite of *patres conscripti*, and the customary high ceremonies were gone through between him and his *father*,—the name which the Indians are taught to apply to the agent of government. Major Tagliawar accordingly gave them plenty of shakes by the hand, and smoked the calumet of peace and amity, and I was the ape to this troop of comedians.

Wabiscihouwa, though wrapped in a wretched buffalo's skin, had perfectly the air and aspect of *a man of quality*. His countenance, his arched eyebrows, his large nose, which he blew with great noise though without a handkerchief,—the motion of his right hand, with which he frequently stroked his forehead and chin,—his thoughtful air,—his eyes fixed as if entranced,—and his imposing manner of sitting, although on the ground, all marked him for a great statesman; he wanted nothing to complete the resemblance but an embroidered coat, a large portfolio under his arm, and spectacles.

The tents of the Sioux are quite different from any we have seen. They are in the form of a cone, covered with skins of buffalos, or elks; the smoke goes out at the top, and almost all are painted in hieroglyphics. For some characteristic features which mark their untutored state, the painter and sculptor might recognise in the countenances of these savages a model of the Roman face; the noses, of the men especially, are quite Roman, while those of the women are perfectly Grecian. The Sioux of both sexes have fine heads of hair, generally black, like their eyes, but almost as coarse and rough as horse-hair. The women, in imitation of those of the Saukis, wear the *catogan*. The men, on occasions of ceremony, or when they are in full dress, generally wear it parted, or in small tresses. These tresses fall upon the shoulders, the breast, the two sides, and the back, and are interlaced with small paste buckles, which the traders give them in exchange for skins. I counted twenty in a single lock of hair.

Their wardrobe and furniture, as well as their canoes and their arms, are very like those of the Saukis. The women would be more attractive than those of the Saukis, if they were not much more dirty in their persons.

This encampment is about one hundred and fifty-four miles from the *Prairie du Chien*. From this encampment as far as lake Pepin, a distance of about fifty miles, the country is pleasant, and diversified by hills, plains, meadows, and forests.

The only two considerable rivers which flow into the Mississippi, within this space, are those of the *Buffaloes* and the *Cypewais:* they descend from the east, and are navigable to a considerable distance up the country.

Near the mouth of the latter begins lake Pepin, which is only a deep valley filled by the Mississippi. But before we enter it, my dear Countess, let us give our attention and sympathy a moment to a subject which is interesting, from the proof it affords of noble qualities in the savages.

A rock, which projects over the eastern side of the lake, precisely where it begins, is remarkable for the same physical and historical features as that of Leucadia. There, the Muse of Mitylene, who was more distinguished for her learning than her beauty, precipitated herself as the only means of curing a passion, which Phaon requited with contempt; here, *Oholoaïtha,* who was beautiful but not less unhappy, resigned a life which was become insupportable to her, separated from her loved and loving *Anikigi.*

If I did not write letters on my rambles, I would write her history, out of which I might make a novel; but a few facts are sometimes much more valuable than whole volumes decked out with fiction.

The tribe of Oholoaïtha was surprised by a hostile band, of which the father of Anikigi is the chief. She escaped the massacre, but was made prisoner. Brought up in the house of the victorious chief, from the age of ten to that of eighteen, the most impressible period of existence, her heart was touched with sentiments of gratitude and love for his son, who had saved her life, and who returned her affection with equal ardour. On the conclusion of a peace, of that kind which both savages and non-savages so often confirm with their lips and belie in their hearts, she was restored to her tribe, and at the same time demanded in marriage for Anikigi. Her father, a barbarous Sioux, and an irreconcileable enemy, obstinately refused to comply with the request of the good Cypewais, who wished at once to gratify his paternal tenderness and the passion of his son, and to consolidate the peace of the two families and of the two nations. Poor Oholoaïtha, seeing the obstinacy of her father, gave herself up to despair, and took the fatal leap: she precipitated herself from this rock, the very day her father intended to sacrifice her to a union which she detested. Heaven knows how many noble minds are concealed under this rude exterior, notwithstanding the vices which their contact with civilized nations has already planted in their hearts.

The Indians devoted her memory to infamy: with them, murder is a meritorious act, but self-murder the greatest of crimes.

Lake Pepin, as you enter it, presents the appearance of an elliptical amphitheatre. It is encircled by little hills of equal height, which, gradually lessening as they ascend, are the *Cunei*; an elevated bank extending completely round it, is the exact representation of the *Podium*. The passages through which the river enters and flows out, are the two *portæ triumphales*—exactly at the north and south, like those of the amphitheatres of antiquity. The waters of the lake formed the *Euripus*, and we were the combatants in the naval games, or *naumachia;* for we found to our cost that the common notion of the savage is not, as is generally thought, a mere prejudice. It is a fact that vessels on this lake are exposed in the daytime to a dangerous sort of whirlwind; we were obliged to resort to some dexterous manœuvres to avoid its consequences. The Indians, who looked at us with astonishment from the banks, were the spectators.

Nature gave the first lessons in architecture; and it is very probable that one of the basins, called lakes, supplied the first model of an amphitheatre. Rome had two of great beauty in the lakes of Albano and Nemi: in the Coliseum, the great amphitheatre of Vespasian, I think I can trace a perfect resemblance to the latter.

Lake Pepin is the head quarters of rattle-snakes. I must detain you an instant to give you some new information, which I have just received, respecting the phenomena of their poison.

The poison of the rattle-snake produces no effect upon pigs; they eat it, thrive and fatten: yet it is fatal to itself; when it is held down with a forked stick, if it can turn its head, it bites itself, swells, and dies. It is an excellent tonic to any one who has courage to swallow it; but it is proved that a wound from its tooth is fatal years after the death of the serpent; nor can chemical agents rob it of its poisonous qualities, although long exposed to the action of the sun, wind, rain or snow.

Four or five miles above the termination of the lake towards the west, we met with another tribe of the Sioux, whose chief is named *Tantangamani*, celebrated as one of the bravest warriors of his nation. He was one of the most ferocious agents of Proctor, and the unnatural father of the unhappy Oholoaïtha.

He came on board the steam-boat to shake

hands with major Tagliawar. He is an old man of hideous aspect, bent under the weight of years and atrocities; but still, the scars with which his naked body was covered,—the dignity with which he wore his buffalo-skin, hung on his shoulders like the *clamis* of the Romans,—his bow and quiver slung across his back,—a club, which added to the imposing gesticulations of his right hand;—and his Indian followers, who, with an air of pride and independance, formed a circle around him, gave him more *éclat* and majesty than are possessed by sceptered kings amidst the splendour of heartless pomp, decked with the spoils of their subjects, surrounded by base slaves who flatter to deceive them, and by mercenary Prætorians, who, like the Romans of Jugurtha and Vitellius, sell themselves to the highest bidder.

He spoke with frankness, though dissimulation is by no means uncommon even among the Indians.

"My father," said he to the agent, "I thank the Great Spirit, that he has granted me another year to behold you once more; for you see that I am very old, and expecting every instant to go to inhabit another earth. I again repeat, that I have been the fierce enemy to your nation, because I had bad advisers, who made me believe that you were coming to deprive us of the liberty of hunting, and to kill our wives and children. But from the time we promised you our friendship, our hearts have been as white as this—(pointing to the agent's shirt.) Give us some assistance; (this is the *amen* of all their speeches) for in this season we can obtain nothing by hunting, and you know that we have no other dependence; be our friends, smoke with us, and in a few days I will pay you a visit at the Fort."

This chief, although seventy, and almost worn out, is still much respected by his tribe, and almost feared. This is the sole effect of the power which true merit exercises over the minds of barbarians, of which this chief is a memorable example; for savages generally neglect their old men, and abandon them to perish with hunger. The Winebegos carry their barbarity so far as to kill them. Probably, however, they consider it a meritorious act to terminate a life, which others spare, only to expose the object of their compassion to the most cruel sufferings, and to a dreadful and lingering death.

I tried to obtain his bow and quiver, by flattering him with the notion that I would immortalize his name by shewing them to everybody in my own country (the moon), and whatever others I should pass through; but finding that this sort of Paradise had but little attraction for him, I offered him in exchange some tobacco and gunpowder. Upon this he immediately grew generous, and gave them to me. Red people give nothing for nothing, any more than white ones.

The place where this tribe was encamped, is called the Mountain of the Gange. Its summit, which is of a flat form, commands a view equal in beauty to those with which I have almost exhausted your admiration. Below me, lay lake Pepin,—the river,—undulating hills and valleys, —forests,—meadows, intermixed with small lakes scattered here and there reflecting every object from their crystal surface,—and lastly, the Gange, which, winding its course along the foot of this lovely mountain, brings the tribute of its waters to the Great River: it was perfect enchantment. I could not satisfy the ardour and impatience of my eyes, and was at length glad to seek repose in the steam-boat, where an atmosphere of Asiatic apathy operated upon me like an opiate. In the midst of these impressive scenes, I heard no other expressions of admiration than—"*Very fine weather!*" "*A very pleasant day!*"

The river Canon, which flows from the west, has its sources in the extensive prairies which separate it from the Missouri. The Indians navigate it in their canoes nearly throughout its whole course.

Between the mouth of this river and that of the St Croix, the Mississippi becomes narrower, and less studded with islands. It is frequently confined between steep rocks, which give an awfully romantic character to its banks. Abrasions, which run horizontally along them, indicate that the waters of this river were formerly more copious; and the traditions of some of the aboriginal savages support this conjecture. Some think that the *Otter's Tail* river, which now flows from the south-east to the north into Hudson's Bay, formerly discharged itself, from the north-west to the south, into the Mississippi, by communicating with the Crows' river, which arises a little to the east of it. These horizontal abrasions frequently assume the striking appearance of friezes, cornices, &c. They were, I have no doubt, the first models of these architectural decorations. Nature is the mistress in everything: art only polishes and perfects.

The river St Croix flows from the eastward. It is a large river, and affords an easy and extensive navigation. The country in which it rises is inhabited by the Cypewais; but the Sioux claim sovereignty over it, which is the cause or pretext for perpetual wars with that nation. This river, I think, received its name from father Hanepin, who probably discovered it on the festival of the cross. It is fifty miles from lake Pepin.

Twenty-two miles higher, at a place called the Marsh, on the same shore, is another tribe of Sioux, governed by *Chatewaconamani*, or the Little Raven. He was gone on a hunting excursion with the principal part of his warriors;—or on the track of the enemy; for when they have no beasts to kill, they kill each other. Perhaps they would prefer to amuse themselves in this way with the whites; but the Americans are become too powerful, and have stationed military posts between their tribes. There is no union among these Indians; and, if I mistake not, the United States think it would be dangerous to them if there were.

War with the savages will ever be defensive. Victories obtained over them would have no other effect than to drive them into their forests, where they are impregnable; whilst the Americans would see their cities and their villages, their fields and cattle, laid waste by fire and sword.

On the 19th we stopped to take in wood. I was told of a cavern, which was only at a short distance from there, and about twelve miles above the encampment of the Marsh.

A small valley on the east leads to it. Cedars, firs, and cypresses, seem to have been purposely placed there by nature, that the approach might bespeak the venerable majesty of this sacred retreat. The entrance is spacious, and formed in lime-stone rock, as white as snow. A rivulet, as transparent as air, flows through the middle. One may walk on with perfect ease for five or six fathoms, after which a narrow passage, which however is no obstacle, except to those apathetic beings whom nothing can excite, conducts to a vast elliptical cavern, where the waters of the rivulet, precipitating themselves from a cascade, and reflecting the gleam of our torches, produced an indescribable effect. You climb to the top of a small rock to reach the level of the bed of this Castalian spring, whose captivating murmur allures you onwards, in spite of the difficulties which impede your progress, and you arrive at its source, which is at the very end of the cavern. It is calculated that it is about a mile in length.

The ancients had yearly *lustrationes*, to purify themselves, their cities, fields, flocks, houses, and armies. The Peruvians used them nearly for the same purpose. The Catholic church has its *rogationes*, by means of which it implores the same mercies of the true god; and in like manner the savages assemble yearly in this cavern, to perform *their lustrationes ;* and, what is more remarkable, at the same season, that is to say, in the spring; and in the same manner, by water and fire, as the Catholics, the Peruvians, and the ancients. They plunge their clothes, arms, *medicine bags,* and persons, in the water of this rivulet; they afterwards pass their arms and clothes, together with their *medicine bags,* through a large fire, which was not extinguished at the time of my visit. This ceremony is always accompanied with a dance round the sacred fire, in a mystic circle, like the *medicine dance.* It appears that this *lustratio* is their corporeal purification.

The cave is appropriated to other ceremonies in the course of the year.

The Indians assemble there to consult either the *Great Manitou* or their particular *Manitous;* and their chiefs, like Numa Pompilius, can make their nymph Egeria speak whenever they want to prevail on a reluctant people to obey them. They perform all their *lustrationes* before they consult the oracle, as the Greeks did before they entered the cave of Trophonius. The Sioux call this cave *Whakoon-Thiiby,* or the abode of the *Manitous.* Its walls are covered with hieroglyphics: these are perhaps their *ex-voto* inscriptions.

This cavern has one great advantage over those of antiquity; credulity is not here an object of traffic. Some religion there must be everywhere, and the one freest from this vice is perhaps the best.

On the 20th we arrived here, where I could not excuse myself from lodging at the colonel's, the commandant of the fort. The extreme politeness with which he opposed my wish to shut myself up, in some independant little room, at first excited my suspicion that his object was to keep a stricter watch upon me; and I confess that I was so malicious as to laugh at this idea, and to make it a subject of laughter to others; but I have since had reason to believe that his intention was to pay me respect, for which I am truly grateful. If any restraint is occasionally imposed upon my curiosity or my enquiries, it is only the effect of that petty jealousy which is to be found everywhere, and particularly in republics; unless they are afraid that I am come to make myself master of these savage regions.

In America you meet with nothing of that hideous police which impedes and molests every movement all over the continent of Europe; and if every individual American choose to exercise the functions of a police officer in his own person, his only object is to know if you are rich, (primo); what rank you hold in society,—for it is utterly false that they are indifferent to that consideration;—what your political opinions are; what business brings you to America; and a number of other trifles, which are rather gossipping than inquisitorial. In America, people are as free and independent as the air they breathe.

However, we may perform the comedy of *Ruse contre Ruse;* and, if the author of the *Caractères Nationaux* is right in the type he gives the Italians, I shall beat the Americans.

Let us rest a little, my dear Countess, for this ramble has been a very long one; nearly nine hundred and twenty-five miles. I hope at least it may have been an agreeable one to you. As for myself, it *ought* to have given me pleasure and relief; but, though the mind may be diverted from its pains for a moment, it soon relapses.

P. S. To give you a proof of my patience, in which you have not much faith, I send you a table of the distances we have just traversed; a task which would exhaust the patience of a hermit. It may be of some use to any of our friends who are inclined to undertake a similar ramble.

TABLE
OF SHORT DISTANCES FROM ST LOUIS TO FORT ST ANTHONY.

NAMES OF PLACES.	Bearings of the bank of the river.	Miles.	OBSERVATIONS.
From St Louis to the mouths of the Missouri,	W.	21	
To the Portage of the Sioux,	W.	12	
To the River Illinois,	E.	9	
To the Great Cape Gray,	E.	13	
To Clarksville,	W.	46	
To Louisianaville,	W.	18	
To the Salt River,	W.	4	
To the Establishment of Mr Gilbert,	W.	13	
To another small Establishment,	E.	8	
To the Two Rivers,	W.	28	
To the Prairie des Liards,	W.	22	
To the Channel of the Foxes,	E.	16	
To Fort Edward,	E.	12	
To the top of the Rapids,		22	
To Old Fort Madison,	W.	10	
To the River Bête Puante,	W.	10	
To the Yellow Hills,	E.	22	
To the River Yawoha,	W.	28	
To the Grande Prairie Mascotin,	W.	16	
To the end of the same,	W.	17	
To the River la Roche, or Rocky,	E.	31	
To Fort Armstrong,	Isle	4	
To the top of the Rapids,		16	
To the Village of the Foxes,	W.	9	
To the Marais d'Ogé,	E.	16	Formerly inhabited by a savage of the same name.
To the old Village Sauvage,	W.	10	
To the Potatoe Prairie,	W.	9	
To the Prairie du Frappeur,	W.	10	Formerly inhabited by a savage of that name.
To the River la Pomme,	E.	18	
To the Chéniere,	W.	10	
To the River la Garde,	W.	10	
To the *Têtes des Morts*,	W.	16	
To the River *aux Fièvres*,	E.	4	
To the Dubuques Mines,	W.	13	
To the Prairie Macotche,	W.	16	From the name of a savage who inhabited it.
To the old Village du Bâtard,	W.	10	A place formerly inhabited by savages, whose chief was called the Bastard.
To the Turkies' River,	W.	16	
To the old Village de la Port,	W.	10	
To the River Owisconsin,	E.	10	
To the *Prairie du Chien*,	E.	6	
To the Pointed Rock,	W.	9	
To Cape Winebegos,	W.	18	
		618	

NAMES OF PLACES.	Bearings of the bank of the river.	Miles.	OBSERVATIONS.
Brought forward		618	
To Cape à l'Ail Sauvage,	W.	10	
To the Upper River Yawoha,	W.	19	
To the River de la Mauvaise Hache,	E.	7	
To the Treille,	E.	10	
To the River Racoon,	E.	10	
To the River aux Racines,	W.	12	
To the Prairie la Crosse,	E.	7	
To the Casse Fusils,	W.	14	
To the Black River,	E.	9	
To the Mountain *qui trempe à l'Eau*,	Isle	10	
To the Prairie *aux Ailes*,	W.	10	
To the River *aux Embarras*,	W.	22	
To the Prairie of Cypresses,	W.	7	
To the Buffalos River,	E.	11	
To the Great Encampment,	W.	8	
To the River Cypawais,	E.	10	
Lake Pepin to the end,		21	
To the River Gange,	W.	6	
To the River Canon,	W.	9	
To the River St Croix,	E.	25	
To the Medicine Wood,	Isle	19	This is a beech, a tree unknown in these countries, and which the savages venerate as a God.
To the *Detour des Pins*,	W.	10	
To the Great March,	E.	13	
To the Cave de Carver,	E.	7	
To the Cave of the Manitous,	E.	6	
To the River St Peter,	W.	6	Where is situated Fort St Anthony.
To the River of the Little Falls,	W.	4	
To the Falls of St Anthony,		5	
		925	

LETTER XV.

Fort St Peter, Mississippi,
June 10*th*, 1823.

How delightful it is to find that the sentiments of friendship can meet us even across the wide extent of sea and land which divides us from our household gods, and can cheer us amid the pains and privations of absence! I have just received your dear letter of the 12th November 1822. The tidings you give me of yourself,—of those belonging to you or to me, and of our common friends, are so interesting to me, that I read it over and over, and know not how to lay it down.

How little did we think, even when we parted, that your letters would follow me into the central wilds of North America, among savages, of whom we had not even an idea. But such is the wayward lot of man.

You enquire kindly about the state of my spirits. The novelty of the objects which surround me, the silence, the immensity of the regions through which I pass, occasionally stop the usual current of my thoughts, or charm them into momentary slumber; but the instant they awake, they fly back to their mournful centre, and leave me once more a prey to melancholy recollections.

You ask me if I have forgotten the use of my pen? My Arguses would tell you that it is always in my hand. When you have read all I have written to you in the short time I have spent in America, you will perhaps beg me to desist. As, however, I have led you into savage lands, I must not let you quit them without making you in some degree acquainted with them.

Let us return to our steam-boat, which has marked a memorable epoch in this Indian territory, as well as in the history of navigation generally.

I know not what impression the first sight of the Phœnician vessels might make on the inhabitants of the coasts of Greece; or the Triremi of the Romans on the wild natives of Iberia, Gaul, or Britain; but I am sure it could not be stronger than that which I saw on the countenances of these savages at the arrival of our steam-boat.

When they saw it cut its way without oars or sails against the current of the great river, some thought it a monster vomiting fire, others the dwelling of the Manitous, but all approached it with reverence or fear.

All the persons on board were in their eyes something more than human. Major Tagliawar, the agent, was astonished at the extraordinary marks of respect with which he was received. The Indians thought he was in the company of spirits;—it matters little whether they took us for gods or devils, for savages pay equal reverence to both; nay, they pray more to the evil spirits than to the good; for, say they, the latter, who are perfectly good, can do only good, but we must take great care not to offend the wicked, that they may do us no harm. If this is not orthodox, it shews at least that the savages are not bad logicians.

Our present ramble, my dear Madam, will begin and end around this fort. I have not been able as yet to go far. But I have no reason to regret either loss of time or absence of interesting incidents.

This fort is in latitude 45°. The river St Peter falls into the Mississippi near the promontory upon which it is built; the two streams make it a peninsula, the former washing it on the S. S.W. side, the latter on the N.E. The fort commands them both admirably, and is delightfully situated. On the south and east it has beautiful and diversified country, and on the north and west immense prairies, whose monotony is relieved by little lakes and groves. This is the last military station of the United States on the north-west of their territory.

Although these frontiers cannot be invaded by a foreign power, unless its armies fall from the skies, yet, being a central point to a great number of Indian tribes, it is a very important post; chiefly as a means of preventing the English from gaining any fresh influence over their commerce or their minds. This is probably the reason that the garrison consists of six companies, and is commanded by a colonel, who is also the military chief of forts Edward, Armstrong, and Arthur, which, on emergency, could send succours to, or receive them from this.

The building of these forts, at such a distance from all possibility of *surveillance* by the government, in any other country would make the fortunes of contractors, and contribute to the ruin of the public finances. Here it does no more than furnish the soldiers' knapsacks a little better: by entrusting the construction of them to their respective commanders, government dispenses with the services of that crowd of engineers who often build and rebuild on an understanding with the contractors. Colonel Snelling's activity and vigilance hardly repose even by night, and one sees walls spring up as if Amphion's lyre had called them into existence.

There are no buildings round the fort, except three or four log-houses on the banks of the river, in which some subaltern agents of the South-west Company live among the frogs. There is no other lodging to be had than in the fort; so here I am following the rule of these Cenobites, to the sound of the drum. I would rather it were the bell of the Paraclete, or of Rancé, or Cominge.

The land around the fort is cultivated by the soldiers, whom the colonel thus keeps out of idleness, which is dangerous to all classes of men, but particularly to this. It yields as much as sixty to one of wheat, and God knows what proportion of maize. Each officer, each company, each *employé*, has a garden, and might have a farm if there were hands to cultivate it.

Every fort built on the Indian territory has an extent of nine square miles. These lots have been sold or ceded by the Indians to the United States. Though these contracts are perhaps defective in the two imperative conditions required by the law *de emendo* of the Justinian code, that is to say, *pretium æquum et consensus (sine quibus non,)* yet it ought to be said, to the honour of the American government, that by this act of acquisition it has shewn that it recognizes the respect due to the property even of savages, who utterly disregard it themselves. Moreover, the chief sovereignty of all this territory belongs to the United States directly, in virtue of the treaty of 1783 with England, and that of 1803 with France.

The first conquerors are the only people who can be accused of usurpation, and as they were justified by *bulls,* it follows of course that nobody is to blame; or, if anybody, it can only be the Indians, as being the weakest.

The colonel has rendered the view of the prairies and forests around the fort much more agreeable, by the introduction of cattle. The country becomes insipid and heartless in time without these animated objects. He has brought oxen, cows, and horses. There are no sheep, owing probably to the too great severity of the winters.

In all the immense tracts we have traversed, from the environs of St Louis to this spot, we have not seen one of those creatures which give animation and interest to the great picture of nature. There is not a single Indian who has a cow, an ox, or a sheep, and very few have horses: this renders it a matter of indifference to them to burn their grass every year, nor do they care if everything else is burnt too; they have nothing to lose, and if the fire approach their camp, their houses are soon transported, either on their heads, like snails, or in their canoes, as the aquatic birds transport their nests when they are threatened by an inundation.

The fort is surrounded by fifteen lakes, all abounding in delicious fish. The one named after Mr Calhoun, the present secretary at war, is the pleasantest, and its conical depth, the character of its banks, and of its neighbourhood, seem to prove that it was the crater of a volcano. It is to the east of the fort. There are two others near it, which communicate; their combined waters are brought through a canal, four miles long, to the edge of a precipice, down which they fall in a most picturesque cascade, which strongly reminded me of one of the Cascatelle of Tivoli. One can meet with nothing grand or beautiful which does not recall some spot of that heavenly country where I first saw the light—that Helen, who is desired and despoiled by everybody—whose charms are continually renewed, and with them her miseries.

"O fosti tu men bella, o almen più forte!"

These two lakes, as well as the others to the east and south, are named after ladies who inhabit, or who have inhabited, the fort.

What a new scene presents itself to my eyes,

my dear Madam! How shall I bring it before you without the aid of either painting or poetry? I will give you the best outline I can, and your imagination must fill it up. Seated on the top of an elevated promontory, I see, at half a mile distance, two great masses of water unite at the foot of an island which they encircle, and whose majestic trees deck them with the loveliest hues, in which all the magic play of light and shade are reflected on their brilliant surface. From this point they rush down a rapid descent about two hundred feet long, and, breaking against the scattered rocks which obstruct their passage, they spray up and dash together in a thousand varied forms. They then fall into a transverse basin, in the form of a cradle, and are urged upwards by the force of gravitation against the side of a precipice, which seems to stop them a moment only to encrease the violence with which they fling themselves down a depth of twenty feet. The rocks against which these great volumes of water dash, throw them back in white foam and glittering spray; then, plunging into the cavities which this mighty fall has hollowed, they rush forth again in tumultuous waves, and once more break against a great mass of sandstone forming a little island in the midst of their bed, on which two thick maples spread their shady branches.

This is the spot called the Falls of St Anthony,

eight miles above the fort; a name which, I believe, was given to it by father Hanepin to commemorate the day of the discovery of the great falls of the Mississippi.

A mill and a few little cottages, built by the colonel for the use of the garrison, and the surrounding country adorned with romantic scenes, complete the magnificent picture.

Let us return to the savages, my dear Madam; we will first try to ascertain the number of their bands, the distribution of their tribes, their ordinary haunts, their population and warlike force.

The Sioux are subdivided into six bands, the Madewakan Tuam, or people of the Spirit's lake. The Wakapetohan, or people of the Leaf. The Wapecothee, or people of the Plucked Leaf. The Sissisthoana or Sussistons. The Yancthoana, or Yanktons. The Pitowana, or the Titons. The former is divided into seven tribes.

ON THE MISSISSIPPI.

The tribe of the Prairie aux Ailes, or Memynoe, governed by the chief Wabiscihouwa, or the Leaf, of whom we have already spoken, is about . . . . 400 strong

Tribe of the Gange, or Gremignieyas,—chief, Tatangamani, or the Red Wing . 200

Tribe of the Marsh, or Ciakántanga,—chief, Cetauwacoamani, or the Little Raven 500

ON THE ST PETER.

Tribe of the Great Avenull, or Wakas-ka-athá, — chief, Wamenitanka, or the Black Dog 400

Tribe of the old Village, or Othoetouni, —chief, Tocokoquipesceni, or Panisciowa 400

Tribe of the Prairie des Français, or Theawatpa,—chief, Sciakape, or the Six 500

Tribe of the Battue aux Fièvres, or Wuiakaothi, — chief, Ki-han, or Red Quilliou 150

The second band forms one single tribe, it is always wandering, but generally makes a halt near the Rapids of the St Peter; its chief is the Wopokian, or the Little Stag. Number 1000

The third band also consists of a single tribe likewise always wandering, it is often seen on the Canon river; its chief is the Kariwassician, or French Raven. Its number is 150

The fourth is divided into two tribes, under two chiefs, Akant-hoo, or the Blue Spirit, and Tatankanathi, or the Standing Ox. They wander about the river of the Blue Earth, or Makatohose. Their number is 3000

The fifth is composed of eight tribes, all wandering about the sources of the St Peter towards the Red river, about the country which lies between these two rivers and the Missouri, &c. The Wanathà, or the Plunger, is chief of the first, the number of which is 1800

He is however a sort of chief sovereign of the Yanctons, and has as great an influence over the whole Sioux nation, from his valour and his exploits, as Wabiscihuowa, from his cunning and policy.

The chief of the second is the Tuimohaconté, or the Little Beaver-Killer. Number 1800

The third, the Ciaka-hapi, or the Lancer 1500

The fourth, the Thaona-hapé, or the Running Original 800

The seventh, the Wawaka-hanà, or the Broken Leg 1000

The eighth, the Waha-koon, or the Medicine Man 1000

The sixth, or the band of Tytons, consists of two tribes, which wander over the country about the Missouri. They are very powerful. The chief of the one is the Cianothepeta, or Heart of Fire; and of the other Ciakahapapi, or the Drummer. Their numbers are calculated at about 28,000

44,950

All these details have been derived from sources to which even my Arguses never had access. They are the purest—indeed, I will venture to say—the only, authentic.

The Assiniboins, a savage people, who wander over those vast prairies which extend from the northern sources of the Missouri to near Hudson's Bay, and who are known under the general appellation of the *people of the plains*, might likewise be considered as Sioux; for, from the information I procured through the same channel,—information which throws great light on the origin of their names,—it appears certain that the Sioux and they were formerly one nation.

A great nation, which came from Mexico, established itself on this side the Cypowais mountains, which separate the sources of the Missouri from the sources of the Colombia, and New Mexico from the western frontier of the United States. These Indians were called Dacotas.

One finds Helens everywhere. The Dacotas had theirs, and she was the cause of as great evils as the beautiful Greek.

Ozolapaïda, wife of Winahoà-appà, was carried off by Ohatam-pà, who killed her husband and her two brothers, who came to reclaim her. Discord and vengeance arose between these two tribes, the most powerful of the nation.

The relations, friends, and partisans of each, took up the quarrel; one act of revenge begat another, until the whole nation was drawn into a bloody civil war, which eventually divided it into two factions, under the names of Assiniboinà, the partisans of the offender's family, and Siowaé, those of the offended;—like the Bianchi and the Neri, the Uberti and the Buondelmonti, &c. &c.

When they wanted greater extent of country they split into two nations, the Sioux and the Assiniboins: but separation and distance did not put an end to their wars, which continued for a long period of time; it is but lately that they have made peace. The event which gave birth to their divisions happened, according to their calculations, about two hundred years ago; and the identity of their language, manners, and habits, adds weight to their respective traditions. I can vouch for the authenticity of these details, though they are perfectly new and totally unknown even to the garrison of the fort.

The Assiniboins always keep together in large bands. When they hunt the buffalo, which is almost their only means of subsistence, they assemble in great numbers, and sometimes form an encampment of a thousand tents. They are supposed to be about twenty-five thousand strong.

The military force of the red men is generally in the ratio of a fifth of their population. This is the body which they call the men of war; but on emergency they all fight,—men, women, and children.

The Sioux are all united by a confederation, but their tribes are independent of each other. Each tribe makes war at its own discretion, and deliberates about its own affairs. They all assemble in a general council on those occasions solely which interest the whole nation. In this case each tribe sends a deputy by whom it is represented in the wood or forest where they hold their meeting. If the resolution of the council is of any importance, and deserves to be registered and transmitted to posterity, a tree serves them as both register and archive; they engrave hieroglyphics, relative to the subject of their deliberations, with a knife or hatchet on its trunk, and each deputy adds the armorial bearings of his tribe.

It appears that four principal or parent languages may still be distinguished in North America; the Algonquine on the North, the Cherokee on the South, the Iroquois on the East, and the Nordowekies, or Nackotahn, on the West. The Sioux speak the latter, which is an additional proof of their Mexican origin; especially as that language is quite different from the others.

It is also said that their religion differs from that of the Saukis, Cypowais, &c. Before we affect to distinguish the differences, we ought to know what each consists in. This, I think, is truly problematical, nor do I see how it can be cleared up, unless religions are all dreams. Without drawing you into dissertations which would only weary you, you will see from what will fall naturally under our observation, what sort of judgment can be formed of their faith. I confess that, from the little I have already seen, I should be tempted to think they have traditions without divinities, ceremonies without worship, and superstitions without religion: the homage they pay to the sun and moon, if it deserve the name of religious worship, is certainly the only one which exists among them.

If we were to judge of religions by external signs, we might come to the conclusion that these savages are Catholics, or at least Christians; for almost all of them, particularly the women, wear crosses. I have counted not fewer than thirty-seven on one woman; she had even one hanging from her nose! This may appear extraordinary, but is, I think, easily explained. The first missionaries sent by the French into Canada, to convert and civilize these people, in all probability sought to win their good-will by presents, of which crosses would of course be the first. The Indians, though abandoned anew to their ignorance and their instincts, were perhaps attached to a sign which reminded them of former hopes, or of the piety of the Black Robes, (for so they called the first Catholic missionaries) and made them their favourite ornaments. The traders, who only try to allure them by the things which please them most, in order to get their furs cheaper, have continued to bring them crosses; and vanity has succeeded to religion, here as in many other countries.

Some travellers have affirmed that the Indians believe in the immortality of the soul. Of this also you shall judge for yourself hereafter; I will only repeat to you here what I myself heard at that awful moment when man, for once in his life, speaks the language of his conscience.

A dying father said to the children and relatives who surrounded him, "I have been brave—be so likewise: I have killed many enemies—kill as many as you can: I have always avenged myself—never forgive the murderers of your kindred." He then recounted to them all his exploits, his battles, his wounds, &c. with as much detail as his situation permitted, and to his last moment talked to them of nothing but his past life, without an allusion to the future; nor did anybody present allude to it.

Another Indian ordered that his dog should be buried with him. As this animal had been faithful to him through life, he wished that it should bear him company even in death. This testamentary disposition seemed indeed to show that he believed in the immortality not only of his own soul, but of his dog's; but system-makers would find themselves surrounded by incongruities they would vainly attempt to reconcile, and by darkness they could never penetrate. I was greatly amused on this latter occasion at the conduct of his wife, who, while she made the customary and proper grimaces and howlings, shewed great satisfaction at the preference he had given to his dog's company over hers. It sometimes happens that these women are compelled either by complaisance, or in deference to public opinion, to follow their husbands to the grave, like the women of Malabar.

I attended some of the meetings of the Indians held in the presence of the agent of government, who is also called the *savage agent*.

These meetings are called councils, and all the tribes or deputations, headed by their respective chiefs, come annually,—generally at this season,—to offer, or to renew, their assurances of peace and amity with the United States. They likewise come to treat of affairs peculiar to each band, or to each tribe respectively, and to make their complaints (if they have any to make) of the traders: they receive any annuities yet due to them from the ceded lands; but their great motive for coming is, to lay their necessities and their miseries before the government, and to receive the presents which it has annually made them for some years past of gunpowder, lead, tobacco, and other articles of necessity or ornament. The object of these presents is, probably, to counterbalance the effect of the captious bounties of the English. Perhaps these measures, which appear liberal and philanthropical, are merely politic; but whatever be the causes, we must admire the effects when they are beneficial to mankind. If the first conquerors of America had employed similar means, their conquests would perhaps have been more secure, and they would have spared the Indians the sufferings, and themselves the infamy, of their bloody victories. It will perhaps be objected that it was the policy of the time to slaughter the savages in a mass, whereas it is now sufficient to look on and let them destroy one another: but it may be permitted to question whether nature or religion sanction conquests which can be obtained at no other price than human butcheries.

When any question is agitated which interests all the tribes who are under the superintendance of one agent, the chiefs and orators of each tribe assemble in the usual council-chamber to debate in his presence and with his assistance. But if the affair regard tribes in the jurisdiction of different agencies, the discussion is carried in the same representative manner before the superintendant-general of the territory. The respective agents then generally form part of the assembly, as being the persons best qualified to give information to the superintendant and the parties respectively.

This is all I have been able to discover as to these different jurisdictions, in the cautious silence which reigns around me.

It certainly is not agreeable to have takers of notes about one, so that I am not in the least surprised at the reserve of these gentlemen, nor at the impediments they throw in the way; but they labour under a strange mistake if they fancy that people will come such a distance, and into such a country, only to shake hands with them and say "How do you do?" They ought to have too good an opinion of themselves to think I can enter into any rivalry with them; it would be madness in a poor and solitary rambler to pretend to compete with national expeditions, provided with sextants, graphometers, *savans*, money, men, horses, flotillas, &c. And, if they are as clear-sighted as they appear jealous and distrustful, they might discover that my character and principles would not allow me to commit them by any indiscretions.

The council-hall is, as it ought to be, a great room built of trunks of trees. The flag of the United States waves in the centre, surrounded by English colours, and medals hung to the walls. They are presented by the Indians to their *Father*, the agent, as a proof that they abjure all cabal or alliance with the English. Pipes, or calumets, and other little Indian presents, offered by the various tribes as pledges of their friendship, decorate the walls and give a remarkable and characteristic air to the room. A table without an inkstand,—for it would be a breach of politeness to write in the presence of those who are ignorant of the art,—three or four seats for the agents, the interpreter and any spectator who may not like to sit, like the savages, on the ground, compose the whole furniture.

The chiefs, the venerable old men whom the renown of their past exploits still renders respectable in the eyes of the young, the prophets, the orators, and the principal warriors, generally attend these meetings.

No formalities are observed, for the Indians use not even a salutation; they touch your hand perhaps if they know you, and consider you as a friend, but always without speaking, and often without looking at you.

There is no demand for masters of the ceremonies, chamberlains, gentlemen-ushers, and the like useful and important functionaries; they come in and go out as they please; they sit or recline as they find it most commodious; neither do they want an ambassador or minister to present them as *gentlemen savages*, or *distinguished*, or *illustrious savages*.

The *séance* opens with a speech of the chief, who rises and addresses the agent. He generally begins with the Great Spirit, or the sun, or the moon "whose purity is equalled by that of his own heart," &c. &c. always finishing with a petition for presents;—*whiskey* is sure to find honourable mention: these are what English lawyers call the *common counts*. The agent replies by the mouth of the interpreter. He begins by a favourable acknowledgment of their friendly sentiments, after which he expounds to them their true interests and the policy it behoves them to follow; he gives them paternal advice, and ends with a flourish about the power, the valour, and the strength of his great nation. Here the scene closes.

The second act begins with the ceremony of the sky blue pipe, or calumet, which the Indians venerate as a Manitou, or Good Spirit of peace; they, however, pay it much less respect than they do to the evil spirit of war, represented by a red pipe.

This calumet is presented by one of the bravest warriors, and by a war chief, who, on this occasion, performs the functions of aide-de-camp of the chief on his right. The agent smokes first, the colonel or commandant of the place (if present) second; the interpreter and other whites follow in succession. The pipe is then passed on to all the red men, beginning by the chief, till it has gone through every mouth.

There is then another pause between the acts, during which the agent and the interpreter are busied in the store-house, preparing for the third and last act. This opens with the ceremony of bringing the presents which *the father* gives them in the name of the *great father*.

The chief receives them without speaking a word or making a sign in evidence of gratitude, or even of the slightest satisfaction. He delivers them to his savages, who depart still more silently than they came, without doing either the *father*, or the strangers who surround him, the honour to cast a look at them. Those who remain in the hall maintain the same air of indifference. The chief afterwards shakes hands with the agent as if to do him a favour, and every one goes his own way. The abbé Casti would not find here either the *Lecca Zampa,* or any other court ceremonies, to represent.

As soon as the tribe returns to its home in the woods, the chief distributes the presents; and those who have killed the greatest number of enemies in the year,—those who have given other proofs of valour,—those who have proved themselves most unwearied and skilful in the chace, are proportionately rewarded. The chief himself is always the last, whatever be his merits, and if nothing remain for him he utters no complaint. The kings among these people think only of their subjects, and they and their families are the poorest among them. If you see a savage, simple in his deportment, sober in his habits, and distinguished by a certain Spartan plainness in his attire, you may conclude that he is a king or a king's son.

Wabiscihuowa, who, though he has not the vices of Agamemnon, has his rank and title; the King of kings of the Sioux was perfectly astonished, and would not believe his ears when I told him that it was not quite usual among our chiefs to give all to their subjects, and leave nothing for themselves; that, indeed, the very reverse sometimes happened. "How," said he to me one day, "you are then more barbarous than those you call barbarians, if your civilization teaches you only to be either stupid slaves or unjust chiefs! we are right then in thinking you inferior to ourselves." I had the mortification to be obliged to hold my tongue before untutored Truth.

Though every meeting is attended with pretty nearly the same forms, though the Indians always preserve the same taciturnity, the same melancholy and sombre countenance, yet very interesting varieties and incidents sometimes occur. Their faces and attitudes are far beyond the reach of the most picturesque or poetical imagination.

I have seen many Hells and Purgatories, Limbos and Paradises, Deluges and Last Judgments. I have seen the *camere*, the *logge*, the *sale* of Raphael and his scholars at the Vatican, and his cartoons in England. I have seen the frescos of Dominichino, Guido Reni, Guercino, Giotto, Cimabue, &c. I have seen Salvator Rosa's Conspiracy of Catiline, and all the most beautiful or most extravagant productions of the Flemish school; but all that is most sublime, horrible, original, and grotesque in them united, cannot equal the strange and extraordinary mixture which is found in the faces, gestures and attitudes of these savages. They would alone suffice to characterize a new world.

Some wrapped in skins with their faces resting on their hands, remind one of the gravity of the senators and magistrates of Greece and Rome: others, when addressing their *father* or their children, unfold their *pallium* with such dignity, their attitudes are so imposing, and their gesticulations so energetic and expressive, that they would be really awfully grand, if one could forget that they are savages.

I was forcibly struck with the resemblance of the chief Wamenitouka to that famous statue of Aristides in the museum at Naples, which has so often held me captive for hours to see,—almost to hear,—him harangue the corrupt Athenians. In the chief Cetamwacomani I beheld that of Cato predicting to the Romans that their vices, their luxury, and their avarice would soon reduce them to slavery. Among those who surround the orator, some listen with signs of approbation, some maintain a haughty and eloquent silence, others appear to attend very little to what he says, and to ridicule both the listening *father* and the haranguing son. Some, resting their right elbow on the ground and smoking their pipe with an affected *nonchalance*, seem as if they despised the whole ceremony; others remaining neutral, like the deputies of the centre, sleep quietly through the business of the nation, and leave care for the future to those who like it. The faces of some are like pallettes filled with every variety of colour, while others, besmeared wholly either with white or black, look like coalheavers or millers; some paint their bodies with winged angels, others with horned devils: every man according to his taste or his devotion. Some decorate themselves with the bones, teeth and claws of wild beasts, the tufts of the buffalo's head, or the feathers of birds; others, with necklaces of glass beads, with ribbons, bracelets, rings and crosses. Some mingle the exotic with the indigenous; others preserve the naked simplicity of nature; and these, though not the most grotesque, are the most interesting.

As they are forbidden to enter the fort with fire-arms, they have only their bows, clubs and tomahawks, which render the whole scene more completely strange and savage.

When the chiefs pronounce a speech, they make frequently very marked pauses, at which all who wish to signify their approbation, call out *uhoa;* i. e. *bravo.* They do the same when the interpreter recites to them, sentence by sentence, the speech of the agent; if indeed they do him the honour to listen and approve it.

Every Indian is at liberty to speak to the agent, as to the common father; but as presumption and gossipping are vices unknown among the Red people, it rarely happens that the agent has to reply to any but the chiefs, civil and military, the orators, or the prophets. Every individual may also lay complaints before him, either in public or private, against the traders; but this is a privilege rarely used, for the Indians will revenge themselves, but will not descend to the office of accuser. There is great dignity and magnanimity in the silence they observe with regard to the traders, who are not ashamed to cheat them in every possible way. This is one powerful cause of their constant and encreasing hostility to civilized people. The Red men, who are most in contact with the whites, are uniformly the worst. The Red women are completely corrupted by their intercourse with the white men. They have all the vices of both races; nor can they find a single virtue to imitate in men who come among them only to sate their sensuality and their avarice.

The North West Company, that is, the English, did worse. In the infancy of the United States, when they had succeeded in getting possession of all the trade with the Indians, they constantly tried to sow discord between the different nations, in order that the rumours of their ferocious wars, and the dread of the tremendous dangers, might deter all competitors from the fur trade; and by this means they obtained the absolute monopoly of it. They were certainly excellent disciples of the British cabinet.

Chance, my dear Madam, is more generous to me than men. It throws facts and information in my way as assiduously as they try to conceal them from me. Never since this fort was begun, three years ago, have so many Indians resorted to it as this year. Within these few days I have likewise had the good luck to witness a presentation, in form, of a great band of Cypowais, composed of a number of tribes, many of whom had not yet done homage to the United States.

Their whole camp was with them, for they always march with arms and baggage, women, children, and dogs. Their houses are wherever they happen to be.

The arrival of their extraordinary flotilla was the most novel spectacle that could be conceived. Never did I see the Mississippi present so busy a scene. Their canoes are of a very elegant form; they are so light and slender, that one wonders how they can carry five or six people, their dogs, their tents, and all their moveables. I have seen them lifted on shore with one hand as easily as a basket. Rods of light wood, not above half as thick as my finger, form all the timbering of them, and the outside is covered with the very thin bark of a tree. It is exactly the papyrus of the ancients; it splits into leaves as thin as paper, and I can write upon it perfectly well. It is the bark of the birch. No nails, nor any metallic fastenings are used. The bark is sewed with threads of other bark, and the joints are then smeared with a kind of tar, which is very tenacious, and resists the strongest heat of the sun. They make it themselves of a resin which they extract from trees, and of some other ingredients: the secret of this composition is kept with great jealousy.

This bark reminds one of the extremely thin planks with which the early Greeks faced their vessels, which were also very light; and the descriptions we find in their poets of the fleets of the Xanthus and the Simoïs, would apply perfectly to the form of the Cypowais canoes. I have got them to make me a model, and to give me a specimen of their tar, which forms part of my little collection of Indian curiosities. It would seem that a breath would upset so frail a bark, and the slightest shock break it; yet in such as these the savages traverse thousands of miles. Their tents are, I might almost say, portraits of their canoes turned bottom upwards. They stick poles in the earth arched towards the top, and cover them with the same bark, which they carry in rolls, like those of papyrus at Herculaneum. Their camps are accordingly as interesting as their fleets.

The Cypowais is one of the most powerful Indian nations, though very inferior to the Sioux. It must indeed necessarily be weaker, from its being more dispersed, and the confederation among its parts less perfect. These are the true aborigines of the country, and their language is pure Algonquine.

They are scattered over those immense regions from lake Ontario to the lake Winepeg, near Hudson's Bay, a tract of about two thousand miles from east south-east, to north-west. It is difficult to calculate the circumference of the country over which they roam. A great part of the Cypowais inhabit the English possessions. Those who came hither live in the American territory, on the high lands of the Mississippi.

Though their noses are rather too flat and too wide, their cheek-bones prominent, and lips thick (like the other Indian tribes,) and their eyes smaller than those of the Sioux, their faces are by no means disagreeable. Their chests and shoulders are better proportioned and stronger, and their whole body better made. Their more rigorous climate and hardier life must greatly contribute to this difference.

All their heads were crowned with garlands of flowers, leaves, grass, or the hair of different animals. These were the favourite *Manitous*, for their superstitions are the same as those of the other Red people.

The Saukis, the Foxes, the Winebigos, the Menomenis, the Sioux, and the Cypowais, all perhaps believe in a Great Spirit; but there is not an individual among them who has not his peculiar Manitou, of his own choice; either an animal, a tree, a plant, or a root; and it rarely happens that two in a tribe have the same. Whether this arise from difference of taste, or whether they think it discreet for every man to have his own god, that he may not be distracted and *bored* with the prayers of others, I cannot take upon me to decide.

One day when I was fishing, a Sioux was greatly offended at my asking him to get me some frogs for bait; the frog, it appeared, was his Manitou—as among the ancient Egyptians; while others of his nation roasted and ate them like all modern nations. An Indian never fires at the animal which has the honour of being his Manitou, even if it is a wild beast coming to devour him. I have in my possession a magnificent skin of a yellow bear, who was on the point of making a dinner of his faithful worshipper, when happily a Dissenter, or *Nonconformist*, came up and shot him. If ever an Indian does kill his Manitou by accident, he begs for pardon, and says, " It is better that you should have been killed by me than by another man, for he would sell your skin, whereas I shall keep it with the greatest devotion:" and accordingly it takes its station among the divinities in the medicine bag. The buffalo is the only animal that is spared by nobody; they all argue that he is the Great Spirit, who presents himself under this shape to provide for all their wants; and indeed every part of the buffalo is useful to them, from the horns, which serve them for a thousand purposes, to the fibres which they use as thread. This doctrine is very fruitful in reflections; I leave it to you to make them. Let us return to the Cypowais.

The assemblies of this nation in the council hall, were more noisy than those of the Sioux, because they were divided into two parties, one of which wished to retain the chiefs now in power, and the other to elect new ones. I should be most happy to give you some account of this comical and truly interesting drama, but I should very likely have allusions fathered upon me which never entered my head. I shall, therefore, only tell you that in the course of their debates I heard bits of eloquence worthy of Athens or of Rome;—that M. B. Constant never employed more resistless arguments against M. de Villèle;—that Peskawè descended from the throne with Spartan dignity, and that Kendouswa extended his hand to him, as he mounted it, with the noble air of a truly generous spirit. I am sometimes astonished at finding the grand incidents of ancient and modern history in these wilds.

General Cass, governor of Michigan territory, undertook, I think three years ago, an expedition across the lakes and country of the savages, in search of the sources of the Mississippi, which Mr Pike had left in great uncertainty; and after fixing them at Upper Red Cedar lake, passed by this fort on his return. He was accompanied by some Cypowais chiefs; and to enhance the glory and utility of his expedition, he used every effort to make peace between them and the Sioux. He succeeded; but the peace was, as usual, as transient as the smoke of the calumet which celebrated it.

Major Tagliawar, animated by a philanthropy which does him honour, and by a truly paternal love for his untutored children, took advantage of the great number of Cypowais now congregated here, solemnly to renew it.

The great hall of the council was full. The Sioux, headed by their chiefs Catewacomani, Wamenitonka, and Penisehiouwa, were seated on the right. The Cypowais, with their chiefs Kendouswa, Moshomenè and Pasheskonoepè, on the left.

After mutual accusations and excuses concerning the infraction of the treaties; afteı some fatherly reproofs and counsels from the Father, Wamenitonka, assisted by a war-chief, lighted the great calumet of *eternal* peace and amity. It devolved upon the Sioux to present it first, since it appeared they had been the first to profane it by their perfidy.

The grave and dignified figure of Wamenitonka greatly contributed to the majesty of the ceremony; on this occasion he assumed a sacerdotal kind of air. He consecrated the calumet, turning the tube first horizontally to the east and west, then perpendicularly to heaven and earth, thus invoking the Great Spirit, or the sun, and the good and evil spirits. He then sent it by the chief of his warriors, to the chief delegated by the Cypowais; he gave it to Pasheskonoepè, the oldest chief, who, after handing it to the agent of government, smoked it himself, and all did the same in rotation, according to their respective ranks. I performed the part of witness; and certainly I witnessed a monstrous act of perjury. The Cypowais repeated the same formalities towards the Sioux, after which all shook hands, as a pledge of their reciprocal *good faith*. The ceremony closed with whiskey, which the good Father distributed to them. The calumets remained as pledges of the sanctity of the treaty, in the hands of the two representative chieftains, who act, I fancy, on that occasion, as keepers of the seals of their respective nations.

When the savages make peace without any foreign mediation, the conference is usually held in the forest. The plenipotentiaries of the high contracting parties assemble there, and the treaty being concluded, it is registered in hieroglyphics in their customary archive, *i. e.* on the trunk of a tree; which comes to the same thing as our *pace celebratâ, die,* &c., *loco,* &c. &c. &c.

The peace was concluded on the 4th inst.;—on the 6th, war was on the point of breaking out again with the greatest fury.

Eskibugekogé, or Flat Mouth, the chief who holds the same rank among the Cypowais as Wabiscihuowa among the Sioux, did not arrive till the morning of the 5th. Ignorant of the intentions of the agent, he took leave of his family and tribe with a promise that he would never touch the hand of one of those dogs of Sioux; which meant that he would never make peace with them. The first person he met on approaching the fort, before he could be informed of what had passed, was Paniscihowa, who held out his hand, warmed with the scene of the preceding evening, and was met by a disdainful repulse.

The Sioux, as ill-disposed as he was cowardly, immediately gave the alarm. All the Sioux who were still in the vicinity of the fort flocked together, they sent heralds at arms to the neighbouring encampments, and the next day they surrounded the camp of the Cypowais in great force. The latter had already concealed their women and children behind the ruins of the old fort, which had served as an asylum to the garrison while the new one was building: and sent a message to the Sioux that, though very inferior in numbers, they did not fear them, and steadily awaited their attack.

At first the agent and the colonel appeared not to choose to take any part in their quarrel. They have perhaps the power of making up a peace among them, but not of preventing a war. They reflected, however, that to suffer them to come to open hostilities, would be to permit an insult to the American flag, and a violation of their territory, declared neutral, sacred and inviolable to all Indians; more especially when they came to treat with their *Father*. They were therefore warned to disperse, which they accordingly did.

Everything conspired against my poor notes; I had already perched myself on an eminence for the purpose of enriching them with an Indian battle, and behold I have nothing to write but this miserable article! In the afternoon, Eskibugekogé shook hands in all the requisite forms, both with the Sioux chiefs and with all who had a mind.

They smoked again perfectly *en règle*,—repeated with great good-will and alacrity the libations of whiskey, and all walked away the best friends in the world.

The next day it was reported that the Sioux had attacked the Cypowais at the falls of St Anthony. I instantly set out on horseback, but it was decreed that I was not to witness that extraordinary spectacle. While the serjeant who commanded the posts was exhorting them to peace, (for fear they should lay waste the settlement,) the express he had sent to the fort returned with troops, and so the affair ended. I had half a mind to ask them to be so obliging as to fight in jest, as they would not fight in earnest. I almost suspected that the savages were in a league with the gentlemen of the fort to disappoint me. But here one may sincerely say, "All is for the best." What frightful carnage should I have witnessed!

This tragi-comedy, however, procured me what I stand so much in need of,—a hearty laugh; and it was at the expense of the traders. These worthy men trembled for at least four days afterwards, at the recollection of the danger they had run,—of losing the advances they had made to the Indians. They thought it scandalously dishonest in them to kill one another before they had killed the beasts whose skins were to constitute the payment. And I do really believe that, on the day of the alarm, they sincerely wished they had been brave enough to go among the Indians and try to pacify them.

One would say, that the pest of usurers and brokers, who are the curse of Europe and the ruin of so many young men of family, has spread to the forests and deserts of America.

You will doubtless be astonished, my dear Madam, at the irreconcileable hatred which exists between these two savage nations. I will tell you all I know about it.

Territorial claims are mere pretexts; their countries, or rather their worlds, are so vast, that there is room for all; and they hardly ever meet, unless they lay in wait for each other for the express purpose of fighting. These wars are only an inheritance they have received from their fathers. The first thing a dying Cypowais recommends to his children, relatives, friends, and all his tribe, is to preserve perpetual enmity to the Sioux; who, on their side, preach the same sort of crusade against the Cypowais. In my endeavours to trace this inveterate hostility to its sources, I succeeded also in throwing some light on the emigration of the Sioux into these countries.

Eskibugekogé assured me that they (the Cypowais) had been at war with the Sioux for more than three thousand moons; with which the great Sioux, Wabiscihouwa's, statement concurred.

Reckoning twelve moons to a year, as they do, more than three thousand moons, adding the complementary days, bring us pretty nearly to the time of the conquest of Mexico by the Spaniards. It was therefore, in all probability, at that period that the Sioux, or Dacotas, flying from the cruelties of the conquerors, invaded the country of the Cypowais, of which they have retained possession; and the Cypowais, massacred or driven from their accustomed haunts, would naturally enough swear eternal vengeance on their aggressors. This sentiment, carefully transmitted from father to son, became a national one, perpetuated through all generations, and now blindly followed as an inspiration or a duty. And as revenge is the predominant passion of all savages, the Sioux are equally inveterate against the Cypowais, and carry on a war of instinct, equally indifferent about the cause or the effects.

Another convincing proof, that the countries now inhabited by the Sioux, the Assiniboins, and other savage nations, who, like them, emigrated from Mexico, formerly belonged to the Cypowais, is, that the mountains which separate these countries from New Mexico, were called the

Cypowaises Mountains; and would be called so to this day, if those most illustrious *expeditions*, which would turn the world topsy-turvy for the sake of being talked of, had not re-baptized them under the name of the *Rocky Mountains*. Before we take leave of the Cypowais, I must tell you a little about their women.

They are much better looking than the Sioux women, and some of them might almost be called pretty. Their persons are fine; their flesh is firmer and in better preservation, and their complexions less red. The cold climate they inhabit has nearly the same effect upon the men. Their mouths and teeth are almost beautiful. Their character appears more simple and less savage; their dress is quite different, and very singular.

When the Egyptians had made sufficient progress in the art of sculpture, to detach the arms and legs of the statues from the block of which their first efforts, the Theuts or Hermes, were composed, they ornamented them with two bands hanging from the shoulders over the bosom; they afterwards added a third, joining horizontally to the ends of the two former. This is precisely the sort of thing which supports a kind of cuirass, of leather or cloth, which covers the bosom and the back of the Cypowais women. Their round and well-turned arms are perfectly naked, and are painted with hieroglyphics to match their faces. Their shoes are of a more antique form than those we have seen; their coverings for the legs, and their petticoats are not much unlike those of the Sioux but are more simple. They wear a great many crosses, all hanging from their nostrils.

Their hatred to the Sioux is still more furious and inveterate than that of the men. This is easily explained. Their camps being nearly always taken by surprise, the poor women are much more exposed to cruelty and carnage than the men; this has also the effect of making them all heroines. During the alarm of the 6th, they all swore, with knives in their hands, to sell dearly their own lives and those of their children, whom they hung over and shielded with their own bodies. I was deeply affected at seeing, even among savages, the force of the tenderest and strongest of all human affections—maternal love.

Au revoir, dear Madam,—I wish it may be farther on;—but I doubt it.

LETTER XVI.

Fort St Peter, on the Upper Mississippi,
June 28*th*, 1823.

THIS is my third letter to you dated from this place; a sufficient indication, my dear Countess, of the difficulties and impediments which I still experience in my progress.

Major Tagliawar had led me to entertain the hope that we should have proceeded together up the river St Peter, which has never yet been explored, the sources of which are occupied by the most wild and powerful tribes of the *Sioux*, and as yet only vaguely defined; while the surrounding territory abounds in buffalos, the hunting of which furnishes the genuine sportsman with the most interesting as well as curious diversion. It was my intention to proceed thence towards the sources of the Mississippi, which are still absolutely unknown; but Mr Tagliawar now feels his health weak, and can proceed no farther. I cannot help fancying that it is intended to lull my projects into lethargy. I am not, however, so easily hushed into inaction and forgetfulness. My constancy against difficulties perpetually increases. The lists are always open; I feel as yet firm in the saddle, and shall sustain, be assured, many a shock and conflict before I surrender. In the meantime, my dear Countess, let us take a social excursion among the neighbouring tribes, to learn something of the manners and customs of these Indians. Let nothing stop or discourage our efforts.

Let us recur to dancing, which among the Indians is a formality of indispensable importance, as with it they open and conclude every description of business, public and private, civil and sacred. It has part in every transaction, like the priest in our own country, like gas in chemistry, like bleeding among the disciples of our celebrated Thomasini.

In order to avoid useless repetition as much as possible, it may be advisable to mention, once for all, that their instrumental music is always the same, and that its tone is seldom changed. With respect to what is properly called vocal music, they have nothing that can be called such; for, when they pretend to sing, they either bawl or scream.

Their instruments consist of tabors, a species of castanets, and small leather or parchment globes, containing within them a few grains of hard seeds. Each dancer holds one of these globes in his right hand, agitating it as he dances, in order to mark the cadence. From the sound produced by them they are called *cicikoics*.

The war-dance can be performed only by warriors. It is this which they exhibit before the agent, when they come in a body to make him a formal visit.

Women and old men station themselves behind the performers, and join chorus in the canticle which each person present utters in accompaniment to the instruments. To give you any idea, however, of the clatter and hubbub of music thus produced, it would be necessary to be either an Indian or a Jew.

They open the dance by advancing in a spacious area, in two files if the party be large, but in one if it happen to be small. A child advances before them with its castanets, or *cicikoics*, in its hand. This is the dreaming or vision-visited child, in whom good and evil spirits sometimes pass the night, making him the depositary of their good or evil presages. The prophet or augur of the tribe collects these presages every morning, and, like the rest of his profession, whether in ancient or in modern times, converts them dextrously to his own purposes; —and while moving in the dance behind the files of the performers, this important personage explains to the brave exhibitants that the *Manitous*, the good or evil spirits, are well acquainted with their valour, and engage to crown it with everlasting glory, if they remain constant in the sentiments of hatred and vengeance against their enemies. After this, my dear Countess, you will see how difficult it is to pronounce on the nature and character of their religion!

Animated by this consoling and heart-invigorating promise, the dancers form in close circle, and set up a sort of hoarse bellowing, while the inspired child, the young demi-deity, with eyes bent down to the earth, utters something which none of those to whom it is addressed comprehend, and which indeed is not understood either by himself or the prophet: for the child is merely the organ through which the *Manitous* speak; and oracles, you are well aware, are never meant to be clear and intelligible to all the world. The moment the child's eyes are raised from the ground, the whole company of these fanatics set up a series of clumsy and antic leapings, marking the cadence with renewed and still more vigorous bellowings. So violent are their movements and contortions that, in a short time, they absolutely reek with perspiration, and the force with which their feet strike the ground is such, as to leave marks similar to those made by the evolutions of a regiment of cavalry.

Under the influence of this mystic and gloomy paroxysm, they devote themselves to hate and vengeance, invoking the *Manitous* in whose presence, in the person of the child, they then consider themselves, to witness their sincerity.

Their music appears to be somewhat monotonous, but still, notwithstanding its uniformity, is not destitute of the power to rouse or to melt the soul; and, from its very extravagance, it derives a capability of exciting in a high degree different passions. Indeed, both their music and their dance strongly recall those of antiquity.

Like them, the primitive Greeks had their parchment globes and their castanets; the latter, made precisely in the same manner as those of the Indians, of shells or the bones of animals. The most popular music of the Greeks was formed, like that of the Indian tribes, by the union of the voice and instruments; and it was expressly this description of music which constituted an indispensable part of the worship they paid to their divinities.

Like the Romans, they mark the cadence by a kind of little bells fixed to their feet,—*podarii*, *pedicularii;* and, like the same people, they have also their *Corypheus,* in the Indian who strikes the tabor or tamborine; and also their *manuductor* in the person who regulates the dance. One circumstance to be observed, modern and peculiar, is, that the Indian *manuductor* carries in his hand a large whip, like a waggoner, or like a negro-driver in the southern States of the Union.

These devotees of Terpsichore distinguish themselves also by the emblems of Mars. They all carry their bow, quiver, and arrows; as well as a plume of feathers on their head, the exclusive distinction of warriors of renown. The feathers are from a bird which the Canadians call *killiou,* and the Indians *wamend-hi.*

These birds are so rare and so highly valued by the Indians in general, that whoever has the good fortune to kill one of them, receives the formal compliments of the whole camp on his success, and is entitled to the privilege of wearing one of its plumes.

Every warrior is authorised to wear as many of them as he has killed of his enemies; and every time he destroys one of these birds, he adds a plume to his previous honours. These feathers have certainly nothing very beautiful about them; but I have attached a value to them on the principle of the Peruvians, who felt no regard or anxiety for gold till they perceived the Europeans so eager to acquire it; and I have directed my efforts with the desired success to obtain some of them.

The Indians dance at marriages, on which occasions the women dance also, and with a grace and agility which you would not expect from their appearance.

But males and females never dance *together* excepting in their religious solemnities. Indian *hauteur* condemns the fair sex to contempt and humiliation as decidedly as we regard it with the most ardent esteem and devotion.

It is unquestionably this contempt for women which retards the civilization and increases the ferocity of these unfortunate tribes. The man who feels no moral sensibility, no moral attachment, towards that being whom heaven has destined to participate in our consolations and our difficulties, in our smiles and our best affections; towards the being by whom we are born in pain and reared with extreme tenderness and self-denial,—who enables a man to live again in his posterity, and whose graces, and love, and genuine friendship, constitute the very extract and essence of human happiness—such a man must inevitably be a barbarian or a brute, and his soul dead to every sentiment of virtue.

When they smoke the calumet of friendship with a stranger on a visit to them, with an ambassador from another tribe or from a civilized state, whose object is to negociate a peace or any description of treaty, they introduce it by a dance and a ceremony, which must be considered as the supposed means of consecrating the calumet before it is presented to the honoured guest. They dance round a sacred fire, and purify it by the rapid motion given it by each person in succession over the flames or in the air, after which it is delivered into the hands of the chief, who then presents it to the stranger with all due formality. This is the dance which appears to me to display most dignity and expression. The war-dance is terrible.

Before marching to meet the enemy, the whole number of warriors form in a circle, fully armed. The chief addresses them by recalling to their recollections the exploits of their ancestors, those performed by themselves, and even, without overstepping the bounds of a modest pride, his own. He excites them by a rude but powerful eloquence to intrepidity, indignation, and carnage. To increase the impression upon their minds, he advances into the midst of the circle, brandishes his club or tomahawk with an air of menace and fury, and strikes with the utmost violence at a human figure sketched in their rough manner on the ground, or at the head of some animal, whichever it may be, representing the figure or the head of the enemy. The whole body of warriors, performing around him the dance of cannibals, imitate his example; and the figure or the head soon disappears under the ponderous and fatal blows successively levelled at it. They then assume all the ferocious and cruel attitudes with which they are habituated to rush upon the enemy. They wield their firelocks, if they happen to have any, their bows, their cutlasses, with the same rapidity and ardour as if the enemy were actually before them. It often happens, however, that under this convulsive excitement the blows meant for the enemy are actually directed against a friend, and that the first blood drawn is not from the enemy, but from their own party.

A bow, which they denominate the bow of *medicine*, or the bow of the *Manitous*, and which is kept hung up in the Great Medicine-hut, closes the ceremony, by being successively passed through the hands of all the actors in the scene. I have a very beautiful one in my possession.

On returning from war, dancing again takes place; and if the spectator be not himself an Indian, the exhibition on this occasion is absolutely appalling.

They dance round pikes and poles, at the ends of which are hung heads, ears, tongues, hearts, and scalps, with the still pendent hair of men, women, and children; and the wretched captives, whom they have spared either for the purpose of slavery or sacrifice, as was the practice with nations of the most remote antiquity, are condemned to witness this scene of horror, recalling to their minds massacre and carnage—presenting before their eyes the bleeding remains of their fathers, mothers, brothers, sisters, wives, and husbands!

Lastly, they dance also on occasion of sacrifices, both public and private; when they give entertainments; and when they administer medicine to the sick.

Public sacrifices are considered indispensable by the Indians when they hold their grand assemblies for deliberating on the question of peace or war. Here also we trace the resemblance to antiquity.

The ceremony uniformly commences with smoking the sacred pipe; and, previously to forming their determination, they invoke their *Manitous*, offering them in sacrifice some defective skin or ragged rug. It seems as if the Indians had adopted the maxim of Lycurgus, who always offered to the gods victims of little value, that the Spartans might ever retain the means of honouring their deities. It is certain that the Indians neither enrich the altar nor its ministers. Their divinities appear to prefer purity of heart to the number and cost of sacrifices.

The gods of antiquity, with their various claims and pretensions, would fare but ill in the worship of the Indians; for they have no bulls, whether black or white, for Jupiter; nor cows or heifers for his stately consort; nor sows, barren or prolific, for his venerable mother; nor lambs, stags, pigeons, rams, pigs, or bucks, nor gilded horns, &c., for the worthless mob of his illegitimate or legitimate offspring; neither calves of gold nor calves of lead.

These sacrifices are offered by every Indian according to his own particular temper or caprice: some offer them to the good *Manitous*, others to the evil; some to one particular divinity, and others to another; and some probably without having a very clear idea to which or to whom: and here again we might trace ancient and modern resemblances.

They perform sacrifices also in spring and in autumn, but most certainly not, as some have pretended, to Ceres or to Bacchus, for the

Indians never rear the vine or cultivate the land, and the names just mentioned are Greek to them; but their objects are self-purification, as has been already noticed, in spring; and, in autumn, obtaining from their respective *Manitous* success in the chase during winter.

The scene of public sacrifices is always on the bank of a river. This is not done for the purpose of furnishing a spectacle to the Naïads, but from an apprehension of surprise by the enemy. This also I consider as the true reason for their encamping either on the banks of rivers or in the open country; as thus they have time for flight or for embarkation when they perceive their enemy at a distance, and feel themselves not strong enough to resist him. What has tended to confirm me in this opinion, although disclaimed by the Indians, (who, like all other men, are desirous to conceal their weaknesses) is, that wherever they can discover a tongue of land between a river and a marsh, there they invariably encamp.

The stage of a private sacrifice is the tent of the individual who performs it. I was a spectator of one of these sacrifices, and enquired what was the motive of it. I was answered that it was an inspiration, but that it was impossible to reveal it. You must, therefore, my dear Countess, try to content yourself with the same answer.

The tent is cleared of all the rags and tatters, the fetid state of which might present an ill-smelling odour to the divinity. Even the profane cinders are removed, and a new and hallowed fire purifies it by the burning of a few herbs or roots, or a little tobacco, consecrated to him by a vow. The peristyle, *atrium*, and the floor or ground of the hut, are strewed with foliage and flowers, like the temple of Vesta, or our modern churches. The ceremony concludes with dancing.

None of the sacred festivals of the Indians are celebrated in the winter months; during which they are wholly occupied in hunting, in feasting on the animals they have killed, and in paying, with their furs, the various traders who follow them like so many harpies through woods and forests, and endure a life which only the love of money can render supportable.

I have been present at one of their dinners. As there was a mystic solemnity connected with it, every individual was obliged to eat, or make some other eat, the allowance set before him; to leave a single morsel on the bark trencher on which the repast was served, would have been an insufferable insult to the divinity to which it was consecrated. One of the guests, after devouring in a twinkling all that was upon his own plate, swallowed nearly the whole of what was placed for me, the greatest part of the allowances of two officers of the fort, and if the interpreter had not possessed the appetite he did, and would have given him (as we did) a little tobacco or powder, he could have induced the cormorant to swallow his also.

It is difficult to imagine, my dear Countess, what these Indian bodies are capable of devouring and digesting in a day: sometimes they will not lie down to sleep till they have swallowed everything eatable that they possess. The Indian, in order to render himself as free and independant as possible, seems desirous to throw off all anxiety and care even for the ensuing day. They are capable of devouring like wolves, and of fasting like camels; perhaps, like the last-mentioned animals, they have also the faculty of rumination.

The entertainment concluded with a dance; and the women likewise performed theirs; but the sister and daughter of the chief, who are far from being the plainest of the tribe, were not present, and did not make their appearance any part of the day. They were said to be unclean, which was explained by a reference to periodical affections, supposed to correspond with lunar renovations. During the influence of these affections, both wives and daughters strictly withdraw from society, abstaining from the slightest contact with the huts or utensils; exhibiting in this respect a correspondence with the practice not only of profane antiquity, but of the Old Testament.

A sick female expressed a desire to have the *medicine* administered to her, and the doctor assented to her request. This is a dance different from what you saw at the *Rocky River*.

A number of those who had been previously initiated in this mystery were speedily brought together, and formed a circle about the patient. Herbs, bark of trees, and roots, were thrown upon her by them as they danced around, and every dancer blew on those parts of the body supposed to be affected with the tube of a pipe, which in all circumstances and ceremonies is an object of veneration, and indeed a *Manitou*. They then shook her, and the doctor blew into her mouth to drive out the evil spirit by which she was possessed; the latter, however, proved stronger than his own, and in the midst of all this infernal bustle and racket the poor woman died. This was, with implicit faith, ascribed to her evil spirit. When the patient recovers it is ascribed to miraculous power.

Although the Indians allege that the sole object of this dance is to remove the disease of the patient, yet I thought I could trace in the ceremony the *proficiscere* of our ritual, and the *extremum spiritum ore excipere* of the Romans.

Thus far, my dear Countess, you have seen not a little of the charlatanism among these Indian physicians; they are by no means, however, destitute of the knowledge of medicines, or of successful remedies; and certainly they kill fewer of their patients than ours, at least when superstition and jugglery do not form part of their operations.

Their medicaments consist entirely of what the great physicians of antiquity, Chiron and Esculapius, exclusively employed—in short, of simples. Experience was, with these great lights and ornaments of the profession, the sole guide; and so it is with the Indians. When Hippocrates began to mix theories with the practice of medicine, its healing power began to wane; imposture usurped the place of simplicity and wisdom; and contradictory reasonings and doctrines involved the clear evidence of facts in the darkness of sectarian and homicidal systems, which ravage the world to the present day.

There are certain herbs and roots made use of by the Indian physicians which are ascertained to be highly salutary and of astonishing efficacy. Every head of a family, moreover, every old woman, indeed almost every individual Indian, possesses a collection of medicinal roots and herbs, which they denominate the *medicine bag*, and which they regard as the sanctuary of a number of divinities. The Jews, the Greeks, and the Romans, possessed their amulets; the Arabs and Turks have them still; and the Negroes possess something of the same kind in their *gris-gris*. We have our bags of relics, the contents of which are more numerous than the roots of the Indians. At Cologne, as I formerly mentioned to you, I saw in a single bag, St Ursula with her eleven thousand virgins, the three royal Magi, and a considerable number of other matters equally holy and efficacious.

The Indians carefully preserve this bag in their huts; and when on a march, or engaged in war, they are never without it. They consider it indeed as a sort of *Palladium*.

They possess remedies for every species of disease, including even siphilitic ones. For even the Indians are not without their Laises and Phrynes; nor indeed, however deplorable it may be, without their Antinouses and Adrians.

They are acquainted both with the high and low systems of surgery; the last of which is exercised even by women. They bleed their patient, or, to give a better idea of the process, they lacerate his skin with a knife, or a sharpened bone, and sometimes even with a gun-flint; then, applying the large end of a horn to the incision, they suck the blood through the other end, discharging it from their mouths as successive repletions require it, till they have drawn the quantity prescribed. Wounds, sprains, &c. are all healed by the application of natural simples, applied internally, or by cataplasm or lotion.

They despise our physicians generally, yet regard with great deference the one residing at the fort, who has cured a considerable number of them after they had exhausted their own medicine-bags. Indeed, it is scarcely possible that he should be without merit, as he is totally without presumption. I have been informed that, in the course of the last year, after having effected a cure of some difficulty, the chief of the tribe among whom he resided entreated him with great earnestness to *leave something of his race* among them, and that the means offered for the accomplishment of this end were worthy of his acceptance. I should have considered this statement as fabulous, if I had not heard from unquestionable authority that the first negro seen in these territories received a similar invitation from the Indians. They regarded him as an evil spirit or devil; and conceived that if they could but succeed in having a family of the breed in their society, the other demons would fraternise with them, or at least would never venture to molest them. You recollect, my dear Countess, my former remark, that the Indians have more respect for devils than for angels.

After exhibiting such a mass of superstition and extravagance ; after displaying such a jumble of credulity and of divinities, what can be said of their religion? How is it possible to form it into a system? Amidst all their ridiculous ceremonies, and absurd and often contradictory doctrines, amidst all the multiplicity and respective peculiarities of their *spirits*, we are not without difficulty led to conjecture that the Indians acknowledge one supreme being. The *Kitechi-Manitou* of the *Cypowais*, and the *Tango-Wakoon* of the *Nardowkies*, or the *Sioux* ;—the *Great Spirit* seems to be the sun ; but it is not known whether they adore it only as the emblem of a God, or as that God himself.

I am at length then, my dear Countess, arrived at the point where your curiosity has been long expecting me, and which I have not reached without hesitation and apprehension ; for we have before us a question of somewhat difficult solution, whatever facility a number of writers may have attached to it. Book-makers have the art of turning everything to account, while a plain observer, like myself, possesses no such advantage. Professed travellers often obtain by their investigations a mighty name, which confers on them the reputation of little less than infallibility, while such a superficial sketcher as myself can scarcely screen himself from the charge of incompetence. However sorry I should be to bewilder you in the mazes of speculation, the worst that I can accuse myself of on the subject on which I am entering will be, that I have added to the number of conjectures. I will therefore proceed to give you my thoughts on the origin of the first possessors of this vast continent.

Different authors have brought them hither from all the different parts of the world. There is no virgin land now in existence to which their origin can be ascribed, unless it be Botany Bay; under the banners, therefore, of one or other of these learned guessers, I have long foreseen the necessity of enlisting.

I was at first induced to join with those who derived them from the Jews; for it must be admitted that that nation, ill-used and persecuted as it has been by the whole world, has some reason for boasting, as it does, of giving birth to all the nations, as well as to nearly all the religions, of mankind. It seemed impossible for me to doubt that by so doing I should be building on an impregnable foundation. But this hypothesis is too general, and perhaps evasive. It is necessary to specify and detail; I adopted, therefore, the idea of those who deduce the origin of these Indians from Asia. And indeed a variety of circumstances concur to authorise it.

Their resemblance in numerous respects to the Asiatic tribes; their principal divinity, the sun, worshipped alike by the Guebres, Tibetians, Indians, Japanese, Chinese, and various others; the facility of passing to this country from the Asiatic territories by the narrow streights of Behring, while immense oceans roll between it and the two other quarters of the globe; all these circumstances, it must be allowed, speak strongly in favour of the Asiatic origin; and a new discovery of the highest interest must be considered as affording evidence nearly amounting to conviction.

The skeletons of mammoths which have been found in the states of Kentucky, and Missouri, and other parts of America, have been ascertained to resemble precisely those which have been found in Siberia and the eastern parts of Asia.

The pens and brains of many men of science were put in exercise upon the subject before the museum of St Petersburg had informed the south of Europe that similar remains had been found in Asia. They imagined at first that the mammoths discovered in America were elephants which had migrated from Africa; but it is now universally admitted that those mammoths are elephants of Asiatic origin.

You perceive therefore, that this very interesting discovery in the animal kingdom has been also eminently valuable, by throwing light on the origin of the nations of America. I availed myself of it with no little eagerness in order to corroborate my conjecture of their being derived from Asia. I had indeed consulted the genealogists, and nearly fixed on the individual son of Noah, whom the American tribes might look up to as their ancestor. I had almost obtained, as I thought, decisive and satisfactory evidence on the subject, when a new incident threw me into new uncertainty.

Some chiefs, from whom I endeavoured to learn from what egg their ancestors sprung, allege that, if not pre-Adamites, as some civilized nations have actually professed to be, they are at least Antediluvians. They stated to me, with an air of confidence that, "when worlds were overwhelmed by a tremendous deluge, their own was spared; and that while a wicked race was totally cut off, they beheld the sun rise every day from the bosom of those waters in which it had perished." The presumption seems not a little in their favour, when we consider that, as God bestowed on Noah only three sons, for the re-peopling of Asia, Africa, and Europe, it seems to be a fair inference that America was not included in the plans of his vengeance; as in that case he would have given the patriarch four.

You must extricate yourself, my dear friend, from this difficulty as well as you can. For my own part, I could merely communicate to you all I know and all I think upon the subject; and in good truth, after all that has been said, it is a little mortifying to find that one knows nothing.—We will now return to the camps and huts which we had left.

The government of the Indians is regulated merely by usages, which are, however, very frequently disregarded.

Each body of Indians constitutes a tribe. Each tribe, as you have already perceived, has its civil chief, who is hereditary as long as the tribe considers the honour to be merited; it has also a military chief, whose elevation is solely the consequences of his services.

Every father of a family is chief of his own hut: if that habitation contain two or three families, the presidency attaches to seniority; but the chiefs of huts are frequently wholly disregarded, and every individual does just as he pleases. Sons have, generally speaking, no respect for their fathers, and fathers no affection for their sons. The apparent agitation and contortions of grief which are frequently displayed by Indians in cases of death, are rather conventional than sincere. There is frequently found among them some particular chief whose talents or reputation give him considerable influence over other tribes, and even over the whole nation.

As each nation, band, or tribe, has a distinct and peculiar name, so has it likewise a particular mark or emblem to distinguish it—as an eagle, a panther, a bear, or a buffalo; and they exhibit them in their hieroglyphics at general or particular councils.

General councils consist of all the chiefs, both civil and military, of the orators, prophets, doctors, diviners, &c. of all the tribes of the nation: particular councils, or those of the tribe, are formed also out of all the above-named descriptions in the tribe; and, in addition, of one member of every family.

But we always come round again to the same point; for the whole of this hierarchy and all these councils are frequently found to terminate in nothing. The Indian knows nothing of subordination, whether civil or military: every man lives in the manner and the place he likes best; goes to war or stays behind according to his own fancy, continues on the scene of warfare, or returns from it at his own good pleasure. He is so jealous of his liberty, that the slightest appearance of command or dependance excites offence and irritation.

As they possess no other property than the four rags which constitute their hut, and the snares and weapons with which they carry on war against beasts and men; and as they never dispute about the possession of a territory for which they have no use, they feel no occasion for distributive laws; and, in fact, have none. And, as vengeance is at once their code and their judge, they dispense also with all laws repressive of malignity and violence.

Every Indian is the executioner of the man who has committed an offence against himself or against his family. No such public officer of justice therefore is required. The offender who dies under the arm of vengeance is never avenged; as were this not the case, vengeance would follow vengeance, and discord succeed to discord, till in a short time the whole nation would be extirpated by its own members.

The homicidal offender is sometimes seized in the very act of guilt, and delivered up to the family of the slaughtered victim; sometimes he delivers himself up voluntarily, and receives the mortal stroke of the avenger with the same coolness and indifference with which it is inflicted.

Sometimes he flies from the rage of his pursuers to distant regions; but it is seldom that he escapes falling by their hands sooner or later. They have an energy and perseverance which impel them onward in the pursuit through the whole of the Indian world: they rush in search of him even into the midst of their enemies; and, in many cases, these enemies will grant a truce on an occasion that calls up the universal sympathy. In some instances the avengers have been treated by these enemies with liberal hospitality, and permitted to sacrifice their victim in the sight and in the tent of these previously confirmed and inveterate foes.

It seldom happens that the offender defends himself against the attack of him whom he has wronged; even in cases in which he has fled to avoid his vengeance, or in which he would be capable of effectually resisting it. The manner of accomplishing their vengeance is regulated entirely by the grief felt for the loss sustained, and by the degree of the avenger's ferocity.

In the exercise of their vengeance they frequently surpass the cruelty of a Nero, a Caligula, or a Maximin. Sometimes even children themselves take part in it. They pierce the victim with pointed and lacerating pieces of wood, tear off pieces of his skin, and bite off parts of his flesh. Even women (and I state the fact with deep regret) sometimes engage in this inhuman work, and shew themselves the most relentless of the tormentors. No one, however, considers the work inhuman, but, on the contrary, it is deemed a most incumbent and sacred duty.

The martyr not unfrequently expires without having uttered a single sigh: sometimes he even stimulates and exasperates the rage of his executioners. What a contrast is thus exhibited in the character of the Indian, who at times displays no equivocal symptoms of cowardice! And, even in the scene we are contemplating, cowardice in the executioners is contrasted with the firmest constancy in their victim.

If the homicide has taken the life of another solely in order to preserve his own, it sometimes happens that the affair is arranged by a family treaty, which is always sealed with presents on the part of the homicide: his life however is in perpetual danger.

What has been stated in the few last pages, contains nearly everything that constitutes what is called government among the Indians, and is common to all the different nations of them.

After having viewed the dying Indian, let us now consider him in the state of actual death, and proceed to follow him to the grave.

The deceased, dressed, or, to speak more correctly, covered, as he generally was during life, placed in a sitting attitude upon a mat or skin in the middle of his hut, with all his weapons at his side; his face is turned towards the east, and decked and ornamented most elaborately.

All his relations are seated around him, and for a certain time observe a profound silence, exhibiting countenances indicative at once of seriousness and grief. Each person then addresses him, some in pathetic tones but without tears, others more emphatically but still calmly, and all uttering some eulogium on his virtues, or some expression of regret for his loss.

I will just give you a sketch of what appeared most interesting in the account given by the interpreter of these addresses.

"Where are you, my beloved husband? You are present, indeed, but you speak not to me. You are now entirely in the society of the spirits, and can no longer interest yourself about your wife, but your wife will never cease to interest herself about you;—look on me once more, if only for a moment; but your eyes are employed in looking upon something much more handsome and pleasing than your wife. Perhaps you will not even have it in your power to remember me. Your wife however will remember you. The sun and moon and stars will ever see me deploring your loss, and I will make no delay in joining you." Catalani could not sing *Ombra adorata aspettami* with more expression, than the Indian widow delivered the above address.

The interpreter told me that she uttered her genuine feelings; of this however I cannot but entertain some doubt, because the poetic style is always more flattering than sincere; and I happen to know that she was very ill-treated by her husband.

Another speaker said, "You are still among us, my brother; your person still has its usual appearance, like our own; not the slightest alteration; nothing wanting but action. But where is that heaving breast, which only a few hours since inhaled the smoke, and then wafted it to the Great Spirit? Why is there silence now on those lips which so lately spoke a language so energetic and expressive? Why are now motionless those valiant arms which discharged the farthest-flying arrows; arms which were the terror of our enemies? You are gone to the place where you were before you came into these countries, but your glory will remain with us for ever."

A third speaker added, "Alas! alas! alas! that form which was viewed with such high admiration is now become as inanimate as it was *three hundred winters* ago. But you will not be for ever lost to us, we will go and rejoin you in the grand region of spirits—again we will unite in the chase—again we will march together against the enemy. In the mean time, full of respect for your virtues and your valour, we come to offer you a tribute of kindness; your body shall not be exposed in the fields as the prey of beasts, but we will take care that it, like yourself, shall be united to your predecessors." By his commencement I imagined this orator to be a Frenchman, but he concluded like a Greek or a Roman. The most singular circumstance relating to these three discourses is, that they contain three different professions of faith.

I asked the interpreter the meaning of the *three hundred winters.* He said that it was not in his power to explain it, and that probably the Indian himself knew less about it, if possible, than ourselves—who certainly knew nothing at all.

All the friends of the deceased, as they arrive, move on by his side, each expressing his regret and the praises of the departed.

When these funeral addresses are concluded, the body of the deceased is wrapped in his rug or skin, and enclosed in the bark of trees, which serves for a coffin; and as, in cases of public or family ceremonies, the Indians always do what is done by others, whatever be their own individual faith, it is customary with all the tribes to place in the coffin all the arms of the deceased, whether they believe that he will follow war and the chase in another world or not; and in that they are very ancient and very modern.

On the following morning at sun-rise, the body is placed outside the tent and raised upon two supporters, and then the scene changes.

All the relations begin to cry and yell as if they were frantic, till they lose their voices, when they set up a sort of low bellowing.

They throw away whatever they are in possession of, without exception, from their ornaments, with which they begin, to their very cooking vessels. One would imagine that they wished to survive the deceased, merely to lament him; and his *friends*, exhibiting at the same time every appearance of grief, collect together the various articles, and take possession of them in order to do honour to his memory.

They prepare a repast of all their provisions. If they have none, which is frequently the case when they are not engaged in hunting, the feast consists of a dog; they sacrifice it to the manes of their kinsman, and the *friends* eat; all the liquors also which they possess are placed outside the tent, and the *friends* drink. Here we may observe something of Roman customs, and something perfectly modern.

Sun-set now arrives, and constitutes another epoch in the etiquette of lamentation, when the screams and bellowings of the morning must be renewed; the *friends* then leave the relatives to cry and bellow by themselves, and retire to sleep.

The corpse remains in this situation, commonly for three or four days, till it has received the customary attentions, and the adieus of all who pass it. Here we trace the practice of the Egyptians, the Greeks, the Romans, the Christians in the age of Tertullian, of several kings, of the popes and cardinals in modern times, and of the Arabs and Chinese. Sometimes, however, it becomes necessary to keep at a considerable distance in paying these attentions; for, in summer, the putrefaction becomes frightfully noisome; and this circumstance attending the ceremony must be considered peculiarly modern.

The due period being completed, the good *friends* again make their appearance, and conduct the coffin to the *Champs-Elysées*. In this procession again, we are reminded of the Roman *Neniæ*, &c.; all present feel, or affect to feel, the desolation of grief; for I am perfectly convinced that affectation is not a little concerned in the matter here, as in other countries, where, as I have already told you, all the contortions of tragic grimace are speedily succeeded by the lively waggery of some broad farce.

The Sioux generally raise the coffins upon four stakes, about ten feet high, fixed in the earth; the other Indians inter their dead, and form over them hillocks similar to those we have noticed at St Louis, but not so large. The face of the corpse is always turned towards the east, a custom which has existed and still prevails among many nations, and which was observed by the Christians of the primitive church.

If the deceased be a person of distinguished renown, a large piece of wood, painted or rather daubed with red, (resembling the *cippus* of the Romans,) is fixed at the side of the coffin, and hieroglyphics are attached to it, transmitting to posterity his achievements and glory; a practice conformable to every age, and to every nation.

The relations, on returning to the camp, recommence their lamentations at the appointed hour. They pierce their legs and arms, some with thorns and pointed pieces of wood, others with knives and arrows. I am convinced that many among them would willingly dispense with this unpleasant formality; but it is the usage, and must of course be complied with. Some there are who wound themselves with no little precaution and skill; and who, in fact, seem to have studied anatomy a little, in order to learn where the flesh is best guarded by the thickness of the integuments; but others, destitute of this convenient knowledge, or eager to display their grief more vehemently than the rest, inflict serious, and sometimes even fatal injuries on themselves.

The lamentations for the deceased continue for more than a month, and periodically, at the rising and setting of the sun. They celebrate the mournful anniversary for some years, reminding us of the *inferiæ* and *parentalia* of the Romans. Only a few days since, I was out with a hunting party, when our ears were assailed by dreadful howlings from a neighbouring forest. I imagined that they were made by wolves; they proceeded, however, in reality from Indians, who were thus lamenting a relation who had been dead more than three years.

I believe I have already mentioned to you that during full mourning they black their faces completely over, and in second mourning black only half of them.

When an Indian dies in the winter hunting season, his body is carefully preserved: for this purpose it is dried and covered with leaves and herbs, which are their medical balsams, and after being enclosed in the bark of trees (thus resembling the mummies of Egypt) it is elevated to a considerable height for more complete exposure to the air. When in the season of spring they proceed to establish themselves in their summer encampment, they go through all the ceremonies which we have detailed, and on these occasions the *friends* generally come off better in their entertainments. They find both provisions and skins, and consequently have much more to collect and much more to eat. The cries and lamentations take place just as if the deceased had expired only a few days or hours before; for, during the hunt, nothing but that is at all attended to. From all circumstances, I cannot help being convinced that, in their various and continued lamentations, there is more of grimace, custom, and formality, than of affection and religion, and that hypocrisy finds its way into every part of the earth.

You have already seen that the Indians divide the year into twelve moons, like the early Greeks; but they give themselves very little anxiety about intercalating, as the Greeks did; so that, properly speaking, they have no year, but merely months or moons.

The year of the Sioux commences at the vernal equinox, like that of Romulus; that of the Cypowais at the summer solstice, as among the Greeks when they instituted the Olympic Games, which were celebrated every four years at the same epoch.

The months or moons of the Sioux have different names from those of the Cypowais: it is proper therefore to take distinct notice of both. We will first mention those of the Sioux, beginning with the first moon.

March . . .	the moon of bad eyes . . .	Wisthaocia-ouì
April	the moon of game	Mograhoandì-ouì
May	the moon of nests	Mograhocandà-ouì
June	the moon of strawberries	Wojusticiascià-ouì
July	the moon of cherries . . .	Champaseià-ouì
August . .	the moon of buffaloes . . .	Yanlankakiocù-ouì
September.	the moon of oats	Wasipì-ouì
October . .	the second moon of oats.	Sciwostapì-ouì
November,	the moon of the roebuck.	Takiouka-ouì
December,	the moon of the budding of the roebuck's horns	Abesciatakiouskà-ouì
January . .	the moon of valour	Onwikari-ouì
February .	the moon of wild-cats . .	Owiciatá-ouì

The Cypowais months are as follow:

June	the moon of strawberries	Hodheïmin-quisìs
July	the moon of blue fruits . .	Mikin-quisìs
August . .	the moon of yellow leaves	Wathebaquì-quisìs
September,	the moon of falling leaves	Inaquì-quisìs
October . .	the moon of migratory game	Bima-hamo-quisìs
November.	the moon of snow	Kaskadinò-quisìs
December .	the moon of the Little Spirit	Manito-quisìs
January . .	the moon of the Great Spirit	Kitci-Manito-quisìs

February .	the moon of the coming of eagles	Wamebinni-quisìs
March . .	the moon of hardened snow	Onabanni-quisìs
April . . .	the moon of snow-shoes .	Pokaodaquimì-quisìs
May	the moon of flowers	Wabigon-quisìs

The Indians have no division of the week. They reckon the days only by sleepings. They divide the day into halves and quarters, measuring the time by the course of the sun from its rising to its setting.

Though the Indians are completely ignorant of geography, as well as of every other science, they have a method of denoting by hieroglyphics on the bark of certain papyriferous trees, all the countries with which they are acquainted. These maps want only the degrees of latitude and longitude to be more correct than those of some of our own visionary geographers.

The polar-star is their only astronomical guide, or at least their most certain guide, when they travel by night. The course of the sun directs them by day. But even though the sun or the polar-star should be eclipsed, they are equally able to distinguish, both by day and night, the four cardinal points; and consequently the direction which they want to follow, whether in the thickest forests or the widest prairies. Their secret is this:—the tips of the blades of grass always incline towards the south, and it is less green on the side towards the north: this is their guide in prairies. The tops of trees also incline towards the south, and the moss which frequently covers their trunks is always found on the north side; the bark is more smooth and supple on the east side than on the west: this is their compass in the forests.

They measure distances only by the number of days required to travel over them; and as they are very well acquainted with the territories they inhabit, immense as they are, they can fix on their maps the precise time requisite for going to attack an enemy's post, or for a new and more excursive chase.

They have also hieroglyphics to express all the numbers for which their language has words.

They know nothing of *milliards* or of millions, because they have neither our desires nor wants; even a thousand is beyond the requirement of any of their transactions. I conceive, however, that, as they can reckon up to a thousand, they would be able to reckon *ten* thousand, a *hundred* thousand, &c.

The marriages of the Indians have been very variously described. I will communicate to you, on this subject, simply what I have myself seen and been informed of on the spot.

When an Indian feels any attachment or inclination for any individual female, he endeavours to obtain her consent to their union. As to sounding the state of her heart, that he considers of little or no consequence. He then asks the consent of her father, which is the more necessary, as the bridegroom goes to reside with the bride: the mother, as among the Greeks, is never consulted on the subject. These preliminaries being completed, the friends of both parties, women on the bride's part, and men on that of her suitor, meet together in the hut of one of his old relations, where a feast is provided for the occasion. They dance, and sing, and eat and drink, if they have the means; and the *friends* of the parties are sure to be present. The company at length retire, leaving behind only three or four of those most intimate with he bride and bridegroom. The bride soon after knocks at the door, and announcing her name, enquires if her betrothed husband is within: the door is opened, and her female friends, like the *pronubæ* of the Romans, present her in form to him, while he stands in the middle of them to pay her the compliments usual on such occasions, and then sits down with her upon a skin. The Romans seated their betrothed females upon the fleece of a sacrificed sheep, to intimate the obligation they were about to enter into to prepare clothing for their husbands and children. The Indians, perhaps, by means of the skin just mentioned, equally indicate the duties about to be entered upon.

The aged relative makes a suitable address on the occasion; after which the husband presents his wife with a small truss of herbage, possibly to hint to her that her sole business will consist in bearing, like a beast of burden, the baggage of the whole family. Thus the Romans presented to their brides the *colum comptum et fusum cum stamine*, to remind them that Caia the wife of the elder Tarquin was constantly employed in spinning. The truss or bundle just mentioned is made up of herbs of such delicate fragrance, and arranged in so ingenious a manner, as in my opinion quite to eclipse the florists and perfumers of Paris itself: I have kept one of them as a very valuable curiosity. The dancing, and eating and drinking are now repeated, after which the wife, attended by her *pronubæ*, returns to the hut of her father.

As Indian girls are not in possession of the *flammeum*, a covering for the head which the Roman brides wore on the marriage-day, they throw over theirs the coverlet which is their usual garment.

The bridegroom follows her the day after, and, instead of asking her father for a dower, which among civilized nations frequently involves families in ruin, and seems to turn the fair sex into a subject of bargain and sale, makes him a number of presents, and again requests the bestowment of his daughter on him. The father grants his request on condition of his remaining with him, and hunting for him for a year or longer. Such are the usages of the Sioux. Among the Cypowais, he is not at liberty to remove till he has obtained offspring by his marriage. Here we see the case of Jacob and Laban.

It might be imagined, that this species of probation was intended to prove the character of the husband, and the sentiments he entertained towards his wife; but I cannot help thinking that it is in reality a speculation of the father-in-law to benefit by the exertions and fatigues of his new relative. And, in fact, a good hunter is in great request with all families.

On the day after their union has been sanctioned by this paternal consent, they offer some sacrifice to their respective *Manitous;* as the Romans, on like occasions, consecrated gifts and offerings to Jupiter, Juno, Venus, Diana, and the goddess of persuasion, denominated *Suada,* whose propitious influence on married life would, in my humble opinion, be of more value than that of all the rest, even among civilized people.

Such are the ceremonies generally observed by the Indians, when they are inclined to transact the matter according to rule and order. But they more frequently marry without any other formality than that practised by the Greeks and Romans in their marriages *per usum;* that is, they take a wife for the satisfaction and services she can bestow on them, and to obtain from her children, who are considered as legitimate, precisely like those of the marriages of antiquity just mentioned. The *patria potestas* is not even consulted on the occasion, or, at the utmost, means are found, by presents, of rendering it a dead letter. And, in fact, as polygamy is very prevalent among the Indians, who sometimes have five or six wives, they would nearly exhaust the whole year in going through their various ceremonies, were they, on occasion of every marriage, scrupulously to perform those which I have just detailed.

The act of divorce is attended with no more difficulty than that of marriage. When both parties have come to an agreement, everything is completed, without recurring to lawyers, who would devour the patrimony of both, or to judges who, after consulting a million of contradictory commentaries, would encumber the text by still adding a new one, and conclude by deciding according to the fluctuation of their own prejudices. The children, if very young, generally continue with the mother, because, without having studied the Justinian code profoundly, or entering deeply into scandalous researches on paternity, the Indians consider the relationship of maternity as more traceable and clear: if the children are grown up, they either remain, or go wherever they please. The only paternal abode they have is the forest, and that has room enough for all.

There are among them some husbands who, without having read St Augustin, Diderot, or Helvetius, and following merely the suggestions of their own minds, mutually accommodate each other by the loan of their wives, and it rarely happens that their wives give occasion for quarrels or revenge. There are, moreover, some tribes or huts in which, as among the Arabs, a single wife is considered sufficient for the whole family, and in which she is treated as a mere article of household furniture, as was the case with the ancient Britons.

A husband who has many wives seldom keeps more than two of them in his hut; the remainder continue with their relations, or sometimes even in the hut of another man. They very rarely quarrel: devoid of affection, they are fortunately also devoid of jealousy; and the eldest of the number becomes the mother-abbess.

It has been repeatedly stated by writers, that

the Sioux are jealous of their wives. This may possibly be the case; but perhaps it is only—on the principle of monsieur de Montespan—that they may be better paid for their wives, their silence, and their virtue.

Others have made statements directly contrary, and asserted that the Indians volunteer the favours of their wives and daughters. I admit that there is no great difficulty in obtaining them; but I am not aware that the Indians whom we have hitherto seen, practice this species of prostitution, except when they desire to obtain, as in a case I mentioned, a race of good or evil spirits. I am informed that the Indians, who are stated to be so far advanced in polite civilization and liberal hospitality, are the *Mandanes* who inhabit the Missouri, and the *Snegs,* a wandering tribe near the sources of the Columbia.

I have mentioned to you, my dear Countess, their manner of making peace: I must now give you some information on their mode of making war, although, as you recollect, they have not been inclined to engage in it in my presence.

The motives from which their wars originate we have already seen; and we have noticed also their councils to deliberate on it, the smoking of their red pipe, the preliminary war-dance, and the weapons they make use of. We will proceed to view them now on their march against the enemy.

Indians generally commence their career of warfare at the age of fifteen. Under the firm conviction that war is the grand duty of their lives, that they are born for no other purpose, little is requisite to kindle in them a sufficient degree of ardour. Their chiefs, however, often represent to them that the bones of their relations, their brothers, remain unburied and bleaching on the hostile territory; that they call aloud for vengeance, which they are bound to inflict; that the Spirit may be heard in the breezes and the winds reproaching them for their cowardice, and that they should hasten to appease their wrath; that the genii, the guardian angels of their honour, urge and stimulate them to the mortal conflict. "Come on, then, my children," adds the warrior-chief, "let us tear asunder with our teeth those who have pierced the hearts of our brethren. Let your youth no longer waste away in inaction. Give free vent to the impulses of your noble valour. Anoint your hair, paint your faces, charge your quivers. Call on Echo to repeat the terror of your shout. Console the spirits of the dead, and stay not your hand till you have avenged them."

Roused by this energetic language (for the

Indians are much more eloquent on the subject of war than on that of peace) the young Indians feel themselves as it were warriors before they have had experience to become such; every delay appears intolerable; and they burn with impatience to imbrue their weapons and their hands in the blood of their enemies. The war-dance increases the exasperation of their rage, and also instructs them how to encounter the foe with most dexterity and success.

The bravest and most experienced warrior of the nation is chosen for their commander, (and in the same manner respectively in bands and tribes,) after which the whole nation marches off in a mass.

It sometimes occurs that a troop of warriors, or young men, excited by some brave leader or some supposed inspired individual, march off against the enemy, without the authority of their tribe, or the consent of their chiefs. Only a few days since, one of these prophets, after having stated that the Great Spirit had commanded him in a dream to march against a party of Cypowais, who were then scouring the neighbouring territory, threw on the ground his belt, (which the Indians consider as a Manitou,) exclaiming, "The first that takes up that belt shall be next in command to myself, and those who follow us will be ranked among the chosen." He marched away with about thirty of his tribe, and as yet no intelligence has been received of him.

Their declaration of war is by attack. The custom formerly was to send a tomahawk, or an arrow dipped in the blood of a prisoner whom they sacrificed on the occasion to the Manitou of War; as the *Fecialis* of the Romans in similar cases threw a javelin into the territory of the enemy: but as the herald-at-arms thus employed never returned with an answer, the ceremony is now dispensed with, and thereby one victim saved.

As they are free from any incumbrance of plunder or military stores, their surprises are effected with great facility; and the precaution, skill, and stratagem with which they are concerted and executed, are of a truly extraordinary character.

When the Indians are advancing to the enemy's territories, they are able to proceed for whole days together dragging themselves forward on their bellies, and in such profound silence that, at the distance of ten paces, not the slightest sound would strike the ear from a hundred men thus toiling out their progress. They kindle no fires, or pipes, and sustain themselves on what they may happen to have about them, or on roots which they find in their way.

Even frogs occasionally cease to be Manitous, and are converted from divinities into provisions.

When they discover their enemy they wind their way like reptiles through brambles, grass, and ditches, and pounce upon their prey when least of all expected. If they perceive that they are discovered, and that they are unequal to making resistance, they disperse in an instant; they conceal themselves in their flight, and re-unite at a spot fixed on as a place of rendezvous previously to their advance. This is a fresh reason for the assertion often made, that civilized nations can obtain nothing but loss by going to war with Indians.

The scenes of horror presented by a hostile encampment completely taken by surprise, baffle all description.

The hatred and rage of the assailants, urged on, as they conceive, by the manes of their slaughtered kinsman demanding vengeance; the fury and desperation of their adversaries, aware as they are of the dreadful fate awaiting them; all these murderous passions let loose a ferocity and occasion a carnage, which I should hesitate to believe possible, if I had not in a certain degree been a witness of the scene myself.

Massacres extend even far beyond the scene of battle with the rapidity of the electric shock.

On the 7th of June, a day of which I gave you some account in my preceding letter, a false report was circulated that *Panischiowa* (the chief) had been killed by the Cypowais at the falls of St Anthony. His mother, on hearing it, instantly seized a little girl of that nation who had been preserved from the period when she had been made a captive in her cradle, and who was the delight both of the family and the camp, and with a single stroke of a hatchet cleft her in two. Panischiowa, however, returned and thanked his mother for this testimony of her maternal love and of her hatred of the Cypowais.

Though the Indians are not cannibals, it is nevertheless true that they sometimes devour their enemies, and they almost always drink of their blood, smearing their bodies with it in evidence and triumph of their massacre.

When they have been successful in an expedition they immediately return to their camp, carrying as trophies the spoils of their foes; as the Romans exhibited their *spolia opima*.

In order to avoid pursuits by any enemy who might possibly succeed to the one they have overthrown, they employ every species of finesse and stratagem, displaying singular sagacity and ingenuity; and, if apprehensive of being followed into their camp, and of being considerably inferior in numbers, they embark with inconceivable rapidity, their town, houses, families, dogs and the whole of their property, and move away to remoter regions, where they may experience greater security.

When they think they are not pursued, they always preserve some of their prisoners that their death may furnish a spectacle to the encampment on their return. The prisoners, who well know the fate that awaits them, are constantly singing on their march the death song: "We are going to die, &c. but you shall see us die without trembling, &c."

On the route, they are so ill-treated that it might be supposed a frame of iron would be necessary to endure it. They are bound with cords made of the bark of trees, which sometimes cut their flesh through to the bone. At night they are extended in a trough made in the earth, and by means of forked branches of trees fixed deeply in the ground, their persecutors nail down, as it were, their bodies, arms, legs and even their necks. This must indeed be torture.

When the victorious band approaches the camp, it announces in loud shouts, and in the customary forms, the success of the expedition, the number of men whom they have lost, and the number of prisoners they are bringing with them.

All who are present in the camp begin then to pour forth the most frightful lamentations and yells; and, ranging themselves in two files, with their knotted staves or sticks in their hands, strike the prisoners, as they pass along between them, with great violence and cruelty; but as they are obliged to husband their ferocity, in order to extend the duration of this delightful spectacle, as to them it is, of human suffering, they apply their blows with critical judgment, and take care not to make them mortal. They paint their bodies with the blood of the sufferers, and the camp presents the image of a great butchery.

A kind of council is now formed at which the prisoners may be said to be tried; sometimes a few of them are spared, and especially women and children. Those who are condemned, are delivered over to their executioners, that is, to the whole camp. The decree of the council is expressed in the following terms: "Let those who are devoted to vengeance be led to the house of death; let the others be conveyed to the house of mercy."

The victims are scorched at a slow fire, their limbs are lacerated and pierced by pieces of pointed wood, and all sorts of cutting instruments. Under the infliction of these frightful tortures, the bare idea of which produces shuddering, some close their eyes, preserving an heroic courage and calmness to the last; others insult their executioners, and lavish upon them expressions of contempt and defiance even to their expiring sigh.

Some of the prisoners are sacrificed to the honour of their Manitous of War, or their infernal gods. Thus Achilles sacrificed them to Patroclus, and the Mexicans to their idol deities. The place of punishment or torture is the centre of the camp.

The herald at arms then proclaims that the prisoners who have been spared are about to be distributed to those who have just claims to them as slaves. The council bestows these on such as have lost some relation in the contest, and the grant is in proportion to the loss.

The children are very well treated, at least when it does not happen that they are made sacrifices to vengeance, like the unfortunate little Cypowais girl given in revenge for the supposed death of Panisciowa. The women prisoners are well off in proportion as they succeed in exciting interest. If any man is spared, it is in order to bestow him on some woman whom the expedition has made a widow. If he be fortunate enough to please her, she becomes his mate; if not, she sacrifices him with her own hands to the manes of her husband.

The dead bodies of the victims are left exposed to birds of prey and wild beasts, and frequently to the dogs of their executioners. Their bones are deprived of the honours of sepulture. Such also was the practice of antiquity. Priam could scarcely obtain from Achilles the body of Hector.

The same council which superintends these honours, decrees also the military honours, and the *Corona Castrensis*, the *Vexillum*, the *Phaleræ*, the *Armillæ*, the *Exuviæ* of the Romans, are the distinctions which the Indians grant to military merit.

The amount of enemies killed forms the test by which this merit is decided; and the manner in which each claimant proves his pretensions is not a little extraordinary.

Every individual marks his own arrows, and the owner of the *fatal* arrow is consequently with ease ascertained. The end of it being fixed to the shaft only by a species of mastic, which is melted by the animal heat of the body into which it passes, and being barbed, it always remains in the wound, though the shaft be withdrawn; it can be found only by cutting open the body pierced by it: sometimes they lacerate and cut open the living subject.

If the enemy has been killed by discharges of fire-arms, or by cutting weapons, the glory is adjudged to him who presents the scalp. This is the hair and skin which cover that part of the skull called the *occiput*, or *vertex à vertendo;* as the hair in that part of the head forms in a circle.

Even though the enemy may have been knocked down by any other person than the man who exhibits his scalp, the honour always belongs to the latter, and for the following reason. The enemy who falls might, as the Indians say, merely pretend to be dead in order to destroy with more ease and security his pursuer; and upon this principle they decide that the person who scalped the fallen foe, by being first to come in close contact with him, incurred the greatest danger, and consequently has a fair title to the honour of the triumph.

There is no enemy, whether killed or only wounded, who, on falling into the hands of Indians, escapes this terrible operation of scalping; and all Indians are so firmly convinced of the fate awaiting this part of the head, that they constantly keep on it a lock of hair which they preserve, as it were, ever ready for presentation to the scalping-knife of the foe. This assertion I make only after very particular attention, and I have found it confirmed in every part of the Indian territories in which I have travelled.

I cannot help thinking, my dear Countess, that you are curious to learn, as I was myself, what extravagant caprice determined the ferocity of these people to this region of the brain; but I am unable to give you any satisfaction, for my enquiries have terminated merely in confirming what I have already stated, that they consider the scalp as the most glorious trophy of their victories and achievements. I can only farther suggest one conjecture, that perhaps they entertain the same opinion as the great philosophers who fix upon this spot as the seat of the soul,—the *sensorium;* and that, consequently, by opening the door for it by the shortest way, they think their enemy must be really and irrecoverably dead, no particle of hope being thus left him from miracles themselves,—not even from those of galvanism.

You have now seen the Indians make war by ambuscades and surprises. The most interesting spectacle, however, is the sight of them when encountering their foe in the open plain, in those immense prairies where, if it were not for their verdure, one would imagine himself in the deserts of Arabia. It is in this situation that intrepidity, subtlety, and address, are more than ever required and displayed by them.

If the two parties be equal in point of numbers, they fight openly; if one be much weaker than the other, and possess no means of flight, they with wonderful speed dig holes in the ground with their nails, and fight within them. While some are intensely working at this operation, the rest surround and protect them.

When the assailants have no more ammunition, they make use of their bows; and their manner of fighting under such circumstances is truly astonishing.

As their arrows, if discharged horizontally, can scarcely strike their enemy, whose head even is not perceivable without some difficulty, they discharge them in the same manner as shells are discharged from bombs; and the parabola which they describe is often so accurate that they enter the body of the foe in their fall. I have myself seen these holes, and Indians obtaining the most brilliant and wonderful success against those entrenched in them. The angel of death is active everywhere; but I was not aware that he could exhibit in his work of destruction such dexterity and address.

Lastly, to conclude what relates to the wars of these extraordinary people, the prisoners who by any means get back to their tribe are no longer considered as members of it; for the Indians consider those who have been taken by the enemy, as dead, and will recollect only those who are determined to conquer or die.

Thus far you have seen the Indians uncivilized, indolent and cruel. I will now afford you a little relief, by exhibiting them in the fairer aspect of their nature or character, as active, sober, and industrious. I will now conduct you to the chase.

This is their principal occupation, I may indeed say their only one; for I know not what characteristic designation to apply to war. It is the chase which supplies exercise for their childhood, their youth, their manhood, and their declining life. It is as conducive to their renown as it is necessary to their existence. A good hunter is among the Indians as much distinguished as a valiant warrior, and is always more wise and less depraved.

When hunting, every Indian is attentive to his duty, and nothing but his duty. He forgets quarrelling, gaming, (which also is one of his vices,) and even his ferocity. Some of the traders, who follow every year in their train, have assured me that the winter Indian and the summer Indian are totally different beings. During summer, he is always in a state of indolence, which degrades and brutifies man in his most civilized and best educated state: the winter he passes in labour, which tames and softens characters the most reckless and ferocious. In hunting, the Indians are indefatigable, though engaged in exercise incessant and most laborious; and the success with which they pursue their various game through both prairies and forests, in lakes and rivers, displays strongly the acuteness of their understandings.

The fatigue endured by the women in the chase exceeds all imagination. They carry the tents; they go in search of the animals the men have killed; they prepare the skins of them, and dry and smoke the flesh: every household duty is included in their department, and frequently an infant at the breast, or in the womb, adds to the burthen of their laborious life. These poor women, even when in the state of pregnancy, are not on that account the more spared. Sometimes, in order to avoid the tediousness and difficulties of parturition, they press their stomachs against an horizontal bar, their head and legs hanging downwards to the ground, and almost immediately after their delivery return to their toilsome and painful occupations.

The animals which the Indians hunt are the castor, the musk-rat, the otter, the marten, the wild-cat, the beaver, the stag-wolf, the badger, the racoon, the grey, yellow, and red fox, the *pecan*, the grey and white hare, a few ermines, the gopher, many descriptions of the squirrel, the prairie dog, the black, yellow, and white bear, and the wolf of various species; the skins of all which are considered as coming under the denomination of peltry. Those which supply skins for the tanner are buffaloes, roebucks, deer, antelopes, elks, *orignals*, (exceedingly rare) mountain-sheep, reindeer, &c. Their flesh serves the Indians for food, and a portion of it is smoked and preserved for the summer, if the chase prove a favourable one; the skins are stored in packages, to dispose of them in payment for articles of indispensable necessity and of luxury, with which the traders supply, or have already supplied them. Indians never dispose of anything for real money, of the value of which they know nothing.

Before departing from the chase they again dance, and purify themselves in the presence of their Manitous, like the ancients before their idols, on occasions of great importance and enterprise; and, like the moderns before the priests and, the altar, previously to their undertaking a voyage or their exposure to great danger. The pigment used by them on these occasions is black.

I should have rejoiced to have had it in my power, and it was my intention, to detail to you regularly some of their most interesting hunts. My constancy is still unshaken, but the symptoms of my being able to extend my active researches much farther are still far from flattering.

I have exhibited the Indians to you exactly as they appeared to myself. On viewing their various qualities, physical and moral in combination, they present a mass of contradictions sufficient, I conceive, to embarrass the judgment of the profoundest observer.

They are very warm in their affections to the dead, and very indifferent towards the living; a father of a family, a son, or a husband, returns home after a very long absence and enters his hut without even raising his eyes towards his relations, and his relations exhibit precisely the same conduct towards him. On the one hand they are extremely avaricious, and always grasping; while on the other they are excessively prodigal, lavishing everything in presents to their friends. They appear to reverence a million of Manitous; and they die without invoking, or apparently even calling to their recollection, a single individual of them. Some offer sacrifices to gods, and others to devils. They complain of never having anything to eat, and devour in a single day what would supply them abundantly for a whole week. They are sometimes indolent and sluggish, sometimes active and indefatigable, vicious and virtuous, sober and intemperate. They never say what they feel, and they never feel what they say; in this respect resembling many other people of all countries and times. Revenge appears to be with them a passion absolutely irresistible, yet presents sometimes moderate and qualify it. They salute you to-day as friends, to-morrow they will lie in wait for you and murder you as enemies. They always expect gratitude from others, but never exhibit any themselves. They promise you favours, but you never obtain them. In their manners, their customs, and their ceremonies, we see traces of the ancients, the moderns, all times, and all nations; but they resemble no other nation in the world. After such a contrast of sentiments and actions, of propensities and devotions, I leave it to those who can compress everything into a system, to decide on the character and the religion of the Indians. I hope they will be more fortunate than he who while attempting to catch the moon in a fountain was drowned in it himself.

With regard to myself I can only repeat what I have already shewn, both respecting the religion and character of these singular people. I will merely add, that the Indian, as long as he remains such, will ever be his own master and sovereign, and bear his independence proudly about him; but that as soon as he becomes civilized, he will be capable of being converted even into the vilest of slaves; that his heart is by its nature the seat of dissimulation and mischief, of inhumanity and cruelty, and that civilization will meet with powerful obstacles in the state or structure of his mind, and only with great difficulty be enabled to make him truly good.

Before I quit the Indian territory, my dear Countess, I will endeavour to learn, and to the best of my power to communicate to you whatever may be most likely to attract your attention and aid your decision respecting these people. My attempts are incessant to grapple with the difficulties which constantly arise to thwart my designs. If heaven should favour my intentions, I should still have to combat a crowd of melancholy recollections. My heart is ever reverting to my beloved and, alas, my deplored Italy! What a conflict is there in a mind ill at ease! It can find rest only in that which agitates it.

LETTER XVII.

Lake La Crosse, or Lake Travers, near the Sources of the river St Peter,
July 26, 1823.

I ADDRESS you now, my dear Countess, from a place which has not yet found its way into the maps. By constantly moving on we get farther than we should have imagined, as by perseverance water hollows out the rock.

Incessantly thwarted in my project of going farther to the north, I was upon the point of changing my direction for the south, intending to traverse by land, with a Canadian interpreter and an Indian guide, the desert tracts which separate Fort St Peter from Fort Council Bluff, on the Missouri; to descend that great river as far as St Charles; to return thence to St Louis, and then follow the Mississippi to its mouths. It is not likely that I should have met with any obstacle to this design; for my Argus observers, considering me by this plan as apparently on my return, and through countries indifferent to them, would have lost all their anxiety and apprehension. But at this period major Long arrived at Fort St Peter, charged with an expedition to the northern boundary territories of the vast empire of the United States.

In this event I thought I perceived an end to all the difficulties which had till then impeded my curiosity. I participated, however, in the *very great surprise* manifested by the officers of the fort at the arrival of an expedition *so completely unknown to the garrison.*

The ardent desire which I had shewn of pushing my rambles farther, was naturally mentioned, and I seized the opportunity of asking permission to follow the major, simply in the character of a wanderer who had come thus far to see Indian lands and Indian people. They first set before me the sufferings, the dangers, &c. which I must encounter; but as I laughed at these childish terrors, they saw that they had no power over my mind, and that the attempts were wholly vain.

They next attacked me on what they thought my weak side,—my purse. After so long a digression from the route which was to lead me direct from Philadelphia to New Orleans,—a digression which has filled the whole time from the month of March,—it might reasonably be supposed to be rather in a declining state; the more so, as the curiosities I had bought of the savages had greatly contributed to diminish its contents. But a little fund which I kept in reserve disconcerted this attack also: I even sacrificed my beautiful repeater that I might have this still untouched; and bought a horse, and all provisions that were said to be necessary, with the proceeds. I contrived, by means of a few little trinkets and articles of luxury I had with me, to give myself the pleasure of offering some slight tokens of my gratitude to the amiable Snelling family, and to major Tagliawar, for the civilities they had lavished upon me during the two months I spent amongst them. When they saw I was determined to go, they even carried their politeness so far as to offer me pecuniary assistance with the most honourable and disinterested confidence; a thing by no means common among an extremely commercial people, especially towards a person of whom they knew nothing but what they had seen.

So many imaginary difficulties were not auspicious. Major Long did not cut a very noble figure in the affair; I foresaw all the disgusts and vexations I should have to experience, and under other circumstances I should have known what to do. But there I was,—and the point was how to carry into effect a plan which had been continually thwarted by others, and which I could not execute in any other way. My first intention, that of going in search of the real sources of the Mississippi, was always before my eyes. I was therefore obliged to sacrifice my pride and my feeling of what was due to me, to the desire of seeing places which one can hardly expect to visit twice in one's life, and of gaining information one can gain nowhere else; and I gave myself up to all I foresaw I should have to endure from littleness and jealousy.

We set out from Fort St Peter on the evening of the 7th instant. The expedition consisted of major Long, as chief, an astronomer, a mineralogist, a physician, a zoologist, an artist, Mr Renville, interpreter for the Sioux, a young Canadian, interpreter for the Algonquine language, twenty-eight men, one officer, and Mr Snelling, son of the colonel.

It was divided into two bodies, one of which went by land with twenty-two horses and mules; the other embarked on the river St Peter in five Indian canoes. The major accompanied the latter detachment, and I followed him with the intention of going sometimes by land and sometimes by water, according to the curious or interesting objects, either route might offer. It was determined that the two parties should meet every evening.

The river St Peter, called by the Sioux *Watpà-menisothé*, tracing it from its mouth, has at first a S. S. W. direction; it then bends to the south, and its constant windings turn to every point of the compass; but as its course, from its sources to the place where it falls into the Mississippi, is almost directly from N. N. W. to E. S. E., I shall distinguish the two banks as northern and southern every time I have occasion to designate them.

After all I have said in my preceding rambles about savages, it might appear that the subject is pretty well exhausted; but besides that the new country which opens before us has fresh sources of interest, it seems that the things we meet with here are admirably calculated to serve as appendices to what we have seen before. If any repetition occur, it will only serve to confirm us in the belief of what had perhaps at first appeared too marvellous.

The first evening we encamped on the southern bank, above the tribe of the chieftain Wamenitonka, or the Black Dog. I had seen this camp extremely populous a few days before, and now we found it a desert; hunger had roused these savages from their habitual indolence, and had driven them to hunt deer and buffalos in more distant forests and prairies. A hut which was shut, and which we opened, afforded us some shelter from the musquitos which attacked us on every side, and against the rain which has attended us ever since our departure. Behind the oak-bark which slightly fastened the door, we found, hung like a curtain, a deer-skin which the savages looked upon as the guardian Manitou of their house. When they return they will probably choose some more trusty *Swiss*, and the deer will lose their confidence and his own divinity at the same time.

The encampment of Paniscihowa on the eastern bank, where we stopped to breakfast on the morning of the eighth, was equally deserted, and for the same reason; but the chief, who is as lazy as he is gluttonous, had retired to the neighbourhood of the fort, to revel in Capuan luxury, and to shelter himself in that sacred and inviolable land from the incursions which the Cypowais, justly indignant at his conduct on the seventh of June, might make upon his *castle*.

We dined at the *Prairie des François*, so called from the first Frenchmen who pushed their discoveries from Canada to this spot, where they were killed by the Indians. It is thirty miles above the fort.

The chief Siacapè has his summer encampment on the east bank. The huts of this tribe are of a singular construction. The walls and roof are of oak bark, interwoven with split rods in so solid a manner, that the most violent hurricane could scarcely penetrate them. Everything here was also deserted. We found only a dog hanged, and thus consecrated to their *penates* or tutelary deities. To render the offering more acceptable, they had decorated his head with a plume of killow of which I stripped him to enrich my *savage* collection.

Next to the women, the dogs are the most unhappy animals in these regions. After being half starved and well worked at the chase, the truck, and the sledge, they end their days as a dinner or as a sacrifice.

On the opposite shore of the river, a meadow studded with little thickets and scattered with bones and *tumuli*, like those I remarked at St Louis and elsewhere, is an image of the Elysian Fields of antiquity; and though one tread on a wild soil, and bones of savages, the pathetic character of the spot strikes one with involuntary veneration, and the mind is agitated by varied feelings which carry it far into other worlds. Here I saw a most singular union: one of these graves was surmounted by a cross, whilst upon another close to it a trunk of a tree was raised, covered with hieroglyphics, recording the number of enemies slain by the tenant of the tomb, and several of his tutelary Manitous. Here presenting a fresh hint to those who are fond of system-making on the subject of the religion of these people, to be cautious in their inductions.

Sixty miles from the fort is a fall, or to speak more accurately, a violent rapid. We pulled up our canoes, dragging them ourselves through the water. This is the first interesting point we met with on this river. Rocks picturesquely grouped, between which the winding stream rushes and breaks with violence; a little woody island in the middle; banks clothed with shady trees on the one side, and broken into steep and rugged rocks on the other, composed a varied and romantic picture, to which I contrived to add a touch of the grotesque. Being obliged to get on board the canoe to cross a deep gulf, my sailors were so deficient either in strength or in skill, that they suffered it to be carried away by the current and dashed in pieces against a rock, upon which I remained perched.

In the evening we halted at the Indian camp of the *Battue au fief*, where I witnessed a most curious contrast. A woman in the deepest affliction was tearing off her hair, which she offered as a sacrifice to the *manes* of some relative, whose lifeless remains were stretched upon a scaffold; while a group of savages were eating, drinking, singing and dancing around another body, exposed in the same manner to the view of passengers, like those of the heroes of antiquity. Here again I must beg you to observe the extreme difficulty of forming any accurate opinion as to their usages or ceremonies.

The next day I quitted the canoe, and got on horseback; the passage of Bois-Franc, in the Indian tongue *Cianthote*, excited my curiosity, and amply repaid it. For thirty miles there is a continual series of trees of every kind, and of delicious fruit-bearing shrubs; little smiling meadows; lakes covered with swans and other aquatic birds; delightful plains, and picturesque hills. It seems a fit haunt for nymphs and dryads; unfortunately, however, we found it inhabited by nothing more agreeable than musquitos and gadflies, which excoriated man and beast. I cannot describe the impression which such a solitude, without a human creature to enjoy its beauty or its riches, makes upon the mind.

We saw hieroglyphics engraven on a tree; they signified that the tribe of the Red Hawk—(the Sussitons) had passed that way with their chief. Everything was recorded; the number of men and of women,—whence they came,—whither they were going,—where they had been hunting, &c. By this means the Indians reciprocally convey much useful information; in the present instance, here was an *avviso* to others not to throw away their trouble on ground which had just been beaten. This passage is a labyrinth; and had we not been accompanied by Mr Renville, who had quitted the canoe party to act as guide, we should not easily have found our way out. The forest extends over the country towards the Missouri to an immense distance. We emerged from it on the west, where we found a vast and magnificent prairie, called by the Indians Wayo-Theè, or the Arrow. A great block of granite, which is visible from a considerable distance on the left, serves the wandering savages at once as a temple and a tutelary deity in their hunting parties. It was painted with a nose, eyes and mouth, as the sun and moon frequently were among civilized nations, until Maria, the preceptor of Copernicus at Bologna, and Bianchini, robbed them of these features. All the tribes which pass that way go to pay it homage and offerings.

At the spot where we encamped, Mr Renville, who has the most perfect acquaintance with the Sioux, being born and having lived among them, pointed out to me a very singular thing, an Indian *Hypocauston,* or *Sudatoria.* When their physicians wish to throw a patient into a perspiration, they shut him up in a little hut between four massy stones of different colours, heated by fire, which they regard as so many divinities. The red is the god of war, the black of death, the green of health, the white of fine weather. The patient remains there until he gives notice, by fainting, that he can stay no longer; it would be a sacrilege to utter a single syllable in order to be let out. It often happens that he is stifled in this manner, particularly if the priests of the *Grande Medicine* have any reason for wishing to get rid of him. An Indian Esculapius is like those of antiquity, both high-priest and physician, so that he is armed with double shears to cut short the life of his superstitious patients. There were also other traces of offerings, which equally indicated the multiplicity of their Manitous.

On the 11th, I returned to the canoes, where we met with nothing very extraordinary except a terrible storm, which upset one, and made us lose a part of our powder and tobacco: it followed us to our camp, where we were deluged by it all night, our tent being open on both sides. I was more thoroughly drenched than any of the others, because the major, faithful to the rules of *bienséance* and politeness, which allot the place of honour to the stranger, had had the attention to place me on one of the two sides of the tent; in order, no doubt, that I might observe the weather at my ease, and reap the glory of struggling valiantly against the fury of the wind, rain, hail, thunder and lightning.

We travelled very slowly by water up the river, which gradually became narrower and more rapid. The major at length saw the necessity of sending back the canoes with a number of the men, who only encreased the dearth of provisions we already began to experience. Though I had laid in an abundant store, which I had thrown into the common stock, yet, at no more than a hundred miles from Fort St Peter, hunger made me envy the hermit of the Thebais the daily morsel of bread brought him by the raven. These soldiers were moreover of no use whatever. The major feared the Sussitons, who are not very friendly to the Americans, but we were too few to make any effectual resistance against a horde of Indians of the most warlike and formidable tribe, and too many for an expedition which had no hostile intentions, and which was already reduced to have its daily portion of food doled out.

I have told you, that they were afraid of the Sussitons. Not to let your curiosity languish, I must tell you the reasons, were it only to throw additional light on the Indian character, and on the resistless power the passion of revenge exercises over them.

One of these Sussitons lost two relations who served in the last war under the English banners against the United States. He resolved to revenge himself upon the two first Americans who fell into his hands. But as some time elapsed without any such opportunity for vengeance occurring, he set out with his cousin; they made a landing by night at Rocky Island, near Fort Armstrong, seven hundred miles from their own haunts; there they lay in wait, and seized the moment when two soldiers of the garrison were walking at some distance from the fort, and killed them both with two well-aimed muskets.

The government, under pretence of holding a council and giving presents, allured a band of the Sussitons to Council Bluff, and seized two of them, who were never seen again. A government founded upon wise and liberal laws ought to be more generous than savages; but either it had no other means of reprisal and of punishment, without engaging in a murderous war with the whole Sioux nation, or its agents acted in an arbitrary and unauthorized manner.

On the 13th we all proceeded by land. A prairie studded with thickets and clumps of trees, which broke the distance in the most enchanting manner, was the first prospect that lay before our eyes. The artificial parks of St Cloud, Versailles, Richmond, or Windsor, are not comparable to this superb work of nature.

In the middle of this terrestrial paradise we found an Indian sarcophagus, about fifteen feet in height. Here Mr Renville shewed us the direction, towards the south west, in which the river of the Blue Earth, *Muskatohose- Watpà*, falls into the St Peter. This is the highest point of the river reached by Father Hannepin and other travellers after him.

The river of the Blue Earth is very celebrated among the Indians. They perform an annual pilgrimage to it, to collect the blue earth of its banks, of which they make dye and paint. At some distance from its sources, in the direction of the Missouri, they dig up a kind of red stone, which hardens on exposure to the air; of this they make their sacred calumets. It is said that these two spots are inviolable, and that the most implacable enemies meet there in peace; but this is a mere fable. The Indian never lays aside the pursuit of vengeance: if ever he refrains from the open expression of it, it is only when he is withheld by superior force.

In the evening we halted near a little wood which lies along the banks of the Lake of Swans. It was the season at which these beautiful birds cannot fly,—the old ones, because they are changing their feathers; the young, because they have as yet only a soft down. We might have had some good shooting, and the *savans* among us might have gained new and valuable Ornithological information, but the major was intent on *making an expedition*, and consulted nothing but his compass: it was sufficient for him to say, "I have been there." On the morning of the 14th we traversed another prairie of a perfectly different character. Little hillocks of the greenest turf formed the undulations of a sea which Vernet or Verdstapen would have vainly tried to imitate. Isolated hills rose in the distance, like the pyramids of Egypt.

At noon we passed the river St Peter at the spot where the river *des Liards, Wagahosà Watpà*, joins it from the south. It is navigable for canoes a considerable way inland.

In the evening, after crossing a region of equal beauty, consisting of alternate prairies and little woods, and wearing the appearance of a cultivated country, we halted near a marsh which was covered with the dwellings of the musk rats. They are formed of rushes and the bark of trees; they rise three or four feet out of the water, and these upper stories are their bedchambers. The part under the water serves them as a winter storehouse, which they fill during summer with the bark of fruit trees. They dig a subterranean passage, the mouth of which is at a distance from the dwelling and in the centre of the marsh ; by this means they escape the vigilance of the hunter; but they fall into the snares which he spreads around them, and into which he entices them by a bait of some favourite food.

The Red Wood was our inn on the 15th. It is so called from a tree which the savages paint red every year, and for which they have a peculiar veneration. It has nothing remarkable to distinguish it from other trees, but every tribe has its favourite images, though they all represent the same divinity, the same object of worship. Whilst one shrine overflows with offerings, another has not so much as a candle burning before it. The fortune of the god, among the antients, often depended on the address of his minister; perhaps it is the same among the Indians.

In this tree they adore the thunder which, as they think, comes from the Rocky Mountains, separating, as we have already seen, Louisiana from New Mexico. This wood is situated on the south bank of the St Peter, and another river which flows into it through the centre of the wood descends from the same point. The natives call it *Ciangagappy Watpà*, i. e. the river of the Red Wood. I was told that the English emissaries came here to offer prayers and incense, and to invoke the protection of this savage divinity, when, during the last war, they stirred up the Sioux against the United States. It is worth while to observe, that the pious British cabinet was accusing Bonaparte of apostacy to Islamism at the very time it was playing the part of the knavish teacher of idolatry in America. Opposite to this spot the *Ciatambè Watpà*, or Brandy river, which flows from the north, falls into the St Peter.

We now reached a valley of the most lovely and interesting character. Never did a more striking illusion transport my imagination back to the classic lands of Latium and Magna Grecia. Rocks scattered, as if by art, over the plain, on *plateaux*, and on hills, were at a little distance perfect representations of every varied form of the ruins of antiquity. In one place you might think you saw thermal substructures, or those of an amphitheatre, a circus, or a forum; in another, the remains of a temple, a cenotaph, a basilicon, or a triumphal arch. I took advantage of the time which chance procured me, to survey this enchanted ground; but I went alone, that the delicious reverie it threw me into might not be broken by cold-heartedness or presumption. My eyes continually met new images: at length they rested on a sort of tomb, which for some time held me motionless. A thousand afflicting recollections rushed to my heart: I thought I beheld the tomb of Virtue and of Friendship; I rested my head upon it, and tears filled my eyes. The spot was of a kind to soften and embellish grief, and I should have long given myself up to its sweet influence had I not been with people who had no idea of stopping for anything but a broken saddle or some such important incident.

These rocks are granitic, and of so beautiful and varied a quality, that the tricking dealers of the Piazza Navona, at Rome, would sell them to the most enthusiastic, and,—in their own opinion,—the most learned antiquarians, as oriental and Egyptian porphyry or basalt, which are now generally admitted to be merely granite more elaborated by time and by water. Nature seems to have lavished all her treasures on this beautiful valley: watered by the river St Peter, it possesses a fertile soil, a salubrious climate, hills and plains adapted to every sort of cultivation, rivers and lakes abounding in fish, shell-fish, and game; delicious groves and forests swarming with deer and with animals of the richest fur, and furnishing every variety of timber for building and cabinet work; and, added to all these riches, magnificent stone, which might be worked with the greatest facility, and fitted for building barns, houses, temples, or palaces. Here might arise the *Urbs Marmorea* of Augustus, as the Europeans found the *Domus Aurea* of Nero at Peru; and the immense blocks of granite scattered here and there with such picturesque negligence, might with small aid from the chisel be raised to rival the pyramids of Memphis or Palmyra. When I awoke from the dream of all that this favoured valley might become, I was struck by feelings I cannot describe at its awful and desert stillness —feelings which perhaps no other scene could awaken. Here Zimmerman or la Fontaine might *indeed* have painted solitude, with less metaphysical refinement and more truth. Perhaps however they would be less read; for in all that concerns human affections and emotions, fashionable caricature and affectation will always be more popular than nature and simplicity.

On the 16th, we came to a prairie, which on the south had no boundary but the horizon, on the north the valley of the St Peter, on the west the winding valley of the river of the Yellow Medicine, *Pepeothaziziapi-Watpà*, which descends from the south-west and falls into the St Peter on its southern shore. On the opposite side is the river of the Jumpers, *Maiioakan-Watpà*, which flows from the north. In this prairie we met two Indians: they told us some buffalos had been killed the day before, but we saw only scattered bones, while our miserable diet was a little biscuit and a semi-diaphonous slice of bad salt meat. The river of the Yellow Medicine is so called from a root of that colour, which imposture and credulity have invested with mystical properties for curing both soul and body. This place is calculated to be about one hundred and eighty miles from Fort St Peter.

Twenty miles from thence, we passed the *Watpà-Danitpà* or Beavers' river, which formerly abounded in those animals, and which descends from the west. At a short distance from its mouth is the *Medeyethàan*, or the Speaking Lake, which is only a narrow basin about sixteen miles in length, filled by the St Peter, which enters it in the north-west and flows out on the south-east. Between this lake and the mouth of the Yellow Medicine, are rapids which interrupt the navigation, and compel those who are ascending to quit the river and travel by land for about a mile.

After passing the river of Precipices, *Skewakan-Watpà*, the river *aux Grais*, *Issonya-hose-Watpà*, on the southern bank, and the Potatoes river, *Stoobodathè-Watpà*, on the opposite side, we came to the lake of the Big Rock, *Hiakiakia-ya-*

Medé, also formed by the St Peter, which runs in on the north, and out on the E. S. E. It is larger and wider than the preceding one.

A numerous party of that tribe of the Sioux called the *Wakapetohan*, or People of the Leaf, who were encamped there, came to meet us and invite us to a feast. I was very sorry that the haste in which it was prepared had unfortunately deprived us of the dish of etiquette—a dog—which they had not had time to flay and season. The hunger by which we were tortured made us feel this as a most cruel privation. We devoured whatever they gave us, and everything appeared to me delicious, even some roots which they call *prairie-potatoes*, and which I had before thought detestable.

The major pronounced a speech, which appeared probably very good to his government, whose power, greatness, and generosity, he greatly extolled, but very bad to the Indians, since it concluded with the information that he had nothing to give them; and accordingly neither the chiefs nor anybody else made the slightest answer. When the interpreter explained to them that "the United States were composed of twenty-four fires, (meaning thereby twenty-four states,) without reckoning the district of Colombia, in which is the seat of the grand congress and of the grand general administration, and the residence of the *great father*, the president;—that they were peopled with so many millions of men, who were thriving by means of commerce and agriculture, and lived in wealth and plenty," &c. &c.—some yawned, others looked contemptuous; and when he added that "the expedition was going to trace the remote boundaries of the American territory," all looked greatly annoyed. Even savages, it seems, are not very fond of seeing other people play the master in their country.

These Indians have a very ferocious and war-like aspect. A great proportion of them are mounted, but, like the nations of the remotest antiquity, have neither saddle nor stirrups; they have only a skin girt over the horse's back, like the *vestis stragula*, or the *strata* of the Romans.

On the evening of the 17th, we stopped at the middle of the lake, just where it takes a northern direction, where a magnificent wood and a miserable little trader's settlement are crossed by the river of the White Herons, or *Hokazambè-Watpà*, which falls into the lake on the southern side. The soft murmur of these limpid waters, the sight of Indian tents and huts scattered here and there, and shaded by majestic trees, added to the charms of this truly picturesque spot.

Three miles above the end of the lake, still keeping on to the northward, we crossed the

St Peter, now a mere ditch. At this point all the canoes stop and unload their merchandize; it is transported hither across a prairie of six miles to the N. N. W., where we arrived on the 18th.

We landed at the only hut; it is an establishment formed by some Scotchmen, who have deserted the English North-West and Hudson's Bay Companies. Mr Renville is one of the partners.

As these gentlemen naturally come in competition with the South-West American Company, they must have sunk at the very outset under the weight of its powerful jealousy; but with the address and cunning for which their nation is so pre-eminent, wherever money is to be made, they have got some Americans to join them and to lend their names, and have christened this the Fur Colombian American Company: they have consequently obtained a licence to trade from the superintendant of the savages. In spite of all their dexterity, however, I think they will be obliged in the end to capitulate with the South-West Company, and to put themselves under its protection.

This situation is extremely advantageous for the fur trade; the traders are quite in the midst of the Sioux, and can push their speculations up to the Missouri and the Colombia, provided that the Russians, who have taken possession of th mouth of the latter river, will let them.

The sources of the St Peter are situated at about twenty miles from this lake, towards the north-west. It would have been interesting to *reconnoitre* them, were it merely to fix the latitude and longitude, and for the glory of being the first to behold them,—but they were not on the route of the expedition, and were therefore neglected.

They spring from the foot of a chain of hills, which the Indians call the Hills of the Prairies, because they run due north and south across those vast prairies lying between the Missouri and the St Peter, from the mountains of the Great Eagle to the sources of Blue Earth river.

I am likewise deprived of the satisfaction of informing you of the exact geographical position of this place (Lake Travers,) for the major carefully concealed it from me: he no doubt had his reasons for this, which I shall not enquire into.

The distance from Fort St Peter is nearly two hundred and eighty miles by land N. N. W. and four hundred by the river, which is very winding.

This lake and the sources of the St Peter are upon the high lands which separate the waters flowing southward from those which take a northward course; and, in fact, the waters of the lake and those of the St Peter cross in opposite directions—the former flows into the Red river, and consequently into Hudson's Bay, the latter by the Mississippi into the Gulph of Mexico.

Lake Travers is on one of the highest points of North America, and is not formed by any affluence or confluence of tributary streams. All around it are prairies and eternal plains; nor can one guess whence it can derive its waters. This surprise is augmented by the total absence of all traces of an extinct volcano, and indeed the shallowness of its bed excludes all conjecture of the kind. Its length from south to north is about fifteen miles; its greatest width two miles. Two islands, frequently inhabited by Indians, form a beautiful ornament to it, and its banks, diversified by wood and meadow, are extremely pleasant.

The great Wanathà, whom I introduced to your acquaintance when I gave you the numbers of the Sioux, came to receive us on our arrival, and invited us to a feast. He had been informed of our coming before-hand, so that a dog had been immolated, and already smoked on the altar of the god of hospitality. Famished as we were, we should have thought it delicious, and should probably not have left even that portion which the Indians distribute after the banquet among the physically and morally diseased, as a remedy for all evils, had not the flesh of the buffalo carried off all our votes. I ought here to remark to you, that the dog, on whatever occasion they sacrifice it, is always an offering to the Manitous, and the eating of it is no less an act of devotion, just as the priests of antiquity lived jollily on the victims offered by true believers on the altars of their divinities. We should therefore have given great scandal by the preference we showed for buffalo flesh, had we not fortunately been at the table of a king, who, like most kings, was not over scrupulous in religious matters, except where his interests required that he should be so.

The major preached him a sermon, as academical as the former, touching the sublime qualities, physical and moral, of his government—for I must do the Americans the justice to say that, as to modesty, they have not in the least degenerated from that which distinguishes the mother country. But as the conclusion of this harangue was not more satisfactory than that of the other, his majesty did not even deign to look at him; and while the interpreter was explaining the doctrines of political economy, he amused himself by laughing, with an air of right royal nonchalance, with his highness the hereditary prince, who was lying on the ground by his side.

The gentlemen of the Colombian Company received us with great politeness, and during the three days we spent there hunger was softened into appetite; but new as they are in these places, and cramped for room in their huts, they are worse lodged than the Indians, who, at any rate, can change their dwelling every day. Beset moreover by the Indian women, who are their wïves, *à la mode du pays*, it is impossible for them to avoid the filth these fair ones import. I had such a horror of their dirt, that I entreated to be allowed to lodge in one of our tents; but the major, who wishes to train me to the virtue of patience, refused to have it pitched; and fleas and other vermin concurred with him in pushing the trial to the verge of martyrdom. He thinks this perhaps a good way of carrying off any bad blood his conduct might occasion.

I leave you, my dear Countess, to give you time to recruit yourself after a ramble through which I have hurried you as rapidly as I was compelled to perform it myself, and the description of which must shew the haste with which I am obliged to put my thoughts on paper. But you, dear Madam, seek the friend, and not the author, in

Yours, &c.

LETTER XVIII.

Selkirk Colony, Bloody River,
August 10*th*, 1823.

Though you must be prepared to follow me a little farther, my dear Countess, and into regions where nature exhibits features less interesting than those we have recently beheld, yet as I lead you towards the cool breezes of the Pole, and as our adventures will be more varied, I hope you will find this ramble less wearisome than the last.

The country we are about to traverse is one eternal prairie, intersected only by rivers and belts of wood, which edge their banks. The horizon is the only boundary of these immense plains, and the direction which every individual may choose towards, or between, the four cardinal points, the only road he can follow. We turned our faces towards the north, and have steadily pursued it up to this place.

We set out on the 24th July from Lake Travers, of which we took leave with a salute of musketry; this same day the buffalos made their appearance. My horse gave notice of their approach by the ardour with which he was animated. He was the finest horse of the party, and as I had often dismounted and walked a little to rest him, he was in the best condition, and the most spirited in this extraordinary chace.

Following the traces of Mr Renville, who is renowned as a hunter, even among the Indians, I gave my horse the reins and let him go in pursuit of the first buffalo we saw. I soon came up with and passed him, though he was two miles off, and having turned him, we drove him towards our people to give them the pleasure of so new a scene, and I shot him before their eyes. At the same time Mr Yeffray, one of the gentlemen of Lake Travers, who was our guide, killed another at a little distance; and in the evening the driver, who carried my baggage in his waggon, brought us a third. For the first time, plenty reigned in our camp;—there was no wood, but the buffalo's dung, which lay scattered about in abundance, formed an admirable substitute. It makes an astonishingly strong fire.

The surprise I felt on a near view of this animal was equal to my pleasure in hunting it; its appearance is truly formidable. In size it approaches the elephant. Its flowing mane, and the long hair which covers its neck and head and falls over its eyes, are like those of the lion. It has a hump like a camel, its hind quarters and tail are like those of the hippopotamus, its horns like those of the large goat of the Rocky Mountains, and its legs like those of an ox.

The following day we found the great chief encamped in this prairie, near the Sioux river, *Ciàntapa-Watpà*, which serves as an outlet to the waters of Lake Travers. He was in a new and very clean tent; he offered us the tongues and humps of buffalos, which are great delicacies, very nicely cured; but he preserved a most invincible gravity and taciturnity. Whenever we turned our eyes, we saw innumerable herds of buffalos. I begged the major to endeavour to induce the chief to give us the sight of a buffalo hunt with bows and arrows, but he replied, with his usual complaisance, that he could not stop.

I let him go on: and Mr Renville prevailed on the chief to satisfy my curiosity. We galloped towards a meadow which was perfectly black with them. My horse, who now regarded neither rein nor voice, plunged into the centre of the herd, dividing it into halves, and turned several of them. The chief, who followed me with Mr Renville, let fly his arrow and shot a female buffalo; she still endeavoured to escape, but the motion of her body in running caused the arrow to sink deeper into the wound, and when she fell the whole barb had entered.

Never did I see attitudes so graceful as those of the chief. They alternately reminded me of the equestrian statue of Marcus Aurelius on the Capitol, and that of the great Numidian king. Altogether it was the most astonishing spectacle I ever saw. I thought I beheld the games and combats of the ancients. I played nearly the same part as the Indians of former ages, who thought the first European they saw on horseback was a being of a superior order; while the chief with his quiver, his horse, and his victim, formed a group worthy the pencil of Raphael or the chisel of Canova. I was so enchanted by this living model of classical beauty, that I forgot my part in the chace, and was only aroused to a recollection of it by the voice of the chief, who pointed to a young buffalo, which I fired at and killed. His majesty did me the honour to say I was an excellent shot. Any one of our *grands veneurs* who should receive such a compliment from one of our kings, would be immortalized, and the court poets would dispute the honour of celebrating his glories. Mr Renville killed a buffalo.

Wolves also appeared on the scene, and formed very curious episodes intimately connected with the principal action, according to all the rules of the Epopea.

These animals are as fond of the delicious flesh of the buffalo as man; but as they are too weak to attack, they employ cunning to entrap him. Wherever they see hunters, they immediately follow in their track and take whatever advantage circumstances may chance to afford. Sometimes they regale themselves upon the offal which is left on the field; sometimes they follow those which they see have been wounded, and which the hunters do not go in pursuit of; on this occasion they showed quite a new contrivance. Three of them joined our charge upon the great herd, and at the moment the females were so occupied in making their own escape that they could not defend their young ones, each wolf seized upon a calf, strangled it, and dragged it off the field: when we had got to a little distance they returned and regaled themselves with their prey. When they are pressed by hunger, and no hunters come to their aid, they have recourse to another stratagem still more surprising. They approach five or six of a herd without appearing to have any design of attacking them. The buffalos, who do not condescend to be afraid, pay no attention to them whatever — they neither avoid nor attack them. The wolves then single out their victim, which is always a female, as the most delicious food, and invariably the fattest of the herd. Whilst two or three keep her attention engaged in front by pretending to play with her, one of the strongest and most active seizes her behind by the teats, and when she turns round to drive him off, those in front fly at her throat and strangle her. Sometimes, however, all their wiles are abortive. But we must rejoin our party; they are getting on, while we loiter wondering at the ceaseless varieties of nature. Mr Renville put me upon their track and returned to rejoin the chief, who meanwhile was procuring a larger supply of victims for his family to flay and cure.

At this place Mr Renville took his leave of the expedition; business prevented his accompanying us farther. I found them encamped near a little wood, which occurred most providentially to furnish us with the means of drying ourselves after a terrible storm which had drenched us to the skin.

On the 27th at noon, we reached the confluence of the Sioux river, and what is called the

Red river; and here I must detain you a moment to point out a geographical error, or rather fraud.

Charles II, king of England, by a charter of the year 1670, granted what did not belong to him; and as men willingly profit by abuses which favour their views, he sheltered himself under the authority of Borgia, that is to say, under the *right of discovery*, which that infamous pontiff had proclaimed. Sanctioned by such a principle and such a charter, prince Robert and his associates, under the name of the Hudson's Bay Company, appropriated not only the exclusive fur trade of these countries, but also all the lands lying near or beyond Hudson's Bay; though that bay had been discovered by the Danish navigator Auschild, before Hudson visited it, and though parliament refused to confirm the charter.

They afterwards affected to consider this property as extending to the sources of the Red river, and over all the lands washed by the various rivers which fall into it; and as the course of the Red river was not long enough and did not receive a sufficient number of tributary streams for the wishes of these gentlemen, they baptized the river we are now considering under the same name; and geographers, who often lay down maps without having been out of their own parish, or with *venal* instruments, have sanctioned the cheat. According to them there are consequently two Red rivers, at no great distance, the one of which flows into the other. This then into which the Sioux river falls, is not the Red river, but the river *Neguiquanosibi*, as the Cypowais call it, or the river of the Otter's-tail, from its having its source in the lake of that name. The Sioux know it under the name *Kakaweuapi-Watpà*, or the river of the Falls, from the number of them which occur on its issuing from the lake.

In the afternoon we descried a herd of deer grazing at a distance. Mr Yeffray followed me, and as my horse with all his speed could not have overtaken them, we had recourse, like the wolves, to stratagem. We crept towards them on our hands and knees, and hung our bridles on our right arms, our horses followed us, and so effectually engaged their attention, that we were enabled to approach them near enough, though on the middle of the meadow, to fire upon them. We killed one. It was a magnificent animal of the most exquisitely beautiful and graceful form. It is one of the same family as the rein-deer, and like them may be tamed and trained for the cart or the sledge. It was a female, and being consequently without horns, was precisely like a fine English horse. Mr Yeffray skinned it, and we carried off as much of the flesh as we could; it is delicious food. You ask which of us had the honours of the chace. We fired at the same instant, on my giving the word; so that the size of the ball alone could decide: and on this evidence the glory was adjudged to me.

Night overtook us, and the distant fires of the camp were our only guide to the expedition. On our arrival we found it in great consternation. Our companions had met a band of Sioux. The major thought he read hostile intentions in their faces; he even thought they had threatened him;—of course everybody else thought so too—like Casti's courtiers, who perfectly agreed with *his majesty* that it rained torrents, though the sun was then shining in all its brilliancy. It was incumbent on me, therefore, to be very much alarmed too; and, for the first time since I had been in America, I girded on my sword in a warlike manner. But as in spite of the major's indiscretion in telling these Indians that we were behind with our horses, (the greatest temptation to their cupidity) they had not attacked us, which they might have done with the greatest ease; and as he had stationed four or five sentinels round the camp, who made noise enough for three times their number, I thought the danger could not be very great, and lay down quietly to sleep under a cart. At midnight, however, I was awakened. The camp had begun its march, or rather flight. The major's agitation was not yet calmed, nor did we halt until the 28th at noon, when we stopped on the banks of the Otter's-tail river, at the point where the Wild Oats river, or *Sau-Watpà*, falls into it from the west. During the night we had crossed two other small rivers, which descend from the east, the Perelle, or *Wayeccei-aoshu-Watpà*, and the Strong Wood river, or *Ciontanka-Watpà*. The heat was terrible, and we felt it the more from the extreme coldness of the nights. Fahrenheit's thermometer sometimes reached 94, 96, and 98, in the day, and fell to 58 in the same night.

I reposed again under the shelter of a cart, for in the woods the musquitos are perfectly devouring. To crown all, I could not bathe; the river is so muddy that one sinks up to the neck in the bottom.

The Indians, who gave us such a breathing, were the very same who had feasted us at the lake of the Big Rock. I rather think the fright they threw the major into was in revenge for his giving them nothing but boring speeches. If they meant it so, they had every reason to be satisfied; for from that time forward he would not suffer us to hunt buffalos, for fear of irritating the Indians; and in order to station advanced posts and vedettes round the camp, he had levied a general conscription on the whole party, which lasted till within a day's march of Pembenar.

You would have laughed heartily, my dear Countess, to hear me call "*Who goes there?*" and "*All's well,*" when I was sentinel. The geese who saved the Capitol did not give the word better. I never thought it would be my lot to mount guard *in English*—but it is the fate of us poor Italians, when under arms, to use all watch-words but our own.

Regions which have never been traversed by any other wanderer, nor by any former expeditions, demand greater geographical detail than is consistent with the limits of a letter, or with my ordinary indolence. I therefore tell you of all the rivers in our route, and I have even the patience and the courage to make you read all their savage names. I am anxious to give the *savans,* the Hellenists, the Orientalists, &c. who swarm in your circles, an opportunity of guessing or inventing an origin for these tribes from some analogy of language.

The rivers we crossed on the 29th and the 30th, days very barren in incidents, are the *Kauta-Watpà,* or river of Plums—where not only there were no plums but no water, and we were dying of thirst; and the *Katapa-Watpà,* or river of Buffalos. This, unlike the former, was appropriately named, so that my horse would have several times disregarded the Major's prohibition, if I had not called him strictly to order. We also crossed a third, the river of Wild Oats; these all fall into the Otter's-tail river on the eastern side. The Cayenne river, or *Kayöes-Watpà*, so called from the name of the people who formerly inhabited its shores, and whom the Sioux have driven in the direction of Columbia;—the river of Elms, or *Kousion-Watpà*, from the number of trees of that species, of extraordinary height, which shade its banks;—and the Bustard's river, or *Magassan-Watpà*, from the birds which frequent it, all flow from the west: the Kayoës river is of considerable size.

On the 31st of July we reached the real Red river, which descends from the east from the lake of the same name, and receives, fifteen miles below the spot where we crossed it, the Otter's-tail river, miscalled the Red river by the Hudson's Bay Company, the sources of which are to the S.S.E. of its confluence.

Geographers tell us that it takes its name from the red sand or gravel which covers its bed; but there is nothing red about it. The origin of its name is widely different: *red*, to be sure, had something to do with it, but a *red* arising from very different causes.

This river, and the lake from which it springs, form the frontier line which separates the territory, or pretended territory, of the Sioux from that of the Cypowais, or at least the line upon which they have always met and still most frequently meet. It may easily be imagined then that the waters of a stream so situated, must have often been " red with the blood of the slain," and that it has thus received from both the contending parties the name of the Bloody river,—in the Sioux language *Maniscia-Watpà;* in the Cypowais, *Sahaguiaigney-Sibi.* The lake is in like manner called the Bloody lake.

Beyond this river we saw no more buffalos. The country becomes less open; the underwood and scattered thickets make them fear the ambushed hunter; but in winter, when they find no food in the vast prairies,—bare of all trees and shrubs, and the grass of which is yearly burnt down by the Indians,—they frequently repair thither to browse on the buds and sprouts, which form their principal food, as well that of the horses, when the terrible frosts destroy all other vegetation.

Hitherto, my dear Madam, you have only seen the manner in which buffalos are hunted on horseback; but, as the Indians are not all mounted, there are other very curious modes. Before we leave these regions, therefore, which

I shall in all probability never see again, let us sit down on the banks of this delightful river, under the shade of these beautiful trees, and study the singular characteristics of this animal; let us also observe its haunts, since fate has led us to them, and we shall have more correct and vivid conceptions of both than we could form from the books of the most learned naturalists.

You have seen that buffalos feed in the midst of wolves without fear, either because they disdain them, or because beasts, like men, must fulfil their destiny. The Indians take advantage of this fact to disguise themselves like wolves, creep near them on hands and knees, and pierce them with their arrows. They choose these weapons for the ease with which they can hide their quivers under their bodies, while, on the contrary, their gun is in the way. Besides, the noiseless stroke of the arrow does not alarm, and enables them to multiply their victims; they spare powder and shot, and always recover their arrows when they flay their prey. When the savages hunt in this manner in a party, each has his arrows marked as in battle, and by this means it is afterwards ascertained who have been the most valiant and successful marksmen; and, if any individual hunts apart, he takes possession of the animal which has been killed by the arrow bearing his mark.

In the season when nature renews their loves, the Indians wrap themselves in buffalo's skins, and imitating their lowing, entice the females, who approach without fear, but meet with wounds and death. Sometimes, under the same disguise, they decoy them into an enclosure, where they slaughter them.

When the ice on a river is not very thick, they go behind a herd and terrify them by firing guns, while one of them, disguised like a buffalo, gets in front and runs across the river to the opposite bank. The whole herd follows; for they are like the sheep of Panurge, where one goes, all go; the ice, which is not strong enough to bear such a multitude, breaks, and the confusion which ensues affords abundant opportunity to the Indians to rush out of their hiding places and seize their prey. The Indians also creep on all-fours through the grass, as we did, and shoot them with muskets or bows.

In whichever way the buffalo is hunted, it is necessary to come upon him against the wind, otherwise he scents his human pursuer from afar, and avoids, even without seeing him.

It is very dangerous to fire at him when asleep, for if he is only wounded, he rises with a bound and rushes on the hunter with resistless force. When he sees one of his favourites wounded, he sometimes combats as if to protect her flight, covers her with his body if she cannot escape, and dies at her side, the victim of heroic love.

The female is faithful to her chosen companion until the birth of the fruit of their union; while he, on the contrary, divides his affections among a seraglio of mistresses. This is a distribution of nature to secure the perpetuity of the species; for, by one of her incomprehensible laws, the number of males in proportion to the females is prodigiously small, although the latter, both by the delicacy of the flesh and the superior quality of the skins, are the only marks for both wolves and hunters; out of a hundred killed, there are not perhaps three males. This month is the season of their courtship. It is very curious to see the buffalo pay his court to the sultana of the moment. He dances round her in a circle like a horse in the *manège*, while she stands still in the centre and expresses her approbation of his suit in gentle lowings.

The Indians, especially those who are called the *People of the Wide Country*, those, namely, who roam to the remotest parts of these immense prairies, and who, as I have already told you, find almost all their wants supplied by the buffalo, venerate this dance as the harbinger of plenty and the palladium of their independence. Indeed, in the absence of all other animals, and in so open a country, they would often be reduced to the extremity of famine were it not for the resources furnished them by this invaluable creature. By a very natural association, it becomes an object of religious observance and celebration, and the dance which they call the buffalo dance, in which they imitate its gestures and lowing, can be performed by none but those who have been initiated into the mysteries of the Grand Medicine.

There are seasons in which the buffalos disappear. They migrate like birds of passage, but less regularly, and sometimes the time of their return is looked for in vain. Then follows a year of scarcity.

The Indians have not yet discovered to what cause to attribute these absences. Sometimes also it happens that they suddenly vanish in a most incomprehensible manner. These peculiarities in the buffalo's movements rouse the Indians from their usual habits of inertness, and of living from day to day, into some exertions to guard against the consequences,—which are not only famine, but total want of tent, bed and clothing,—by preserving the flesh and the hides. They prepare the latter better than our tanners, with no other implements than the bones of the animal. The flesh they cut into very long and slender strips, which they dry in the sun or smoke, and roll them up into balls so closely that they keep perfectly well for years.

We must proceed on our way, dear Madam. It is hard to leave these beautiful limpid waters, falsely said to be red; but perhaps we shall find them again higher up, for the project of wandering on in quest of the sources of the Mississippi has always been the principal whetstone to my ardour and perseverance.

You must have been puzzled to guess how I have found time for this long chat with you. Everybody, you know, has his good genius. Mine upset two waggons belonging to the expedition in very troublesome places, so that I gained all the time the Major lost.

The 1st of August was tremendously hot, though the night had been very cold. This was the more unwelcome, as we were without water all day. The river *Ciokan-Watpà*, i. e. the river of the Marsh, at which we hoped to slake our thirst at noon, was partly dry; even mud would have been very acceptable, but there was none. In the evening, when we reached a stinking ditch, we acted the *pendant* of Domenichino's wonderful picture of the Hebrews thirsting in the desert. We fell upon this ditch *pèle-mèle*,—men, dogs, and horses. One threw himself flat on his belly and dipped his mouth into it, another his cap, another his hands or his hat. We quarrelled for precedence, but the horses had decidedly the most powerful means of enforcing their pretensions, of which I retained convincing proofs in my right foot for at least ten days afterwards. The mud decorated our faces most beautifully, and the filthy water left us a pair of mustaches; to complete our graceful air, we were almost all lamed by the kicks we got from our horses. What an accommodation it would be to expeditions of this kind, if the Jews of Amsterdam would lend them the tip of Moses' rod, which they keep in their *sanctum sanctorum*. Perhaps, on *moderate terms*, they would.

On the 2nd, we crossed the river called the Two Rivers, *Nipa-Watpà;* and on the 3rd arrived at the celebrated colony, called Pembenar, from the name of a river which descends from the west and falls into the Red river at this spot. The Indians call it *Wettacia-Watpà*.

Reckoning from the confluence of the Otter's-tail, the Red river also receives on the same side (the west) the Tortoise river, *Atkasia-Watpà*,—the river of Salt, *Meniscouya-Watpà*, and the *Menissiceya-Watpà*, or river of the Park, so called from one of the Indian enclosures I described to you above.

This colony, or its skeleton, has been the scene of every species of fraud, crime, and atrocity. It is one of those hideous monsters which avarice and selfishness give birth to wherever they direct their steps.

It is a pity, my dear Madam, that I am not a *traveller dans les règles;* I should have a fine field for eternal narrations in these remote settlements, which are as little exposed to the view of morality or authority as of the world at large; but as it is, I can give you nothing but a slight sketch. You will be the better able to judge of the incidents I am going to relate to you, if I first trace out the scene of action.

The Red river divides the colony, which extended to this spot, but which began sixty miles lower down, directly on the north, near the place where the river of the Assiniboins falls into the Red river from the west. From this confluence the Red river flows on thirty miles farther, still in a northerly direction, and falls into lake Winipeg. This lake at its farther extremity in length, (which is three hundred miles from the south to the N. N. W.) discharges itself into Hudson's Bay by a great outlet or natural canal, which flows to the N. N. E. for about two hundred miles, and which the English called Nelson river, from the captain who first built a fort at its mouth.

The Hudson's Bay Company, in spite of the great concessions it had claimed and obtained in virtue of the charter I have mentioned, had not extended its commerce much above lake Winipeg before the year 1806: but its members, jealous of the thriving state of the North-West Company, which, as you have seen in my third and fourth rambles, was daily gaining ground, at length devised means to check its progress and to push their own speculations. The project of a colony was found to offer the most certain means of accomplishing both these ends. The times were propitious; for a great number of people were quitting England, Scotland, and Ireland. It was the policy of the English government to favour the scheme, in order that this torrent of emigrants might not encrease the population of the United States, already a source of alarm to England.

But to impose on the credulity of adventurers and speculators, something brilliant must be got up to dazzle and excite the imagination. Accordingly, lord Selkirk, a Scotch earl, of high birth and great fortune, was made choice of, and pretended to be associated in the enterprise. He was publicly given out to be possessed of greater wealth and higher qualities than he actually possessed; he was proclaimed a *tender father* of other colonies formed by him in Canada; colonies which *(par parenthèse)* had all failed. In 1811, the company pretended to sell him a vast tract of land on the Red river. To this land their title was still worse than that of Charles II, inasmuch as the charter granted only "the lands within the entrance of the streights commonly called Hudson's Streight;" nor had the aboriginal inhabitants ever given their consent to the occupation of them.

This farce was very well calculated to impose on the blind; but the North-West Company, who were very clear-sighted, and had their agents in the very centre of government, were not so easily gulled. They quickly perceived that the great lord was only a puppet moved at the will of the Hudson's Bay Company. They beheld this scheme in the light of a premeditated attack upon their interests, and an attempt at establishing an exclusive and arbitrary monopoly.

They could not however prevent the foundations of a settlement being laid by Mr Miles Macdonnell, and a few Highlanders from lord Selkirk's Scotch estates. This took place in 1812, near the confluence of the Assiniboin, where the North-West Company had for many years had a fort; but they immediately set to work to undermine the new settlement in every possible way, and, in the first instance, by exciting the animosity and jealousy of the savages against the settlers. But as the savages now received a double share of bounties, and as the company discovered that half measures are good for nothing, a large meeting of the partners assembled in 1814 at Fort William on lake Superior, one of their large establishments, where they concerted a plan for the destruction of the rival settlement.

From its very origin the North-West Company had obliged every Canadian in its service to marry *(à la mode du pays)* one of the Indian women, hoping by this means to attach them for ever to these deserts and forests, and to raise up a breed of obsequious emissaries and slaves. They succeeded; and it was to this execrable race, called the *Bois-Brulès*, from their complexions,—of a darker brown than that of the savages;—and to leaders, the most honest of whom had been two or three times under sentence of the laws, that the execution of this plan was entrusted. From that time the mask was thrown off, and war declared on both sides.

I will spare your benevolent heart the recital of horrors committed by both parties, from which humanity recoils. It is sufficient to know that the colony was beaten and dispersed in the June of 1815; and that, having rallied, it was finally destroyed in the same month of the following year. Governor Semple, the successor of Mr Macdonnell, who had been made prisoner the preceding year, was massacred, together with twenty of his men, and the fort taken and pillaged.

Meanwhile his lordship had arrived in Canada from England. He asked for troops to go to the succour of his colony, which he declared to be under the protection of government, and to arrest the offenders who had polluted the English territory by such horrible crimes. But the governor-general, who lent a more favourable ear to the golden arguments of the North-West Company than to the feeble voice of his lordship, would grant him no assistance. Lord Selkirk then instituted legal proceedings, but means were taken to place men upon the judgment-seat who were parties interested in the cause.

Two powerful enemies may mutually injure each other, at the same time that they labour, without suspecting it, in favour of a third party, who perhaps is the friend of neither, and who keeps vigilant watch on all their errors. In this case, Machiavel, I think, advises them to unite; so thought the two emperors Alexander and Napoleon, at Erfurth, and the Hudson's Bay and North-West Companies prudently followed their example. They saw that the Americans rejoiced at their dissensions, and were ready to take advantage of them; and by an act of oblivion, concord, and alliance, they have concealed from the public and the government their crimes and the falsehood of their pretended rights. But who committed the massacres? The Indians. And the brutal violations? The Indians. And the pillagings, &c. &c. It was all the Indians, who had never appeared on the scene. To keep up appearances, two or three of the unfortunate *Bois-Brulés* were given up to the authorities, who wished to make a parade of justice; for, as La Fontaine says, "according as you are powerful or wretched, the judgments of courts of justice will make you black or white." And so the affair ended.

The United Companies, however, found that this colony was very convenient and useful. It was a nursery for men, of whom they stood in great need for the numerous stations of their immense trade, which extends its ramifications as far as the Colombia; as well as for their transports, their internal navigation, &c. &c. These men too, they would pay as slaves, whereas Canadian labour was very costly.

But the English, Scotch, and Irish, had already discovered that the only fortune to be made in this colony was a bare maintenance, and that of the poorest kind; that sometimes food was not to be got; that if the soil was good, the locusts, or the storms, or the frosts, destroyed all the produce in the bud; that though only in the fiftieth degree, the cold was as intense as in Siberia; that men were frozen to death, and that trees and rocks were split by the frost. It was necessary therefore to look about among other nations, and they accordingly caught some good and credulous Germans and greedy Swiss, by means of the grand Prospectus, which you will find annexed.

A part of these poor people died of cold or of distress; others escaped, as they could, through fatigue, hunger and danger, and took refuge in the United States. I met some myself at the lake of the Big Rock, who were in a deplorable condition, as also at Fort St Peter, where the colonel and his officers assisted them in a truly philanthropic manner, and had the goodness to allow me a share in the heart-cheering satisfaction—(the only substantial one on earth, and the best offering to the divinity)—of alleviating the sufferings of fellow-creatures. The few who remain watch, eagerly for any opportunity of escaping. But this is a step which cunning and avarice have rendered very difficult, by means which I will endeavour to explain.

Whenever any money makes its appearance the Company carefully get it into its possession. It has adopted a curious "circulating medium." They pay and are paid in handkerchiefs, stockings, breeches, petticoats, shirts, shifts, &c.

and if they make a fortune it must be all in clothes.

These trumpery things are fixed at an exorbitant price, so that if they could succeed (which would be very difficult) in turning them into money, they would get not more than a fifth or sixth of what they cost. It is thus rendered impossible for them to get away. These poor people have thus been reduced to a level with the savages, without sharing their advantages or enjoying their independence. This is a stretch of cunning which avarice alone could enable men to reach.

The colony was at first, as you have seen, established near the confluence of the Assiniboin, also called by the Hudson's Bay Company the Red river; but during the great troubles, detachments of it had been transplanted hither on account of the greater fertility of the soil, and the greater vicinity to the buffalos. The only people, however, now remaining are the *Bois-brulés*, who have taken possession of the huts which the settlers abandoned.

Two Catholic priests had also established themselves here, but as neither the government nor the Company gave them any means of subsistence, they went away; and the church, constructed, like all the other buildings, of trunks of trees, is already falling into ruins.

Their departure is the more to be regretted as not only does it deprive these regions of every source of instruction, which could be derived from these ecclesiastics alone, but the *Bois-brulés* will relapse into their former state of barbarism, by losing whatever good they had gained from their evangelical precepts. To be just, we must admit that the French missionaries, when not Jesuits, have always and in all countries, distinguished themselves by their exemplary lives, truly conformable to their vocation. Their religious sincerity, their apostolic charity, their persuasive mildness, their heroic patience, and their freedom from all fanaticism and asceticism, in every country they have visited, deserve to be recorded in the annals of the Christian church. So long as the memory of Del Verde, Vodilla, &c. shall be held in execration by all true Christians, so long will those of Daniel, Brebœuf, &c. be regarded with that veneration with which they are so justly recorded in the history of discoveries and missions. Hence the predilection of the Indians for the French; a predilection which they find almost instinctive at the bottom of their hearts, nourished by the traditions their fathers have bequeathed to them in favour of the first Apostles of Canada, then New France, and which have travelled by way of lake Superior to this point.

Lower down, at Fort Douglas, there is still a bishop, Monsieur Provençais. His merit and virtues are the theme of general praise. I was told that he does not mingle politics with religion, that his zeal is not the offspring of ambition, that his piety is pure, his heart simple and generous. He does not give ostentatious bounties at the expense of his creditors; he is hospitable to strangers; and dissimulation never sullies his mind or his holy and paternal ministry. But as he cannot, of course, preach to Catholics in a manner to please the Company, it is much to be feared that the unfortunate inhabitants will soon be deprived of their excellent pastor.

Yesterday Charles II's charter was mutilated nearly by one half. The Major took possession of this place. The boundary which separates the territories of the two nations was formally laid down, in the name of the Government and President of the United States. A number of *Bois-brulés* were present, and seemed to ridicule the ceremony.

There is a great division of opinions and inclinations among them. An address which they have been recommended to present to their new masters, for a judge, a priest, &c. is still without signatures. They will be the partisans of whoever will pay them best; I think, therefore, they will most probably desert to Fort Douglas; some indeed are already gone thither. The English, individually, are avaricious, but their government and public bodies, when they have an end to accomplish, know how to unite the resistless power of gold to the magic influence of their intrigues; whilst the Americans are yet very backward in this art.

It would be very interesting to know whereabout we are with relation to the North Pole, but the Major conceals this from me with more care than the priests of Thibet conceal their Grand Lama. I know, however, that by an agreement between England and the United States, the boundary of the two territories on this side is fixed at the fiftieth degree. We are about two hundred and sixty miles from lake Traverse.

I shall conclude this letter by a scene which is interesting and perfectly new. The *Bois-brulés*, who call themselves the *free people* when they are not in the service of the Company, are compelled to live the same sort of life as the savages, in order to obtain the means of subsistence; and when urged by hunger, they unite in numerous bands to hunt the buffalo, in which they are sometimes joined by the hunters in the regular pay of the Company. Sometimes their toils are fruitless, but the day before yesterday they returned very rich, after two months absence.

A hundred men on horseback opened the march, a hundred and fourteen carts, heavily laden with dried meat, formed the centre; women and children, carried or dragged by large dogs, brought up the rear; for the whole family accompanies them, and during their hunting season they all grow fat and strong; but they return to the village, and soon lose their good plight. It was a curious sight, the details of which I leave to your imagination. They ranged themselves in order of battle at the place where we were encamped, and the fair commenced.

Several of these poor devils soon saw their carts emptied: either the Company which had advanced him some money, or one man who had let him have powder and shot, or another who offered him the clothes he wanted in exchange; or the tinker, the carpenter, the barber, the apothecary, the tax-gatherer, all fall upon him at once. The meat disappears, his numerous family remains around him, and the usual state of misery and famine returns.

The dogs deserve a few minutes of your attention. They are a great resource in this country. In winter they perform those labours on the ice and frozen snow, which the horses, who perish of cold and hunger, cannot endure. During the summer, when they are not hunting and their owners have no food for them, they put them out to board with jobbers, who feed them on bad fish, with which the river abounds, and thus swell the number of creditors who await the return of the owners from the chase.

I have seen some very numerous boarding-schools of this sort: the order and discipline which prevail there are curious and surprising; they might serve as models for some of our establishments of education. But a still more curious thing is, to see these poor animals go a-fishing themselves when they find that the dinner-bell is inconveniently delayed. They onclude that they have nothing to hope for from the head of the establishment; they therefore betake themselves to the banks of the river, and dart with the rapidity of lightning on the fish which swim near the shore, or on any which by chance may have carried off the fisherman's hook and line, and float dead upon the water.

And now my dear Countess, rest awhile; for if I succeed in bending my steps towards the point which has been the object of my constant wishes ever since I entered these wild regions, we shall have long walks and much fatigue to encounter.

PROSPECTUS

OF A

PLAN FOR SENDING

SETTLERS TO THE COLONY

OF THE

RED RIVER

IN

NORTH AMERICA.

EARL SELKIRK, a Scottish nobleman, of high rank and large fortune, has purchased a great extent of very fertile lands, situated upon the banks of the Red River, which falls into the great Lake Winipeg, in North America. These he possesses with all the seignorial rights attached to them, in full and absolute sovereignty. Lord Selkirk is desirous of peopling these beautiful and fertile countries with honest and industrious inhabitants, and particularly with Swiss and Germans. To effect this object, his lordship has commissioned, and invested with full power, Captain R. May, of Uzistorf, a citizen of Berne, in the British service, to engage persons in Switzerland to repair to his colony. Captain May fulfils a pleasing duty in communicating this information to his countrymen, persuaded that such of them as may avail themselves of the present opportunity, will find, in the country to which they are invited, whatever can contribute to their comfort, success, or happiness, provided they are industrious and economical.

This colony is situated between the 49th and 50th degrees of north latitude, about two hundred and thirty leagues south of Hudson's Bay, not far from the sources of the Mississippi. The climate is mild and very healthy; the winter is not colder nor longer than in our mountainous countries, but the summer is much hotter. The country consists of extensive plains, interspersed with mountains, not high, by no means rugged, and generally covered with beautiful forests.

These immense plains are clothed with the most luxuriant herbage, thus forming fine natural meadows, easy of cultivation, the settler having nothing to do but to throw up the turf with the plough or spade, after which he may immediately sow or plant; the soil is remarkably fertile, the first crop producing from thirty-five to forty-five times the quantity of seed. Every species of corn, potatoes, pulse, vegetable, hemp, flax, tobacco, and all kinds of fruit-trees, even the most delicate, grow and thrive there in perfection. Wood, either for fuel or building, in short for all the purposes of life, is in the greatest plenty. These immense meadows maintain a prodigious quantity of game of every description, and particularly innumerable herds of wild oxen, which any person is at liberty to kill, or to take alive and tame, thus providing himself with as much meat and leather as he may want. The country abounds in lakes and rivers filled with excellent fish, at the disposal of every one, both for food and traffic. Numerous salt pits afford to the settler an easy and abundant supply of this essential article of life and rural economy. The country also produces the sugar-maple, from which is prepared a sugar equal to the cane. In short, whatever is necessary to life may be attained in great plenty, with much facility and little labour: so that few counties offer so many natural sources of comfort, wealth and happiness to new settlers.

The number of families is, at present, about three hundred. A fortress, more than two hundred houses, saw and flour-mills, are already built; and, as there is no deficiency of artisans of every description, any one, on his arrival, may procure whatever is necessary to his establishment. European cattle, pigs, sheep, even those of the Merino breed, have been conveyed thither, and thrive remarkably well: the Merinos, in particular, encrease with great rapidity; and as in these immense meadows every planter is at liberty to graze his flocks or mow the grass, he may multiply this breed of sheep to any extent he pleases. It is easy to form an idea of the sources of riches which this single article offers to the planter. Excellent native horses may be purchased of the Indians, in any number, at eight or ten crowns each. In short, the country supplies in profusion whatever can be required for the convenience, pleasure, or comfort of life. It is also provided with great facilities for the sale of its produce. The first market open to the settlers, is that of the new comers, who annually and constantly flock thither from all parts, and who, for many years to come, will consume nearly all that the settlers can produce. Besides this, the English Hudson's Bay Company has entered into an engagement with Earl Selkirk, to purchase from the settlers of this colony all the provisions or commodities it may want for its immense fur trade, and to pay for them the same prices as in England; and, as in that country provisions are very dear, it is easy to conceive the profit and advantage which this arrangement offers to the planters. The same Company has engaged to become the agents of the colony, to export and convey, on the most moderate terms, all the productions of the colony, such as hemp, flax, wool, tobacco, &c. in its ships to England, to sell them there for the settlers, and to remit the amount, either in money or goods, at their option.

The conditions on which the planters are received and engaged are moderate, and not burdensome.

As to the conveyance of the Swiss to the colony, each individual of either sex, above fifteen years of age, is to pay twenty-one louis, at fifteen livres, of which, however, only ten louis ready money are to be paid at the time of sailing; the remaining eleven louis may be paid by instalments, and at the convenience of the person after his arrival at the colony, during a term of four or five years, at an interest of five per cent.

Each child between ten and sixteen, is to pay seven louis ready money, and afterwards eight, as above.

Each child between two and ten to pay five louis, and afterwards six, as above.

For this sum, Earl Selkirk engages and promises—

1st. To convey the planters from Switzerland to Rotterdam at his own expense; to provide and have ready for them, a good ship, supplied with good provision and in sufficient quantity; the embarkation to take place on their arrival at Rotterdam and the vessel to sail immediately. Captain May engages to accompany the planters to Rotterdam; to take care of them during the voyage; to conduct them on board the ship, distributing and arranging them in such a manner as to secure them sufficient room; to inspect the provisions, taking care that they are in sufficient quantity and of good quality; in short, to adopt every measure and precaution essential to their comfort during the voyage, which, he assures his countrymen, he will exert every effort to render as agreeable as possible.

2nd. On their arrival at Hudson's Bay, where they will disembark, they will find a sufficient number of boats and boatmen, supplied with necessary provisions, ready to receive them and convey them up Nelson River and Lake Winipeg to the colony there, as they will be distributed in the houses of the settlers already established, till they have built their own, for which they will receive every instruction, and the requisite supply of wood.

3rd. Such persons as are too poor to purchase food, will be supplied with provisions during the first year, or till the first crop. These, with their industry, will enable them to live, provided, however, that they contribute as much as possible to the support of their families, by hunting and fishing, for which they will receive instruction and whatever else is necessary; otherwise they will have no claim on this assistance.

4th. They shall be supplied with grain, potatoes, and other seed necessary for the first sowing and planting of their lands; for these they shall pay in kind, at the first crop.

5th. They shall be supplied on credit, and at the most reasonable prices, with whatever they may want for their first establishment, whether furniture, kitchen-utensils, or implements of husbandry, &c. They shall be allowed sufficient time to repay the amount of these advances, and the interest at five per cent.

6thly. To every father of a family, to every young married couple, and to every adult, desirous of having an establishment of his own, shall be assigned a hundred acres of land, to become for ever his property, and that of his descendants, without any purchase-money or charge whatever; for which an annual and regular rent, equally moderate, reasonable, and easy to the settler, is to be paid in kind, according to tho following proportions:—

For the first year, nothing.

For the second year, twenty English bushels of wheat.

For the third year, thirty English bushels of wheat.

For the fourth year, forty ditto.

For the fifth and following years, fifty ditto;—
making half a bushel per acre; which, considering the great fertility of the soil, is certainly very moderate, and by no means burdensome to the settler, particularly as this is the only ground-rent or charge which he will have to pay to the proprietor of the land: besides, he may release himself from this charge whenever he pleases, by a single payment of five hundred bushels of wheat, in consequence of which he will be for ever freed from this rent, and possess his land exempt from all claims whatever.

Should a settler bring property with him, and wish to purchase land instead of renting it, Earl Selkirk will sell him a lot, which cannot be less than one hundred, nor more than five hundred acres, at seventy-two *baches* per acre, which he will assign to him as his property and that of his heirs for ever, free from all rent charge; and he may choose his lot wherever he may think proper.

If the whole purchase-money is paid before departure, twenty per cent shall be deducted for prompt payment; otherwise a third of the sum shall be paid before departure, the other two thirds to be paid in three instalments, with an interest of five per cent upon the sum remaining unpaid; one every year for three years.

The number of settlers for the ensuing year may amount to five hundred persons, including fifty young unmarried women, healthy, strong, and robust, to be married to an equal number of Swiss young men, who are already settlers at the colony.

A contract shall be regularly drawn up between Captain May, in the name of Earl Selkirk, and each settler. This contract shall contain whatever each party engages to perform, that every one may know what he has to do, and what to expect. Each party shall have a duplicate, signed by the said Captain May and the respective settler, in presence of two legal witnessess; and this contract shall be written or printed on stamped paper.

The departure shall take place at the end of April, next year. Whoever intends to engage is requested to apply by letter, post-paid, or personally, as soon as possible, to Captain May d'Uzistorf, at Berne.

Berne, May 20th, 1820.

(Signed) R. MAY D'UZISTORF,

Captain in his Britannic Majesty's service, and
Agent Plenipotentiary to Lord Selkirk.

LETTER XIX.

Julian Sources of the Mississippi
and the Bloody River,
August 31st, 1823.

I WRITE to you from the midst of deserts, under the vault of heaven; a large maple is the only roof which shelters, the only closet which secludes me: the solitude—the deep silence around me, is interrupted only by unknown birds or strange and savage beasts. In this remote and central wilderness, my heart and mind are filled with the most delightful emotions. Like another Colossus of Rhodes, I can almost touch with either foot two of the most interesting spots on the surface of the globe: I find myself in a place which has been the object of so many researches, but which has till now never been pressed by the foot of civilized man. This moment, next to that which taught me to appreciate the treasure of friendship that I have lost, is the finest of my life.

The situation of Pembenar clearly pointed out to me that towards the south-east I should perhaps find what had been the object of my wanderings in these wild and remote regions; and I immediately resolved to follow that direction. But I had great difficulties to conquer. Not an individual in that place knew either the way, or even the Red river above the point at which the Robber's river falls into it. Everybody represented to me the dangers which I was going to brave among the Indians, who are generally described as being very ferocious, and who are still very unfriendly to the Americans. I however found two Cypowais, who, having lost one of their companions at the Cayenne river, were going precisely to Red lake, to stimulate and rouse his relatives and their nation to avenge him on the Sioux, (the Yanctons,) who had killed and quartered him. One of the *Bois-brulés*, or *Fire-brands*, offered to accompany me as far as the Robber's river with his train of dogs, to carry a small quantity of dry provisions which I had purchased, and my small luggage, and to act likewise as my interpreter. I instantly engaged the whole. I smothered the rising apprehensions which some were eager to excite in my mind in order to intimidate me from my design, and on the 9th ult. left behind me Pembenar, the Major, and my horse. I sold the last, as useless and burthensome in an excursion through unknown regions, thick forests, lakes, and deep rivers. With no slight regret I quitted this faithful friend Buffalo, the fearless companion of so many chaces and dangers: I should have been not a little glad to have kept him and taken him back with me to Italy. He would have been a living memorial to me of interesting events, and would have excited the jealousy of my *Bucharest*, whom, if he be still in existence, I should thus have punished for having broken my thigh: could I have enclosed him in my portfolio, he would unquestionably have returned with me. I can safely assert, that this beautiful animal would appear a second Bucephalus were he mounted by another Alexander, and would be thought by no means the most contemptible of senators if he belonged to another Caligula. I substituted for him a small mule, used to the country, which I hired of another *Bois-brulé*.

I cannot but gratefully acknowledge the kindness felt for me in this situation by colonel Snelling's son, who shewed the most friendly concern and apprehensions for me. He also left the Major at the same time, not without violent altercation, and went back to Fort St Peter, by way of lake Traverse. He quitted me in tears, exclaiming, " What will my father say ?" With considerable regret I parted from Dr Say, one of the naturalists attached to the expedition, the only one who deserved the designation. He is Professor of Zoology at Philadelphia, and distinguished at once by modesty and merit.

The expedition was intended to descend as far as lake Winipeg; pass up the river Winipeg, and that of the woods; ascend Rain river, and from Rain lake descend to lake Superior; then to cross lakes Huron, St Clair, and Erie, to Buffalo canal, and return by that and the New York road to Philadelphia. I now leave these gentlemen to the care of a good providence, and return to the subject of my own concerns and progress.

The two first days after our separation I experienced only a few difficulties in passing along places infested by wolves, in which my Indian guides had to strike out for themselves the quickest road to accelerate the completion of their vengeance. Their natural compass was as exact as the most finished production of art and science: I have already mentioned with what facility they discover their proper route both by day and by night, even when the stars are concealed.

On the third day my poor dogs, which were by that time exhausted by fatigue, found insurmountable obstacles in the marshes and woods. We were compelled, therefore, to load my mule with nearly the whole of my baggage; and I consequently proceeded in the style of St Francis.

The interpreter informed me that it was necessary to follow blindly and implicitly the savages whom we had connected ourselves with; for on the least contradiction they would have left us on the spot. I therefore in every possible way consulted their humours: we halted when they pleased; we smoked when they desired it, although I never smoke myself but for form and ceremony; they partook whenever they liked of everything eatable that I had with me; and, even more than that, I frequently regaled them with heath-cocks, which I killed in considerable numbers on our way. The Indian, having neither powder nor ball to throw away, and rarely aiming at game when on the wing, is but little expert at this description of sport. My companions were, therefore, extremely astonished at the dexterity with which I brought down my game at almost every fire; and I of course exerted my best efforts to justify the name which they had bestowed upon me, and inspire them with an imposing opinion of my powers. I was desirous, like the first Spaniards in America, to appear as a superhuman being in their eyes, in order to excite their respect and submission: but the most subtle and refined malice has now succeeded to that species of simplicity which formerly distinguished them; and they have become more cruel and ferocious in proportion as they have discovered that white men regard them as an inferior *caste* to themselves, appropriate their lands under pretence of defending them, and, while affecting to confer favours by engaging in commerce with them, degrade them into mere slaves of their own avarice. They denominated me the *Great Warrior;* and when an explanation was asked of them, at my request, they answered that they had dreamed I was such; and their dreams are ever considered by them as infallible. You must now, therefore, regard me as *Kitcy Okiman.*

On the fourth day I killed a young white bear, and one of the Indians killed another: the dam had apparently incurred the same fate, for we sought for her in vain. With a little bread I should have had a feast for an epicure, for heathcocks and the cubs of bears are high dainties: but all Pembenar was unable to furnish me with a grain of wheat or an ounce of flour meal.

The white bear is the only wild beast of these

regions that is dangerous. He almost always attacks the traveller, and when hungry never fails to do so. One of these animals, last year, rushed into the canoe of two *Bois-brulés* while they were resting near the bank, and seizing one of them, dragged him into the forest, while the other, whose musket had become wet, was totally disabled from assisting him. Fortunately, however, a party of Indians were hunting near the spot, who ran to his assistance and killed the bear while still grasping his prey. The unfortunate man was merely wounded, and gave me the recital of the circumstance himself, and likewise sold me the animal's skin. The black bear, on the contrary, is extremely timid, and always on the approach of man betakes itself to flight. Next to the buffalo it is the most valuable of all animals to the Indians. Its skin, its flesh, its fat, its tendons, even its nails and teeth, are all convertible to purposes of utility.

Nature has distinguished this animal by peculiar characters. He feeds entirely on fruits during summer and autumn, and it is at those seasons that the Indians go in search of him in places where fruits are abundant, and destroy him. When the cold weather commences he proceeds to hide himself in the hollow of some tree, or in a hole which he digs for himself in the earth. Here he remains completely motionless, apparently under the influence of the soundest sleep, for the whole of the winter. He sustains himself by sucking his paws, from which the fat with which his body is covered seems to pass for his nourishment. The Indians discover his abode sometimes by means of dogs which scent him, sometimes by the place which his breathing marks in the snow, and they destroy him without his making the least resistance or even motion, so that a single pike or lance is sufficient for the purpose. In the spring, the season when he quits his den, he in the first place exerts himself to regain possession as it were of those natural powers which have remained suspended or paralysed during the whole winter. He cleanses himself by purgative and diuretic simples, which nature points out to him with more clearness than they are indicated by our physicians and botanists. As, however, so long an abstinence, and this succeeding purgation, must necessarily have weakened his stomach, and it is consequently necessary for him to follow a light regimen, he commences with fish.

The manner of his conducting his fishing is truly extraordinary. Sitting on his hind paws on the bank of a river or a lake, he continues so perfectly motionless that he might be mistaken for a burnt trunk of some tree, which frequently deceives even the keen and practised eye of an

Indian himself. With his right paw he seizes with incredible celerity and skill the fish which unsuspectingly pass under his eyes, and throws them on the bank. When he has obtained a plentiful supply for his table, he regales himself on a portion of it, and conceals the rest, that he may have sure recourse to it, as appetite serves, during the day: he appears perfectly to know that morning and evening are the only times for fishing. He afterwards proceeds to a more substantial fare, to the flesh of beasts which he hunts, or finds dead, and at length he returns to his diet of fruits. Thus, at successive periods of the year, he is a *piscivorous, carnivorous,* and *frugivorous* animal.

On the fifth day we arrived at Robber's river (called *Wamans-Watpà* by the Sioux and *Po-wisci-sibi,* by the Cypowais), so denominated because one of the Sioux, in his flight from the vengeance which had been denounced against him for murder, kept himself concealed, and *robbed* on this spot for many years, escaping the observation of his persecutors and enemies, by whom he was completely surrounded. We passed along its bank for two or three miles, to the place where it falls into the Red river, and there my Indian attendants discovered their canoe, which was concealed among the brambles.

I had been informed at Pembenar, that a number of *Bois-bruilés* had proceeded to this confluence in order to erect huts for their winter-hunting establishment, and that some one of them would certainly be able to accompany me, and act as my interpreter, as far as Red lake, and, if I desired it, still farther; but we found none there. The Cypowais had driven them away, as we were informed by one of the latter, and they were gone to establish themselves about a hundred miles lower down. On the other hand, my interpreter from Pembenar could not possibly continue with me: besides his having to conduct back the mule, other powerful reasons operated to prevent him. I was therefore compelled to decide; and I delivered myself over to the care of my two Indians.

We had not again proceeded up the river more than two miles before they stopped, and presented an offering of dry provisions and tobacco to *Miciliki,* the Manitou of Waters. This was a stake painted red, and fixed under a kind of *sacellum,* like those of antiquity, and the ceremony is by no means modern. They were, for this once, more generous towards their deities than Indians in such circumstances generally are: the reason is, that their offering was at my expense.

The frequent rapids which we had met with

in the course of five or six miles, and which had compelled us to walk continually in the water, and over pointed and cutting rocks, in order to preserve our canoe from injury, had very much fatigued us, and our appetite also induced us to make a halt: we accordingly did so, and after eating my repast, I went to sleep beneath a tree, recommending myself to the care of providence.

I was awakened by discharges of fire-arms, and on starting up perceived five or six Indians on the opposite bank of the river, apparently desirous to cross it. On seeing me they seemed struck with astonishment and terror, and fled with precipitation: one of our Indians was wounded. Those who had fired at them were Sioux. I was already known among the Indians of that nation, as the *Tonka-Wasci-cio-honsca*, or *the Great Chief from a far country;* and my tall stature and noble horse had rendered me the more remarked by them, as these are two things of which they are extreme admirers. When they again saw me on this spot, they concluded that the whole expedition was there, and fled with all haste for fear of being recognized. This was the idea that first presented itself to my mind, and I instantly acted upon it. We jumped immediately into our canoe; I performed to the best of my power the labours of the wounded Indian, who had his left arm shot completely through, and his right shoulder grazed. The ball, however, had not touched the bone of the arm, and the wound in the shoulder had injured only the integuments. The juice of some boiled roots was applied as the healing balsam; the down of a swan-skin, which I had purchased at Pembenar, was substituted for lint, my handkerchief served for a bandage, and the bark of a tree called *owigobinigy*, or white wood, answered the purpose of securing the arm in a sling. We kept on our course till evening, and saw nothing more of them.

My intrepid champions saw nothing but Sioux. The slightest sound from wind or water, the shadow of a tree or of a rock, everything was the Sioux. I discovered that they were plotting against me, for they carefully avoided my looks. I had not the slightest doubt that they meant to leave me on the spot, and determined therefore to make them re-embark, it being more easy to guard them in the canoe. About midnight we stopped. I had but little to fear, being left without my canoe, for I was already well aware that their intention must be to continue their course by land, by a route which would conduct them in two or three days to Red lake; whereas, were they to proceed by the river they would require more than six. However, I considered that no precaution ought to be neglected by me;

I therefore drew the canoe to land, and fastened it to a tree by a cord, one end of which I tied to my leg, and then laid myself down by the side of them in such a manner that they could not rise, even if I should be able to sleep, without waking me. These precautions, and my musket and my sword between my legs, ready for immediate use, kept them quiet the whole night.

On the following morning they embarked without difficulty. But this was only with a view of reaching a certain point, whence the route by land was shorter. I might have used violence against them if I had chosen, for certainly I had no fear of them; I had even taken the precaution of putting water into their musket barrels: but I should only have exasperated their nation, in a territory where it was now absolute and despotic, and where I could expect no assistance but from my own energies and the care of providence; I therefore suffered them quietly to go off. They intimated to me, what I was before well aware of, that they were going to leave me. They invited me to follow them, and to leave the canoe, provisions, and baggage, concealed in the brushwood. I deliberated with myself on the subject for a moment: I considered that the river was my best and surest way, that I was in possession of a canoe, provisions, a musket, a sword, and ammunition; whereas, by accepting their invitation, I should be following barbarians who had the cowardice to abandon a stranger confided to their guardianship at Pembenar by their most intimate friends, one who had treated them as brothers, saved them from the hands of the enemy, healed their wounds, and assisted them kindly with all his means. I should, with wretches of this description, be exposing myself in inextricable forests, in the midst of swamps and lakes, and abandoning to the mercy of a thousand accidents, my baggage, my provisions, and materials for the presents, which are indispensable passports through a savage country. My determination, therefore, was soon fixed: after having vainly endeavoured to make them comprehend that both *Manitous* and men would punish such atrocity, I commanded them by words and signs peremptorily to be gone.

I imagine, my dear Countess, that you will feel the frightfulness of my situation at this critical moment more strongly than I can express it. I really can scarcely help shuddering, as well as yourself, whenever I think of it. Fortunately, I was not at the time overpowered and confounded. Woe be to us, if in exigencies like this, despair takes possession of our minds. In that case all is completely over with us!

To the indignation which I could not help feeling at the conduct of these wretches, the most perfect calm succeeded; and I soon even changed tragedy for comedy. I began by smiling at my singular adventures; and was soon inclined to think that I had been wrong in refusing credit to those of Robinson Crusoe. A good breakfast, which strengthened both my stomach and my mind, was the first step in my new career as a hero of romance. I then carefully put my gun in order, to be able to defend myself against the attack of white bears, which abound near the Red river. With respect to the Indians, I was already so accustomed to see them, and often even to despise them, that they gave me not the slightest apprehension of danger; and this circumstance did away with one important obstacle (as I should formerly have felt it) to the resolute continuance of the course I had adopted.

The solitude I now experienced, which romance-writers would not have found so pleasant and delightful as that which they have been pleased to exhibit in their fictions, impressed me at first with ideas the most dreadful. But this, perhaps, was merely designed to try the strength of my mind, and elevate it above the standard of the vulgar.

Never was I offered by providence a more favourable opportunity for entertaining self-esteem without vanity; and my modesty was indulgent enough to permit me freely to enjoy it, with a view to my rendering myself still more worthy of it. But your mind is too much agitated about my fate to enter into these reflections—you are too eager to know what befell me—I proceed therefore to lift the curtain.

I must, said I to myself, leave this place some way or other; and I jumped into my canoe and began rowing. But I was totally unacquainted with the almost magical art by which a single person guides a canoe, and particularly a canoe formed of bark, the lightness of which is overpowered by the current, and the conduct of which requires extreme dexterity. Frequently, instead of proceeding up the river, I descended; a circumstance which by no means shortened my voyage. Renewed efforts made me lose my equilibrium, the canoe upset, and admitted a considerable quantity of water. My whole cargo was wetted. I leaped into the water, drew the canoe on land, and laid it to drain with the keel upwards. I then loaded it again, taking care to place the wetted part of my effects uppermost, to be dried by the sun. I then resumed my route.

You sympathize with the embarrassment in which you conceive I must have been involved, with all my difficulties and want of means for continuing my course. I bore all however with great philosophy, and with a resignation which I believe you will readily admit is not very natural to me. I could scarcely help incessantly smiling. I threw myself into the water up to my waist, and commenced a promenade of a rather unusual kind, drawing the canoe after me with a thong from a buffalo's hide, which I had fastened to the prow.

The first day of my expedition, the 15th of the month, was employed in this manner, and I did not stop till the evening. It was natural to expect that I should be fatigued; but I was not in the least so. While thus dragging after me my canoe, with a cord over my shoulder, an oar in my hand for my support, my back stooping, my head looking down, holding conversation with the fishes beneath, and making incessant windings in the river, in order to sound its depths, that I might most safely pass; I must leave it to your imagination to conceive the variety and interest of the ideas which rapidly passed in review before my mind!

I quitted my cenoa and hid it. I was completely wet, as was inevitable. I would have kindled a fire, but the Indians had carried off my steel; and I could not succeed in doing it with my gun. I was unable therefore to dry myself for the whole night; and when, on the morrow, I resumed my progress, my clothes, as you may suppose, seemed to have no dread of getting into contact with the water, for they were as completely soaked as they had been when taken out of it the evening before.

The weather on the second day of my progress was very disagreeable. A storm which commenced before mid-day continued till night. Notwithstanding this, however, I did not relax an instant but to take my food. I saw the hand of providence in the physical and moral vigour which supported me during this dreadful conflict. In the evening I had no access to a more comfortable hearth than on the preceding one. My bear skin and my coverlid, which constituted the whole of my bed, were completely soaked; and, what was worse, the mould began to affect my provisions. I was almost tempted to think that it was all over with my *promenades*, and that I began to *travel*, and that not very *comfortably*.

On the morning of the 17th, the sun's beams

gilded the awful solitude by which I was surrounded, and I eagerly availed myself of their influence. I laid out my provisions, baggage, gun, and sword, and stretched myself also at full length under his rays. The powder, which had fortunately been closely confined in tin canisters, was the only thing that escaped the water.

Necessity makes man industrious, and the necessity I was now under to become so was great indeed, as otherwise it was impossible for me to continue my progress. The river became narrower and deeper the farther I ascended it, as is the case with all rivers originating in lakes. It was thus absolutely indispensable for me to learn how to guide the canoe with the oar. I set myself, therefore, to study this art in good earnest; and in the afternoon, when I struck my tent, I exerted myself first to pass several deep gulfs, and afterwards to traverse short stages or distances of the river: but the fatigue I endured was extreme; and I preferred returning to my drag-rope whenever the river permitted my walking in it. As appearances seemed to threaten rain, I covered my effects with my umbrella, stuck into the bottom of my canoe. It was singular enough to see them conveyed thus in the stately style and manner of China, while I was myself condemned to travel in that of a galley slave: nor could I help reflecting on those unfortunate victims of despotism which the *Restoration* has condemned to drag the vessels on the Danube. As it was of consequence for me to avail myself of everything that could promote cheerfulness and keep up my spirits, I could not help smiling, which I am sure, my dear Countess, you would yourself have done, at the sight of my grotesque convoy. This night was less painful; my bed was dry; and, but for the millions of gnats, which incessantly attacked me, and almost flayed me alive, I am convinced that I should have enjoyed sound and uninterrupted sleep.

Whenever I awoke, the view presented to my imagination by my actual circumstances was truly frightful; but my mind, instead of yielding to despair, rose in firmness with the exigence of the occasion; and the death-like silence, interrupted only by the depressing notes of night birds and the howlings of bears and wolves; the darkness, through which the moon pierced in these vast and gloomy forests, only to exhibit doubtful and startling images; instead of appalling or alarming me, only inspired me with a pensive feeling equally new and pleasing: a state of mind strongly felt, but perhaps almost impossible to be communicated.

The morning of the 18th awakened me to my

active duties, and I proceeded in my course; and before mid-day fell in with two canoes of Indians.

Being alone in a canoe of their nation, with three muskets, (for those of my two Indians were in my possession,) I might naturally have been apprehensive of exciting their most dangerous suspicions. But, heaven be praised, I entertained no apprehension whatever. I called to them with confidence, while they, struck with wonder at so extraordinary an object, halted on the opposite bank of the river. What astonished them most was my superbly conveyed baggage. They could form no idea of what *that great red skin* (my umbrella) could possibly be, nor of what was placed beneath it; and, observing me walking in the water, they perhaps imagined me to be their *Miciliki*. Some Catholics, from the tallness of my stature, would have thought they saw our Saint Christopher: if the latter carried the infant Jesus, I might be well said to carry the cross. At length, however, they politely replied to my *Aniscicin nigy*, (Good day, my friends); but they could not recover from their surprise, and approached me with great hesitation.

I made them comprehend what had occurred to me, and that I wanted one of them to accompany me as far as Red lake. At first they started immense difficulties; but a woman was captivated by the beauty of my handkerchief, which was hanging from my pocket; a lad was fascinated with the one I had about my neck, and an old man muffled up in a miserable ragged rug, which through its innumerable holes displayed nearly one half of his person, had already cast his rapacious glance on mine; pretending to search for something in my portmanteau, a bit of calico which casually came to hand excited the full gaze of one of the young girls; and my provisions, which they had already tasted, strongly stimulated their gormandizing appetite: I satisfied the whole of them, and the old man decided to accept my proposal. He took the helm of my vessel, and we set off.

This assistance extricated me from a situation which certainly was by no means pleasant, and it was so much the more valuable as it would have been impossible for me to proceed alone, because the river was constantly encreasing in depth. Notwithstanding this, however, my mind was in a state of incessant agitation as I proceeded, and I perceived its attention completely occupied about something which it left behind it with regret. It was no difficult matter for me to detect this secret. My mind was, in fact, adverting to the four days of its solitude and independance, and had addressed to itself some such language as the following, "You have experienced complete solitude, you have tasted genuine independance, you will from this time never enjoy them more. The independance and solitude represented in books, or to be found among civilized nations are vain and chimerical." I, at that moment fully comprehended why the Indians consider themselves happier than cultivated nations, and far superior to them.

It is difficult to meet with a rower as strong as my patriarchal companion, and we advanced at a rapid rate, without stopping, till the evening. Our table was furnished with a couple of ducks: I had fire to make a roast, and I shot them accordingly. Though my bed was without a coverlid, (the cunning old fellow having left in his own canoe the one which I had given him,) yet wrapping myself, like the Indians, in the skin I wore about me, I lay down to rest very comfortably. In the course of the night I was waked by my cautionary cord; and, at first, I imagined that my pilot was also going to desert me, but it turned out to be occasioned by some large animal who had taken a fancy to my provisions. I gently seized my gun which I always keep at my side, and in an instant brought him down.

My Indian, confounded by the report of fire-arms, thought he had been attacked by the Sioux, about whom, not improbably, he had been dreaming, and immediately betook himself to flight. I called out to him, I ran towards him to convince him of his error and restore his confidence, but the forest and darkness concealed him from my view, and thus in a moment my solitude and independance were renewed. However, I could still have smiled at the adventure, if such an expression of feeling had been at all seasonable.

I waited for him in vain for the remainder of the night. Two discharges of the gun however, which I fired off immediately one after the other, (considered by them as a signal of friendship,) brought him back to his quarters with the dawn of day.

We searched for the animal I had fired at, which it seems retained strength sufficient to drag itself to a few paces distance among the brushwood, to which traces of blood guided us; it proved to be a wolf. My companion refused to strip the animal of its skin, a superb one, viewing it at the same time with an air of respect, and murmuring within himself some words, the meaning of which will probably surprise you. In fact, the wolf was his *Manitou.*

He expressed to it the sincerity of his regret for what had happened, and informed it that he was not the person who had destroyed it.

On the 19th, my Mentor wanted to play me the trick of handing me over to the charge of another Indian whom we fell in with; but I gave him a frown, and he went on with me. We again made a good day's progress, to which I contributed by rowing to the best of my ability.

Night arrived without his pausing in his exertions. He gave me to understand that it was indispensable for him to reach the destined place without delay, and appeared excessively eager to rejoin his canoes.

Much fatigued, and shivering under a cold moist air, with which the night-dews in this country pierce to the very bones, I lay down under my bear-skin to sleep. A distant sound awoke me, and I found myself alone in my canoe, in the midst of rushes. On turning my head I observed three or four torches approaching me. My imagination had at first transported me to the enchanted land of fairies, and I was in motionless expectation of receiving a visit from their ladyships, or of being addressed like Telemachus, by the nymphs. They proved however to be female Indians, who came to convey my effects, and to guide me to their hut. My Charon, who from purgatory had conducted me to Hell, had applied to them for this purpose, and then hastened his return to his family who were waiting for him where he first met with me. I was now at Red lake, at the marshy spot whence the river springs, and about a mile from an Indian encampment.

I was conducted to a hut covered with the bark of trees, like those which I have already described to you as belonging to the Cypowais, but on a larger scale. I there found fourteen Indians, male and female, nineteen dogs, and a wolf. The latter was the first to do the honours of the house; however, as he was fastened, he could not attack me so effectively as he was evidently desirous of doing, and merely tore my pantaloons, which were, indeed, the only pair I had still serviceable. This wolf was one of their household gods.

The first two of the Indians that my eyes glanced on were my former treacherous companions: I appeared not to observe them. I desired the women to hang up my provisions to the posts which supported the roof, to preserve them from the voracity of the dogs; and, not having any power to help myself, I lay down in the corner assigned to me in this intolerably filthy stable. When I got up again, you will easily believe that I did not rise alone: thus I incurred an addition of wounds and inflictions on a body which the pointed flints and cutting shells of the river, and the boughs of trees, thorns, brambles and musquitos, had previously converted into a Job.

On the morning of the 20th, I desired to be conducted to a *Bois-brulé* for whom I had brought a letter from Pembenar. I was told that he resided at a distance, and that the waters of the lake were in a state of great agitation. I could not even obtain the favour of having him sent for, for this happened to be the day when it was the bounden duty of all the members of the hut to devote themselves to yelling, eating, drinking, and dancing, in commemoration of the Indian killed at the river Cayenne. I quitted the place, and offered the only handkerchief that I had remaining to the first Indian whom I met, and he immediately went off with my letter.

The funeral ceremony presented nothing more extraordinary than what we have already seen, excepting the pillaging of my provisions in honour of the hero of the fête; and the convulsions of the father and mother composed to quietude by the blowings and exorcisms of the priests, and the wounds inflicted on the arms and legs, the contortions, yellings, and howlings of his relatives.

The Indians of this tribe, amounting in number to about five hundred, and presided over by a chief denominated the *Great Hare* (Kitci-

Wabouse,) do not inter their dead; they burn them, and scatter their ashes to the winds, in order to enable them to reach heaven with greater facility; and even though only a thigh, a leg, or a foot, should be burnt, they believe the whole body goes with just the same certainty to paradise: they conceive that this single member cannot continue separated from the rest of the body, and that by means of its celestial power it attracts to itself all the others which are possessed of a merely human nature as long as they remain on earth. This explains why the ceremony in question was so noisy and violent: they manifested by the vehemence of their yells the grief they felt from having in their possession no member of the deceased to burn.

A party of the relatives and friends was gone on an expedition for discovering whether the Sioux had left no remains whatever on the spot where the tragedy had been acted, while my old friend the pilot, as herald-at-arms, had proceeded to rouse the vengeance and implore the succour of some Cypowais Jumpers, who were scattered in various spots about the forests. The doctrine of these Indians is strikingly singular, it is perhaps held by them only, of all mankind. For they seem to recognize rather the immortality of the body than that of the soul.

My *Bois-brulé* had now arrived. He was one

of the numerous progeny scattered over the country by the vice and immorality of the *fur* traders. He is the son of a Canadian, and a female Indian of the tribe of the Cypowais.

The chief then addressed himself to me through this interpreter:—"*Great Warrior*, my people have deserted thee, and thereby excited thine anger. But they entertained no evil design; they consider thee to be brave, and cannot possibly intend thee ill. Thou hast thyself been witness of the infraction of treaties committed by that nation of assassins, (the Sioux); my people therefore had a double motive for quitting thee; it was incumbent upon them to come as soon as possible, and rouse our vengeance, and he who was wounded suffered very great pain. They took the shortest way in their power. We have offered nothing to thee because thou hadst more provisions than we had, and better than ours; and then thou wast angry. We have this day eaten a little of them because we were in want, and thou art generous. If thou hast need of us, tell me so. Smoke with us the calumet of peace, and grant me a small portion of tobacco." I accordingly gave him a little, smoked, and then left him without making any answer. Had I prolonged my stay, for ever so little time, Indian hospitality would have ended in consuming the whole of my provisions.

My *Bois-brulé* resides about twelve miles distant from this encampment to the south of the lake. The wind was too high for a canoe made of bark, and the lake too violently agitated; we were compelled, therefore, to disembark, and passed the night under an immense plane tree. This plane is, perhaps, the Colossus of the whole vegetable kingdom. The Indians adore it as a *Manitou;* the ancients would have done the same, and though I am myself a modern, I admire it as one of the most prodigious and most beautiful productions of nature.

We arrived at his hut on the morning of the 21st. Misery might be said to be personified in his family, and in all by which he was surrounded; a wife (the daughter of a father whom she has never seen,) nourishing an infant at her breast, but nearly destitute of nourishment herself, and five naked and famine-struck children, constituted the whole of his property. The uncertain fishery of the lake, and a small quantity of maize, in its green and immature state, furnish the whole means of their subsistence. They are neither civilized nor savage, possessing the resources of neither state, but every inconvenience and defect of both. The worst part of the case is, that this *Bois-brulé* has a great deal of natural talent, which serves only to render him more dangerous. He has been taught both to read and write, and has obtained that species of education which just serves to strengthen the innate evil propensities of the man, when unaccompanied by that moral training which is their proper curb and correction: in fact, the obliquity of his character has quite ruined him in the opinion of the traders who have successively employed him; and his crimes obliged him to abscond from Pembenar, where I was informed that I ought to be more on my guard against him than against the Indians themselves. I mention all these circumstances to you, my dear Countess, because, with the truest and noblest friendship, you are desirous of participating, as it were, in every description of danger incurred by me, and in order that those of our mutual friends who may be inclined to engage in the field of adventure like myself, may learn how to meet and overcome the various enemies they may have to encounter.

I immediately saw that from Scylla I had fallen into Charybdis. I had recourse therefore to two expedients, which I conceived to be best adapted in similar circumstances to baffle the mischievous machinations of grasping and greedy minds,—I mean generosity and menace. I began by sharing with him the small stock of provisions and linen that I had remaining, to assuage his indigence, the wants of himself and his family; and then told him, in a firm and elevated tone, that, when occasion required, I should not hesitate to shew my teeth and exert my power; that moreover every person at Pembenar well knew that I had confided myself to his guidance, and that the commandant of Fort St Peter, and the government of the United States, would consider him responsible for whatever might befall me in passing through the Indian territories. He then changed the manner and character of his discourse. All the immense difficulties and invincible objections which he had at first mentioned, and which I had pretended to hear with the greatest indifference, almost immediately vanished. He offered his services with alacrity to assist me in surmounting the obstacles which really existed, and sealed his promises by doing me the honour to say, "You are a man of ten thousand." But we will now return to the Red river, from which we have somewhat, though not unnaturally, digressed, and which we have surveyed hitherto rather through the imagination than the senses.

It presents no other extraordinary feature than the very frequent winding of its course, in which perhaps it is scarcely exceeded by the Meander itself. It waters a country uniformly level, and the rapids which we have seen do not lower its level but by the height of its banks.

After Robber's river, as you ascend, no other river flows into it. This is more particularly to be noticed, because the English Hudson's Bay Company, according to their theories, have created on their map other Red rivers, with many more tributary streams flowing into it than this has.

At the distance of about forty miles from the lake, its banks are lined with impenetrable forests; above, the view is agreeably varied by smiling meadows and handsome shrubbery. On flowing from the lake it passes among rushes and wild rice. It is an error of geographers, founded on the vague information of Indians, that it derives its source from this lake; indeed, a lake which is formed by five or six rivers which flow into it can never be considered as itself the source of any single river. We shall soon have occasion to look farther for this source.

The lake, by means of a streight, is divided into two ports, one to the north-east and the other to the south-west. Let us proceed to make the circuit of the last, which is certainly the most interesting.

It receives on the western side the river Broachers, *(Kinougeo-sibi,)* and that of the Great Rock, *(Kisciacinabed-sibi;)* to the south, the river *Kahasinilague-sibi*, or Gravel river, near which the hut of my *Bois-brulé* guide is situated; that of

Kiogokague-sibi, or Gold-fish river; and that of *Madaoanakan-sibi*, or Great Portage river; on the south-east, Cormorant river, *(Cacakisciou-sibi.)* A large tongue of land on the E. N. E. forms a peninsula about four miles in length, and of varying breadth, ending in a point towards the west. At a little distance, towards the north, there is another encampment of Indians, consisting of about three hundred persons, the chief of whom is the Grand Carabou, *(Kisci-Adike)*. The streight is situated to the N. N. E., and there is a small island in the midst of its waters dividing them into two. To the north we find another tongue of land, which serves also to separate the two lakes, and reaches as far as the streight, commencing at the spot whence, as we have seen, Red river, or (more properly speaking,) Bloody river, proceeds. The other lake receives, on the east, Sturgeon river, *(Amenikanins-sibi)*. By the channel of this river, and by means of two portages there is a communication with Rain river, from whence one can easily communicate with lake Superior, to the south; and with the waters of Hudson's Bay, by the lake of Woods, to the north. The waters which flow into lake Superior on this side, may be considered as the sources of the river St Lawrence.

These two lakes are about one hundred and thirty miles in circumference; and Red river traverses about three hundred from the lake to Pembenar; but in a straight line the whole distance scarcely amounts to one hundred and sixty.

How much has it cost me, my dear Countess, to write you these details! Perhaps as much as it will you to peruse them; for, like all women of spirit, you are fond of the brilliant and romantic. But our geographical friends would accuse me of negligence if I forgot them in a country completely unknown to them, and where no white man had previously travelled. Our political friends also would equally complain, particularly our two F . . . , our B . . . , and our S . . . ; for they also require similar details, in order to avoid error in their frequent divisions and distributions of the world.

In the course of an excursion which I made to the south-west, I discovered eight small lakes, undistinguished by names, which all communicate with each other, and of which Gravel river is the outlet. These lakes seem to have been negligently scattered by nature through a territory sometimes gloomy and sometimes gay, varied with hills and dales, and presenting to the eye landscapes the most delightful and enchanting. I resolved to pass a night amidst scenes so uncommonly charming, that I might enjoy as long as possible the exquisite impressions they made upon my mind and senses. I dedicated these lakes to the family to which I am united by the most cordial friendship; and accordingly gave them the names of Alexander, Lavinius, Everard, Frederica, Adela, Magdalena, Virginia, and Eleonora. The purity of the waters of these lakes I considered a correct image of that of *their* minds; and their union reminded me of the affection by which the members of this happy family are so tenderly connected.

The whole of this territory abounds with innumerable maple, or sugar trees, which the Indians divide into various *sugaries*. The sap of the trees flows through incisions made in them by the Indians in spring at the foot of the trunk. It is received in buckets of birch bark, and conveyed to the laboratory of each respective sugary, where it is boiled in large cauldrons till the watery parts are evaporated. The dregs descend, and the saccharine matter remains adhering to the sides of the vessel. When this process is completed the sugar is made.

This commodity is, to the Indians, a most valuable resource: they barter it for articles of indispensable necessity; it supplies them with a salutary and excellent nourishment; and when taken in ptisan, or pure water, proves an efficacious remedy for complaints of the stomach and bowels. It is the favourite application of their quack doctors and clerical impostors, who attribute the virtue of this wholesome product and its balsamic effect to their own miserable jugglings. I find myself occasionally indisposed by eating too copiously of the wild fruits of the country, forgetting under the sensation of hunger the wise precept of the Salernian school respecting both "quantity and quality." In these cases I take a thin decoction of sugar, a few simples which have been recommended to me, and especially wild cherry wood, and my cure is completed.

I returned to the encampment of *Great Hare*, to engage an Indian to attend me, together with my *Bois-brulé* guide, during the continuance of my excursion, and to purchase the canoe which was the scene of my tragi-comedy on Red river: for I was desirous of having it conveyed, if possible, to my rural cottage, and preserve it with my other Indian curiosities as a memorial and trophy of my labours in these my transatlantic *promenades*.

All the principal men of the tribe were assembled, constituting the grand conclave or council of *Medicine*. As I belonged to neither of the five distinct societies or worlds known by savages, being neither French, English, Spaniard, American, nor Indian, and consequently ought to be regarded as the member of an unknown world, and could not be considered as profane, I was permitted to enter.

They were engaged in blessing their favourite and magic roots. The *Great Man of Medicine, Piscientha Onicy Asciatophy;* gave out the tune of their psalms, and each individual among the initiated chanted his verse in turn. The roots passed through the hands of every person, being in the last instance returned to those of the *Great Man*, who completed their consecration. This was followed by eating; for this process accompanies every form and ceremony; and in this I also participated. I was still in the camp when one of these devotees, if I may call them so, died of poison. At the above repast each person had his separate allowance placed on a bark trencher; the portion of the deceased had been seasoned with one of those medicines which he had himself joined with the rest in blessing. He was a person held in suspicion by the *Great Man of Medicine.*

In cases of this description vengeance is perfectly silent and inactive. No one speaks of the matter; not even relatives. The deceased victim is lamented only in secret. His heart is burnt privately, and the ashes are preserved by their medical or priestly juggler, and distributed to the true believers, as occasion requires, as amulets of sovereign virtue. I saw the unfortunate victim myself; he died calmly; and the other inhabitants of the hut, men, women, and children, were at the time proceeding on their own respective occupations with a coldness and indifference absolutely appalling, not even turning on the dying man a single look. This event, my dear Countess, recalled to my recollection a number of others which made me sigh and shudder at the baleful effects of imposture and superstition. I then quitted the scene in a state of great dejection and humiliation, with a thousand painful reflections rushing on my mind.

The river of Great Portage is so called by the Indians because a dreadful storm that occurred on it blew down a vast number of forest trees on its banks, which encumber its channel, and so impede its navigation as to make an extensive or great *portage* in order to reach it. The river thus denominated, however, is the true Red, or rather Bloody river. It enters the lake on the south, and goes out, as we have seen, on the north-west. This is the opinion of the Indians themselves, and it is not difficult to find arguments in support of it.

According to the theory of ancient geographers, the sources of a river which are most in a right line with its mouth should be considered as its principal sources, and particularly when they issue from a cardinal point and flow to the one directly opposite. This theory appears conformable to nature and reason; and upon this principle we should proceed in forming the sources of the river of Great Portage. By the name *Portage,* is meant a passage which the Indians make over a tongue of land, from one river or lake to another, carrying with them on their backs their light canoes, their baggage, and cargoes.

I left Red lake on the morning of the 26th. The commencement of *Portage* is between the river so called and Gold-fish river. It is about twelve miles long; and I therefore engaged another Indian, with his horse, to effect it more conveniently. The country is delightful, but at times almost impenetrable.

Half-way in my course I was stopped by a fine little lake, surrounded with cypress-trees. It has neither entrance nor exit. Its waters are gloomy, like the objects reflected by them; and a cavern, where the water is motionless, as it is indeed in every other part, recalled to my mind the Sybil's Grotto at Cumæ: as, however, I am no Eneas, I did not consider it prudent to enter. This lake had no name, and I gave it the appellation of the *Lake Avernus* of the new world.

In the evening, after extreme fatigue and experiencing a dreadful storm, we arrived at the end of the portage, near a small lake, to which we gave the name of the *Lake of Pines*, from the immense number of those trees by which it is surrounded. Its waters, which by their continual foam and bubbling, appear to gush upwards out of the earth, after a course of four or five miles, go to form the eight lakes which, as has been observed, discharge themselves into Bloody lake by Gravel river.

On the ensuing day, the 27th, I discharged the supernumerary Indian, with his horse; for, having no provisions but what we could procure by means of our guns, we were already three too many. We crossed the small lake strictly in the direction from north to south; and here we commenced another portage of four miles.

The Indian carried the canoe, the *Bois-brulé*, as much of the effects as he was able, and the rest I undertook myself. You smile, my dear Countess, at our laborious and humble procession, and indeed I cannot help joining you. As, however, I have condescended to be considered an animal of burden, I shall not expect to be ever again accused of *impatience*. We proceeded at a brisk pace, and my air and carriage were not contemptible for a man who was hitched and hooked on every side in thorns and briars. Even Delille, who converts everything into rose and jessamine, would have changed his tone in my situation. Not a word of complaint, however, did I utter!

At the end of this *corvée* we found the Great Portage river. We embarked and proceeded up its current, crossing two lakes which it forms in its course, each about five or six miles in circumference, and containing patches of wild rice—unfortunately for us not yet ripe. A family of Indians, whom we found there, collected from several spots a few ears for us, but these only served to make us still more acutely feel the sense of privation, and stimulate our appetite more strongly. We gave these lakes the name of *Manomeny-Kany-aguen*, or the lakes of Wild Rice.

After proceeding upwards of five or six miles, always in a southerly direction, we entered a noble lake, formed like the others by the waters of the river, and which has no other issue than the river's entrance and discharge.

Its form is that of a half-moon, and it has a beautiful island in the centre of it. Its circumference is about twenty miles. The Indians call it *Puposky-Wiza-Kany-aguen*, or the *End of the shaking Lands;* an etymology very correct, as nearly all the region we have traversed from the lake of Pines may be almost considered to float upon the waters. The foot sinks in with the turf it treads on, and the latter resumes its level when the foot removes. This lake is situated at a very small distance from high lands, which divide the waters flowing northward from those which take a southerly direction.

I passed on this spot a part of the day of my arrival and the whole of the succeeding night. We had excellent sport among the wild ducks, which abound and build their nests there. We also dried and smoked some of them, in order to preserve some stock of provisions, of which we were frequently in want. On the morning of the 28th we resumed our navigation of the river, which enters on the south side of the lake.

About six miles higher up we discovered its sources, which spring out of the ground in the middle of a small prairie, and the little basin into which they bubble up is surrounded by rushes. We approached the spot within fifty paces in our canoe.

But now, my dear Countess, let me request you to step on quickly for a moment, pass the short portage which conducts to the top of the small hill, which overhangs these sources on the south, (the only hill I have met with since those I pointed out to your notice on the river St Peter,) and transport yourself to the place where I am now writing. Here, reposing under the tree, beneath whose shade I am resting at the present moment, you will survey with an eager eye, and with feelings of intense and new delight, the sublime traits of nature; phenomena which fill the soul with astonishment, and inspire it at the same time with almost heavenly ecstasy! This is a work which belongs to the Creator of it alone to explain. We can only adore in silence his omnipotent hand.

In this situation the mind of man rises in rapture towards the Author of all the wonders which surround him. Here the most determined infidel would be compelled to admit the existence of a Supreme Being. That sublime temple, before which all the monuments of antiquity sink into insignificance, and which ages to come will never be able to equal, the august temple of the Vatican, where the deity and religion display themselves in all their majesty, would not excite in your mind sentiments of faith and piety so perfect and profound as those inspired by the present enchanting, transcendant, and prodigious creations of divine omnipotence!

We are now on the highest land of North America, if we except the icy and unknown mountains which are lost in the problematical regions of the Pole of that part of the world, and in the vague conjectures of visionary mapmakers. Yet all is here plain and level, and the hill is merely an eminence formed, as it were, for an observatory.

Casting our eye around us, we perceive the flow of waters—to the south towards the gulf of Mexico, to the north towards the Frozen Sea, on the east to the Atlantic, and on the west towards the Pacific Ocean.

A vast platform crowns this distinguished supreme elevation, and, what is still more astonishing, in the midst of it rises a lake.

How is this lake formed! Whence do its waters proceed? These questions can be solved by the grand Architect alone; man can merely suggest conjectures; and those of the *savans* are sometimes the weakest and most erroneous, because the most presumptuous, and, from their extreme subtlety, unsubstantial; and even when they understand nothing of the different phenomena before them, they always consider themselves obliged to talk and theorize as if they had comprehended all. I will, myself, inform you in the first place of what I have materially and actually seen on the subject, and then offer the inferences naturally flowing from the facts.

This lake has no issue: and my eyes, which are not deficient in sharpness, cannot discover, in the whole extent of the clearest and widest horizon, any land which rises above the level of it. All places around it are, on the contrary, considerably lower. I have made long excursions in all its environs, and have been unable to perceive any volcanic traces, of which its banks are equally destitute. Yet its waters boil up in the middle; and all my sounding lines have been insufficient to ascertain their depth; which may be considered as indicating that they spring from the bottom of some gulf, the cavities of which extend far into the bowels of the earth; and their limpid character is almost a proof that they become purified by filtrating through long subterraneous sinuosities: so that time may perhaps have effaced the exterior and superficial traces of a volcano, and the basin of the lake have been nevertheless its effect and its crater. Whither do these waters go? This, I conceive, may be more easily answered, although there is no apparent issue for them.

You have seen the sources of the river which I have ascended to this spot. They are precisely at the foot of the hill, and filtrate in a direct line from the north bank of the lake, on the right of the centre, in descending towards the north. They are the sources of Bloody river. On the other side, towards the south, and equally at the foot of the hill, other sources form a beautiful little basin of about eighty feet in circumference. These waters likewise filtrate from the lake, towards its south-western extremity: and THESE SOURCES ARE THE ACTUAL SOURCES OF THE MISSISSIPPI! This lake, therefore, supplies the most southern sources of Red, or, as I shall in future call it (by its truer name) Bloody river; and the most northern sources of the Mississippi—sources till now unknown of both.

This lake is about three miles round. It is formed in the shape of a heart; and it may be truly said to speak to the very soul. Mine was not slightly moved by it. It was but justice to draw it from the silence in which geography, after so many expeditions, still suffered it to remain, and to point it out to the world in all its honourable distinction. I have given it the name of the respectable lady whose life (to use the language of her illustrious friend the Countess of Albany) *was one undeviating course of moral rectitude, and whose death was a calamity to all who had the happiness of knowing her;* and the recollection of whom is incessantly connected with veneration and grief by all who can properly appreciate beneficence and virtue. I have called the lake, accordingly, *Lake Julia;* and the sources of the two rivers, *the Julian sources of Bloody river*, and *the Julian sources of the Mississippi*, which, in the Algonquin language, means *the Father of Rivers*. Oh! what were the thoughts which passed through my mind at this most happy and brilliant moment of my life! The shades of Marco Polo, of Columbus, of Americus Vespucius, of the Cabots, of Verazani, of the Zenos, and various others, appeared present, and joyfully assisting at this high and solemn ceremony, and congratulating themselves on one of their countrymen having, by new and successful researches, brought back to the recollection of the world the inestimable services which they had themselves conferred on it by their own peculiar discoveries, by their talents, achievements, and virtues.

I cannot inform you of the precise latitude or longitude of this interesting spot; for I have no instruments with me by which I could ascertain them; and to speak candidly, even if I had, I could not perhaps satisfactorily avail myself of them. Astronomy was but slightly touched on in my education, which was merely general, but had not an appointed object. This is one of the faults of our country, for the education of every individual should have some principal and determinate object in view; and, as you well know, my dear Countess, my occupation related rather to what men ought to do and to avoid on earth, than to what may be explored or guessed in the heavens. Moreover, perhaps the case

case is best as it is: for, since Mr Melish is far from agreeing with Mr Schoolcraft, and Major Lang with Mr Tardieu, even respecting the degrees of countries well known, there is reason to believe that a correct sextant is not easily to be met with: I have at least, therefore, not led the world into error on the subject. However, as I calculate that from Pembenar, which is in the fiftieth degree, I have proceeded almost always longitudinally as far as Bloody lake, I presume these sources are not far distant from the forty-ninth.

My Indian and *Bois-brulé* are now announcing to me, for the third time, that my table is ready. Occupied by the most grand and interesting objects in nature, with a mind absorbed by the sentiments which these solitary and venerable regions inspire, and those also arising from my associations with the name by which I have just designated them, I had nearly forgotten the very means of my existence—I now go to my Indian repast.

LETTER XX.

At Sandy Lake,
Sept. 20, 1823.

In my last letter, my dear Countess, I left you at the Julian sources of Bloody river and the Mississippi. We have seen the greatest part of the first, let us now follow the second. I hope, if heaven prove propitious to my wishes, to conduct you to the mouths of it. We shall, in that case, be the only individuals who ever traversed the whole of its course, as we were the first to discover its sources.

The Julian sources of the Mississippi run directly to the south of the small basin which has been noticed, by a narrow strait of three miles length, into Turtle lake. If I had not been afraid of adventuring my canoe amidst the almost impassable brambles and brushwood which impede its portage, I should have commenced the navigation from the very spot on which they spring.

I find it impossible to become weary of examining and admiring the least objects of attention furnished by this scene. The majestic river, which embraces a world in its immense course, and speaks in thunder in its cataracts, is at these its sources nothing but a timid Naiad, stealing cautiously through the rushes and briars which obstruct its progress. The famous Mississippi, whose course is said to be twelve hundred leagues, and which bears navies on its bosom, and steam-boats superior in size to frigates, is at its source merely a petty stream of crystalline water, concealing itself among reeds and wild rice, which seem to insult over its humble birth. I could not but be struck with the valuable lesson here furnished to haughty upstarts, or help recurring in imagination to the slave in antiquity, who, placed behind the car of triumph, repeated in the conqueror's ear, "*Respice post te et hominem esse memento.*" In short, my imagination, which had figured to itself precipitous mountains, down which the waters of this monarch of rivers rushed in mighty waves, was struck with astonishment at finding one eternal flat of swampy ground.

The Tortoise lake, called by the Indians

Mikinakosa-guay-guen, took its name not, as geographers tell us, from its form, but from a tortoise of extraordinary size, which the Indians found there about a century ago: they fed it with everything they could offer it most delicious, and long worshipped it as a great Manitou.

Neither traveller, nor missionary, nor geographer, nor expedition-maker, ever visited this lake. A great many of the stories which find their way into books are invented by the Red men, either to deceive the whites, or to conceal their own belief or their own weaknesses. You never hear an Indian talk about his gods, or about the worship he pays them. Theological disputations, claims to religious ascendancy, despotic intolerance, do not disturb their communities or their families, every man goes to the heaven of his own creation by the way his conscience or his instinct points out. The Indians themselves have confessed to me that, when they go down to the traders' settlements, they amuse themselves with gulling their credulity by a number of fables, which afterwards become the oracles of geographers and book-makers.

This lake is like a labyrinth. The quantity of streights and little bays formed by the numerous islands and peninsulas, renders it almost inextricable. Setting out from the most northerly point, where the Julian sources of the Mississippi enter the lake, you steer direct to the south for two miles, then turn to the east through a streight formed by an island and a tongue of land; then turn to the south again, then to the west, constantly doubling capes and promontories, and at length you reach the point, towards the S. S. E. where the Mississippi resumes its course. The lake, including all its numerous bays, is perhaps more than a hundred miles in circumference. It has no other outlets than the entrance and issue of the Mississippi. The volume of water of the river is so considerable even at its first issuing from the lake, that it already affords a safe navigation for large boats; which leads me to think that the lake is fed by subterranean springs; indeed the whole surrounding country is, to use the Indians' expressive word, completely "*shaking*." The whole substratum here is water, just as in the kingdom of Naples it is fire. But the former of these phenomena is much more surprising than the latter, for it is the property of fire to ascend, but it is impossible to understand how so vast an extent of elevated country, which has no higher land around it, can remain thus saturated with water.

The Mississippi turns almost immediately to the east, then to the north east, in which direction it flows into a pretty little lake, which I have taken the liberty to consecrate to you, by christening it *Jeromine*. The river flows out of it again on the E.S.E., and, after a course of seven or eight miles, passes through another, which I called *Monteleone*, in memory of that illustrious man, and as a mark of my grateful remembrance of the friendship with which he honoured me, and of which death alone could rob me. It keeps the same direction for about fifteen miles, describes a point towards the east, and then takes its course towards the south-west for fifteen miles more, to the confluence of the river which the Indians call *Scisaïaguay-sibi*, or the Heron's river, from the number of these birds which inhabit it: it flows from the north-west. I stopped there the night of the 2nd instant.

My Indian guide, who had hunted in all these desert tracts, informed me that this river was a truly delightful and charming one, and that by availing ourselves of its course and of one portage, we might return to Turtle lake by a short cut, saving not fewer than twenty miles. He moreover led me to hope that, by silently ascending it, we might meet with some bears, (as they abound on its banks, which furnish great quantities of wild fruits,) and kill them from our canoe. I determined therefore to make known to the world this short passage; and we set out on the morning of the 3rd accordingly.

This river is indeed a touchstone of sensibility. It traverses a number of small basins of the most luxuriant and variegated description. But the beauty of the lake whence it issues is what principally strikes and fascinates the attention. It is certainly one of the most exquisite spots in nature. It consists of two basins; the first, which we enter on the south, is triangular; we then clear a small streight on the north, and see before us the other basin, in the form of an ellipsis or a circle. Its banks are of a majestic character, from the stately and spreading trees which overhang them. I have given it the name of *Torrigiani*.

We disembarked on the north side and made a portage of four miles; we however left behind our little baggage, which we hung up in the trees, and carried with us only our arms and our canoe. We passed through a gloomy forest, which abounded in martens, and at the end of the portage we came to another lake of an oval form, which I called *Antonelli*. We traversed its breadth from south to north, a space of about four or five miles; and then, after clearing a narrow pass, dreadfully encumbered with trunks of trees and wild rice, we found ourselves again in the Mississippi, precisely at the point where it issues from Turtle lake. Here we passed the night; and it very nearly proved the last night of our lives. A dreadful storm had almost crushed us under the trees, which it mowed down like so many tulips in a garden, or uprooted with the same ease as if they had been carrots. We scarcely had time to save ourselves with our canoe in the midst of a spot of prairie, to which, by a sort of miracle in these forests, we very fortunately had access. Had we lost our canoe, we should have been completely ruined; for even Indians would have been unable to extricate themselves safely from such a watery labyrinth without a canoe.

The place from which we had fled for security in the night, we found in the morning strewed with immense trees. The forest of the portage, which we again traversed, was equally encumbered by fallen trees, and the clear and tranquil water of the lakes had become foul and agitated. This terrible convulsion was not improbably the effect of an earthquake. But on a tract of territory so boggy and shaking, it was scarcely possible to distinguish such an event with accuracy. My Indian, for the convenience of drying ourselves, kindled a flame under the trees which had crossed one another in falling, and we soon had a noble bonfire, which comprehended in its blaze some portion of the forest; and which not improbably is burning yet.

Near the lake Torrigiani, on the right, as we

were returning, my Indian attendant satisfied my curiosity upon a point by which it had a long while been excited.

It seems difficult for a traveller to publish his adventures without mentioning the castor or beaver, even though his travels may have been limited to Africa, where this animal is not to be found. I should wish to avoid repetitions, but I do not distinctly recollect anything that has been stated by these ingenious gentlemen on the subject, or even what Buffon wrote about it in his closet. I will communicate to you only what I have myself actually seen, and been from good authority informed of, respecting these astonishing creatures. If I mention circumstances which others have narrated before me, you may consider it as affording additional evidence of what you were previously acquainted with; and if what I advance be new, you will, I hope, give me credit for adding to your information.

A small river flows into the lake on the western side. The beavers have barricadoed the mouth of it by a dike, completed in a manner which would not disgrace a corps of engineers; the water is thus kept back, and forms a pond, in which they have erected their habitations. It is proper to notice that the river in question is never dried up, as otherwise they would not have fixed upon it for their purpose.

The stakes fixed in the earth, and the trunks of trees which are laid across them, are of considerable thickness and length. It is difficult to conceive how such small animals are able to transport such bulky articles. But what is more astonishing is, that they never make use of trees blown down by the wind, or levelled by the strength of man, but select them themselves, cutting down such as are peculiarly adapted for the intended building, and doing this always on the banks of lakes or large rivers, in order to avail themselves of the opportunity of conveying them by water to the place intended.

While five or six are occupied in cutting or sawing with their teeth the bottom of the trunk, another stations himself in the middle of the river, and indicates by a hissing sound, or by striking the water with his tail, which way the top inclines towards the fall, that the operators without interrupting their labour may conduct it with proper caution, and preclude all danger. It is worthy of remark, that they never gnaw the tree on the land side, but always on that of the lake or river, in order to ensure its falling into it.

The whole tribe then combine their exertions,

and float the trunk to the place where it is wanted. Here, with their teeth, they point the stakes; with their claws dig deep holes for them in the earth, and with their paws introduce and drive them in. They then place branches against them, and fill up the interstices with mortar, which some prepare while the others are cutting down the trees, or engaged in different departments of labour; for the tax of labour is carefully distributed, and no individual remains unemployed. The mortar used by these wonderful animals becomes more hard and solid than the finest Roman cement.

When the dike is completed, and has been proved fit for the purpose designed, they effect an opening at the bottom of it, by way of flood-gate (which they open or close as may be required,) that the stream may not be too much impeded. They then commence building their habitation in the midst of the mass constituting the dike. They never begin to erect the habitation previously to forming the dike, lest the latter operation should fail of success, and they should consequently lose their valuable time and labour.

Their mansion, formed equally of wood and mortar, consists of two stories, and is double; its length is in proportion to the number of the tribe for whom it is intended.

The first stage, or story, is a magazine in common for provisions, and is under water; the second is divided into dormitories, each family having its distinct chamber; this part of the building is above the water.

Under the foundations of the building they form a number of avenues, by means of which they enter and quit subterraneously, so as not to be perceived by the most keen and watchful Indian; these all terminate at a distance from their dwelling, and in part of the mound constituting their dike, or in lakes or rivers, near which they usually form their establishments, that they may have it in their power to select that direction which may be most convenient and least dangerous in the various incidents and exigencies of their lives.

Beavers are divided into tribes, and sometimes merely into small bands, each of which has its chief; and order and discipline exist in these distinct societies to a greater extent probably than among the Indians, or even among some civilized and polished nations.

Their magazines are invariably fully stored with provisions in summer; and no one is permitted to break in upon this stock until the scarcity of winter begins to be experienced, unless circumstances render it imperatively necessary to violate this rule. In no case, however, is any one permitted to enter without the express authority and indeed the presence of the chief. Their provisions consist, in general, of the bark of trees, principally of the willow and poplar species. On some occasions, when bark is not to be found in sufficient quantities, they collect also the wood of those trees, which they divide into distinct parcels with their teeth.

Each tribe has its peculiar territory. If any foreigner be taken in the act of marauding, he is delivered over to the chief, who, on the first offence, chastises him with a view to correction; but, for the second, deprives him of his tail, which is considered as the greatest disgrace to which a beaver can be exposed: for the tail is the carriage on which he conveys stones, mortar, provisions, &c. and it is also the trowel (the figure of which it represents exactly) which he uses in building. This violation of international rights, however, is considered among them as so great an outrage, that the whole tribe of the mutilated culprit take up arms in his cause, and proceed immediately to obtain vengeance.

In this conflict, the victors, availing themselves of the customary rights of war, expel the conquered from their home, take possession of it themselves, appoint a provisional garrison for the occupation, and eventually establish in it a colony of young beavers. In this connection, another circumstance relating to these truly wonderful creatures will appear not less astonishing.

The female beaver whelps usually in the month of April, and produces as many as four young ones. She sustains, and carefully instructs them for a year, that is, till the family are on the eve of a new increase; and then these young beavers, compelled thus to make room for others, build a new home by the side of the paternal mansion, if they be not very numerous; but if there should be too many to admit of this, they are obliged to go, with others, to a new spot, forming a new tribe and a new establishment. If, then, about this season the enemy should happen to be driven from his quarters, the conquerors install in them their own young ones of the current year, provided they be duly qualified for emancipation, or, in other words, capable of managing for themselves.

The Indians have related to me as a positive fact another circumstance respecting the conduct of these animals; but it is so extraordinary, that I leave you to credit it or not, as you may think proper.

They allege, and some will even assert themselves to have been eye-witnesses of such a fact, that the two chiefs of hostile tribes sometimes terminate the quarrel by a single combat, in presence of the two opposing armies, instances of which have occurred in various nations; or by a conflict of three with three, like the Horatii and Curatii of antiquity.

Beavers practice the usage of matrimony, and death alone separates the parties. They inflict heavy punishments on their females for infidelity, and sometimes even death itself.

In cases of sickness, they mutually and anxiously take care of each other; and the sick express their pain by plaintive sounds and tones like the human race.

The Indians hunt the beaver in the same way in which I formerly described them to you as hunting the musk-rat: indeed the latter animal may be considered as a beaver of a secondary order. It is of the same shape, only smaller, and resembles it in many of its qualities, but its fur is very inferior in beauty and fineness. It may be added, that in winter the Indians make holes in the ice which covers the ponds surrounding the habitation of the beavers, and, carefully watching for the moment when they lift their heads up to take breath, instantly shoot them.

Great Hare, at Bloody lake, confidently assured me that, on reaching the spot where two tribes of beavers had just been engaged in battle with each other, he had found upon the field fifteen, dead or dying: and other Indians, both Sioux and Cypowais, have equally declared that they have occasionally obtained capital prizes on the like occasions. It is perfectly correct that they are sometimes taken without a tail. I have seen one in that state myself, which corroborates the history of the punishment inflicted by them on obstinate offenders. In short, these animals are deemed so very extraordinary, even by Indians, that they consider them as men metamorphosed into beavers; and killing them is regarded as conferring upon them a very essential service, as it is conceived to be a restoration of them to their original state of being. Here, again, my dear Countess, is a puzzle for those who are desirous of compacting the religion of these tribes into a system! But it is time for us now to return to the Mississippi.

We rejoined it on the evening of the 3rd, at the place where we had quitted it the evening before, and again passed the night there. Our household gods seemed to have expected our arrival, for the fire we had kindled there was still burning.

On the 4th, we struck our tents very early, and arrived in the evening at Red Cedar lake, so called on account of the number of those beautiful trees, whose dark green foliage overshadows its islands and banks.

The Mississippi, from the mouth of Heron's

river, receives no other, but may be said to flow constantly through the midst of water, for all its banks are submerged and shaking, though varied by prairies and forests. Its bed is always very deep, and its course gentle and uniform. It traverses or forms four superb lakes, the largest of which is seven miles in circumference, and the smallest four. I have called them *Providence* lakes, on account of the fields of wild rice which Providence has formed there, and the ears of which resemble those of the land of promise. After passing through the streight of the last of those lakes, the river enters Red Cedar lake to the south, and flows out of it on the left, at E. N. E., at the end of a bay formed by a tongue of land which projects into the lake at S. S. W.

On the right of the entrance of the lake, accident discovered to us a very remarkable and indeed astonishing echo. It was night, and my Indian and *Bois-brulé* called out in loud voices, as usual, in order to learn the situation of the flying camp of the Indians who inhabit this lake. Their calls were repeated times without number, gradually diminishing in loudness, and at length fading through the distance into extreme faintness.

This lake is the *non plus ultra* of all the discoveries ever made in these regions before my own. No traveller, no expedition, no explorer, whether European or American, has gone beyond this point: and it is at this lake that Mr Schoolcraft fixed the sources of the Mississippi in 1819. For the more complete celebration of this fortunate discovery, this illustrious epoch, he rebaptized it by the name of lake Cassina, from the name of Mr Cass, governor of Michigan territory, who was at the head of the expedition. Mr Schoolcraft was the historiographer.

The geographers who had previously comprised this lake in their maps, might fairly protest against this conduct as usurpation, for he has infringed on the right which they unquestionably possess of calling it Red Cedar lake, or the lake of Red Cedar, a name long since consecrated by usage, and *inveterate usage* (you know) *is held equivalent to law.* You will perhaps, remark, that I have myself baptized a tolerable number of lakes. Mine, however, must be admitted to have been fair subjects for the ceremony. They were not only not to be found in any map, but they were unknown to all the world; and I trust that flattery has no share in my inaugurations of them, as I applied to them only such names as were consecrated by my veneration for the dead or my friendship for the living.

This lake is also to be considered as a large

lake, if we are to comprise in its extent that of two others with which it communicates by two streights on the W. and E. S. E. Some islands which intercept the full view of it, are of an immense size, though they might appear small to the eye of the observer who merely passed for a moment into its first basin, and, after breakfasting there, returned almost immediately by the way he came, satisfied with being able to say, "I have been there," and with having had the portrait taken in a sort of miniature. But those who advance farther, and examine with more attention, experience no small surprise on discovering the vast expanse of water before and around them, sufficiently convincing them that in those regions, yet more than in others, that element covers more than two-thirds of their surface; while the picturesque and enchanting scenes, continually presented to the eye, excite the most intense delight and admiration. Mr Cass represented merely what, as I before intimated, must be considered as a miniature delineation (taken from his encampment on the western bank of the lake, where I encamped myself,) of the western island, which is in fact of great extent. As soon as the hasty sketch had been taken, he returned to join the expedition, which he had left, for the greater part, at Sandy lake, as we shall see at the close of the present letter.

The figure of the first basin is varied by bays and promontories, and four islands divide it into numerous arms. One of these islands is about twenty miles in circumference, and inhabited by about a hundred Cypowais Indians. According to the opinion of those Indians, the circumference of this basin must be considered as about eighty miles. That which joins it on the E. S. E., of an oval form, and surrounded by gloomy pine and cypress trees, is about eight miles. The third, to the west, which is nearly triangular, is little less than thirty miles. At the bottom of this last lake, on the west, is found the entrance of a considerable river, which the Indians call *Demizimaguamaguensibi*, or the river of lake Traverse. It issues from the lake, (the second of that name,) twenty miles above its mouth, on the N. W. This lake communicates, in the same direction, by a streight of two or three miles in length, with another lake, which the Indians call *Moscosaguaiguen*, or Bitch lake, which receives no tributary stream, and seems to draw its waters from the bosom of the earth. It is here, in my opinion, that we shall fix the western sources of the Mississippi. The waters beyond the high lands which surmount this lake flow towards the north into Hudson's Bay.

The Julian or northern sources of the Mississippi, are about a hundred miles distant from Red lake; about that distance, therefore, from those fixed by Mr Schoolcraft; and the sources of Bitch lake, or the western sources, are, I conceive, fifty miles distant. We resume the course of the river.

On issuing from the Red Cedar lake it turns to the east, and continues in the same direction as far as lake Winipeg, which is about fifty miles in circumference. It traverses this lake, and issues from it in the direction of E. S. E. At some distance from this, it forms a small lake four or five miles round; and twenty-five or thirty miles farther on, in the direction of S. S. W., it receives the river Leech, *(Cazaguaguagine-sibi,)* which is the first tributary river to be found below Red Cedar lake for the space of seventy miles, and which flows down from the west.

Its depth and its progress are always the same, and these regions may be almost as truly said to bathe the river, as that to bathe them; for, to whatever part of the bank we direct our view, we see nothing but water and shaking bog. On the night of the 6th, in order to avoid getting in contact with the water, I constructed a pile formed of three layers of the branches of trees, over which I spread my bear-skin; but all my precaution was insufficient to secure me from the springs which bubbled up around me; and whenever I turned, I felt myself rocking as with the movement of a cradle, and as if floating, like another Apollo, in the isle of Delos.

While you read these pages, your friendly regard will perhaps take alarm at every leaf you turn over; and you will be apprehensive that I shall sink under the fatigues incidental to so very laborious and novel a mode of life. You will be comforted, however, by the assurance that I have scarcely felt even a head-ache, though, when I wake in the morning, I am completely drenched by the dew from above, and by the bubbling of the springs below me; though I always sleep in the open air, and am therefore, completely exposed to the inclemency of the season, and the attacks of musquitos, gnats, emmets, and reptiles; though my gun only can be depended upon for food, and the river for my drink; though, in short, I am surrounded *by all sorts of miseries.* You may hence, my dear Countess, judge of the elevation of these regions, the purity and elasticity of the air of which can impart spirits and vigour sufficient to counteract such inconveniences and dangers.

On the night of the 7th I slept at the mouth of this same Leech river. The lake whence it issues is a new Colchis, where a second Jason found, like the first, a golden fleece; where Mr Pike fixed the sources of the Mississippi, fourteen years before Mr Cass fixed them at Red Cedar lake. This circumstance could not fail of exciting my curiosity, and I determined, in consequence, to go and view the scene which had given birth to the conjectures of the first of my two predecessors.

We arrived on the evening of the 8th at lake *Sogahyguen,* or Muddy lake. Like those of *Providence,* it is completely covered with wild rice. Only one river discharges itself into the Leech before it reaches the lake. The Indians call it *Bagatwa-sibi,* or the Owl. It flows from the north. By means of this river and a few *portages,* a short cut may be taken to reach Cedar lake.

On the 9th we arrived at Leech lake, *(Kaza-gas-guaiguen,)* at *Macuwa* or Bear island, where we found a considerable band of *Cypowais plunderers,* so denominated from their plundering and murdering the first Canadians who pushed their commerce to such a dangerous distance.

This band is very numerous and warlike. I found it divided into two factions, one of which is actuated by the spirit of legitimacy, the other by its opposite. The *Pokeskononepe*, or Cloudy Weather, a usurper, contests the crown and empire with the chief *Esquibusicoge*, or Wide Mouth, who possesses them by hereditary right: but as these Indians beyond all others require for their head a daring and active man who can conduct them to victory over the Sioux, by whom they are frequently harassed, instead of an idle and profligate poltroon, always reposing under the shade of his genealogical tree, and destitute of all merit but that allowed him by his flatterers, *Cloudy Weather* has the majority on his side. The government of the United States acknowledges both; *Cloudy Weather*, because he declaims in their favour; and *Wide Mouth*, in order to detach him from the English, to whom he is friendly; but principally, I imagine, from the policy of keeping alive division in a band powerful in force but precarious in attachment. From the observation I have myself made, I must acknowledge I am tempted to believe that the whole affair of apparent disunion may be a mere farce originating in Indian craft and subtlety, having for its object to turn to the best account the solicitations and liberality of both these nations. And in fact they receive the rich repasts and grand galas of both with the same customary phrases of friendship, devotion, and *fidelity*. When an option will become absolutely necessary, they will probably side with the party most skilful in intrigue and most liberal in bribes: they will most likely, therefore, take part with the English. The fact is, that the two chiefs reign respectively over their peculiar partisans, or perhaps it may be said more truly, are respectively their slaves.

On my arrival among them they were in no little commotion on another subject, involving the two parties in new contention. *Cloudy Weather's* son-in-law had been killed a few days before by the Sioux, and they had at the same time received intelligence of the affair at Cayenne river, and of what had happened to my two Indians on Bloody river. *Wide Mouth* demanded an immediate war, and was desirous of forming an army, of which he himself never constituted any part. *Cloudy Weather,* who is not deficient in sense, suspected that this warlike ardour, this extraordinary eagerness and zeal, were assumed with a view to remove him out of the way, and turn his absence to his injury; and therefore, although the principal person aggrieved, strongly recommended *prudence* and *moderation.*

I had no sooner disembarked than he immediately called a council of war, which is composed of the chief officers of the army, and came to me to invite my attendance. It is to be observed, that all these Indians had seen me at Fort St Peter.

He began by observing, that the *Great Spirit* had sent me for the express purpose of giving them salutary counsels; that as the friend of their father (the agent) it became me to fulfil the duties which the circumstances required of me; that division existed in their camp; that his heart was torn with grief for the death of his son-in-law, while at the same time he was aware that it would ill become him to sacrifice his beloved Cypowais for the sake of his own personal vengeance; that he had every need, therefore, in such a conflict of mind, of consulting with *that man of another world, who had smoked with them the calumet of friendship, and been a witness of the peace which the Sioux had sworn to with them*, &c. &c. My reply was soon made. I told them that, being a stranger to the Americans, to America, and to the Indians, I neither ought nor designed to interfere in their affairs, and more particularly in their quarrels; but that, as it was the duty of every one to answer as well as he could those who confidingly asked his advice, I must declare mine to be that, as they had in Mr Tagliawar a father who loved them, and who represented the government, they should do nothing without his consent; and that such was too the will and command of the *Great Spirit*. The council approved of what I said; and *Cloudy Weather* offered to accompany me to Fort St Peter to consult his Father.

A few moments after, *Wide Mouth* sent to request my attendance. I went accordingly. I found him lying at full length in his tent, like old Silenus, in a state of intoxication, surrounded by his partisans. He began a discourse, and seemed to intend introducing into it a number of subjects, but I cut short his address, and merely observed that wars in general served only to gratify the views and passions of the ambitious or despotic few; that the public good was often solely the pretext for them, but the people always became their victim; that as to anything farther on my part, I had nothing to do with them, that I had neither time nor inclination to involve myself in their quarrels, and that I referred them to the proposition I had just suggested to the other council. This indeed they could scarcely fail of having been informed of, for I had reason to know that even Indians have among them the same neutral class as abounded in Greece of old, and as may be found indeed in all parts of the world—cameleons of all colours—renegadoes of all parties.

The royal chief, ill satisfied with my observations, and desirous of counteracting truth by imposture, consulted the oracle respecting the event of the war he wished to engage in: and the oracle was favourable, as might naturally be expected; for the decision was given by one of his own priests.

I cannot repress my astonishment at finding the usages and ceremonies of antiquity every instant copied or renewed among these Indians. Their oracles spoke precisely by the same means as did the oracle of Delphos formerly. Instead of the Pythian priestess, one of their priests is seated on a perforated tripod completely concealed under a bell-formed cover of birch bark, which has a round opening at the top, through which the divine annunciation issues. Beneath the tripod a tube, also made of bark, communicates under ground with a stove, over which a kettle filled with water and aromatic herbs is kept boiling, the vapour of which passing through the tube has the effect of heating and sublimating to what are deemed prophetic visions the brain of the officiating priest, who utters the cries and ravings of a demoniac, and borrows on those occasions a language intelligible only to the *Coryphæi* of the Indian sanctuary. My *Bois-brulé* himself, though well acquainted with the Algonquin language, understood not a single word that was delivered. It is a remarkable circumstance, that professional jealousy excludes all foreign priests from this ceremony, conformably to the practice both of ancient and modern times; and I had some difficulty in persuading them that I was totally unconnected with the priesthood, in order to be permitted to be present at it. I have been informed that similar means are sometimes used for applying vapour baths to the sick; and, occasionally, even for suffocating the individuals whom the *Grand Medicine* junta wish to get rid of.

I was a spectator of the funeral ceremony performed in honour of the manes of *Cloudy Weather's* son-in-law, whose body had remained with the Sioux, and was suspected to have furnished one of their repasts. What appeared not a little singular, and indeed ludicrous in this funeral comedy, was the contrast exhibited by the terrific lamentations and yells of one part of the company, while the others were singing and dancing with all their might. I was scarcely able several times to refrain from laughing: but the ceremony having some resemblance to the usages of the ancients, who also on such occasions paid and employed together *Tibicenes* and *Præficæ*, my respect for antiquity and our antiquaries enabled me to preserve my gravity. At another funeral ceremony for a member of the *Grand Medicine*, and at which, as *a man of another world*, I was permitted to attend, the same practice occurred. But, at the feast which took place on that occasion, an allowance was served up for the deceased out of every article of which it consisted, while others were beating, wounding, and torturing themselves, and letting their blood flow both over the dead man and his provisions, thinking possibly that this was the most palatable seasoning for the latter which they could possibly supply. His wife furnished out an entertainment present for him of all her hair and rags, with which, together with his arms, his provisions, his ornaments, and his mystic medicine bag, he was wrapped up in the skin which had been his last covering when alive. He was then tied round with the bark of some particular trees which they use for making cords, and cords of a very firm texture and hold (the only ones indeed which they have,) and instead of being buried in the earth, was hung up to a large oak. The reason of this was, that as his favourite Manitou was the eagle, his spirit would be enabled more easily from such a situation to fly with him to Paradise. Here, again we perceive another trait of antiquity, and a rich relish for our antiquarian amateurs, whom, I think, I must at length have completely satisfied. The oak is also among the Indians the tree consecrated to the eagle, that is to say, to Jupiter.

Mr Pike, who was at the head of the expedition despatched by the government of the United States in 1805, to discover the sources of the Mississippi, fixes them at this lake, although the river Leech which flows into it on the N.N.W., ascends more than fifty miles higher up; and although various other rivers, the courses of which are as yet unknown, equally flow into this lake. But it was in winter; the cold was excessively severe, and it is no pleasant or easy matter to discover sources through ice. It is impossible to doubt, that, at a different season of the year, and with a less embarrassing party, Mr Pike would have pushed his discoveries farther. He was a bold and enterprising man; and his expedition to New Mexico, and his glorious death in the field of honour, merit a place in history. He will always be entitled to the distinction of having been the first who extended his researches so far in regions so wild and repulsive, and that at a time when there existed no fort whatever on the Mississippi.

This lake is interspersed with innumerable islands and peninsulas, the latter of which form a number of deep bays, that appear to be so many separate lakes. That which is to the north of the Indian camp exhibits the perspective of a theatre, the promontories which gradually advance from each side representing so many scenes. The lake has a great number of issues, which, by means of various portages, afford the Indians facility in traversing, with their canoes, either in or out of them, all the surrounding territory; and cross cuts which preclude the necessity of those wearisome and almost endless circuits, that would require to be traversed in entering upon it by the Mississippi and the mouth of Leech river.

By ascending the last-mentioned river about fifteen miles, and then crossing two lakes and effecting two portages, we may go in one day to Red Cedar lake; and the last portage terminates at its small basin.

On the west, we rejoin Raven's Plume river, which flows into the Mississippi, and ascends nearly as far as Otter's-tail lake.

On the south we descend to the Mississippi by Pines river; and on the south-east by the river Willow, which Pike has denominated *Pike* river.

The day and night of the 12th were the most dreadful of my whole life. I tremble whenever I even think of them; thank God, however, I did not tremble at the time. I was aware that, if I exhibited before the Indians the slightest indication of fear, it was all over with me. I carefully preserved, therefore, my self-possession, and an intrepidity, I flatter myself, of no easy attainment.

A number of these Indians, who *drink at two fountains*, had just been visiting the English agents at Romaine island, on lake Huron; and among the presents distributed among them they had received some barrels of whiskey. This was soon circulated through the encampment, almost every member of which soon became violently heated and maddened by it.

It is the usual practice of the female Indians, when they see cases of intoxication in their own tent, or in the camp, to preserve to themselves the strictest sobriety, that they may be enabled to prevent or mitigate the frequently dreadful consequences of intemperance in the men. But, on this occasion, the women were more completely inebriated than the men, and with the exception of a few young persons, all were plunged in the most frightful state of intoxication.

The hell of Virgil, and of Dante, or even that painted by Orcagna, at St Maria Novella in Florence, in a style so deeply impressive, are only faint sketches in comparison with that full display of terror and death presented in the tragedy now acted; a tragedy exhibiting in all their horrors the Bacchantes, the Furies, the

Eumenides, Medusa, and all the monsters of history or fiction.

Hatred, jealousy, long standing quarrels, mortal antipathies, all the ferocious passions, were in most exasperated excitement and conflict. The shrieks of the women and children, mingled with the yells of these cannibals, and the bayings of dogs, added the tortures of hearing to all the agonies which appalled the sight.

Standing on a mound of earth with my cutlass in my girdle, my gun in my hand, and my sword half unsheathed at my side, I remained a spectator of this awful scene, watchful and motionless. I was often menaced, but never answered except by an expressive silence, which most unequivocally declared that I was ready to rush on the first who should dare to become my assailant. My *Bois-brulé* had concealed himself, and I had great difficulty in rallying him to my side, where he at length appeared to feel more confidence and security than elsewhere; for he became convinced that there was a greater probability of escaping the threatened catastrophe by courage and resolution than by indecision and terror.

But it became necessary for me, for a few moments, to quit my intrenchment. The life of the chief, *Cloudy Weather*, was in danger. I was his host, and he was the father of the beautiful *Woascita,* who, by giving me timely notice, in two instances, of plots formed for my destruction, and thus kindling into stronger power the fierce and menacing expression of my countenance, had been twice my preserver. I darted forward with her and my *Bois-brulé,* who was now become a hero, and we saved him by disarming of their knives the two assassins who had attacked him, and against whom, merely with a small piece of wood, he defended himself like a lion. We pushed him into his tent, and committed him to the care of a warrior chief, one of his intimate friends, who was enjoined to protect him and prevent his going out. He found however a knife, which had been concealed; and, whether from that impulse natural to Indians, which often occasions them in their passion to make a victim of the first man they meet, or whether through real mistake, he rushed on his friend and stabbed him with repeated thrusts: we however returned instantly at the call of Woascita, and fortunately in time to prevent the completion of murder.

On this occasion I was exceedingly surprised and affected, my dear Countess, by a display of genuine magnanimity and generosity.

The son of the wounded savage, about eighteen years of age, entered the tent, and surveying with an expression of terrific dignity the assassin of his parent, with heroic self-possession thus addressed him:—"Thou hast *stabbed* my father . . . thy own friend . . . I ought to avenge him, and I could do it . . . but thou wouldest not have done this, hadst thou not been intoxicated . . . I pardon thee." In this young Indian, the son of *Bear's-heart*, I perceived Rome and Greece united. He was the hero of the day. He was not only able to resist the temptation of a liquor so exceedingly attractive to Indians, but he contributed greatly to mitigate the effects of its deadly influence. I embraced him with sentiments such as these savage people had never before excited in me. The noble conduct of this young man is also one of those circumstances which infuse such contradictions into the character of Indians, and almost preclude the power of defining them. In order to testify my admiration of his conduct, I gave him a liberal quantity of powder, the most valuable present that, situated as I was, I could possibly bestow upon him. I would have conferred on him an empire, had I been able; but my destitution was even greater than his own.

On examination, the ensuing day, twenty-four were found to have been wounded, seven of them mortally, and two dead, one of whom was my poor Indian from Red lake.

My *Bois-brulé* also had received a wound in

one of his hands. He was desirous moreover now of going back to his family, and not without reason, for the provisions I had left them must have been all consumed, and without his exertion it would be impossible for them to obtain subsistence. I gave him fresh proofs of my gratitude, as far as lay in my power. I purchased a canoe for him to go back in, and then went forward in my own, with *Cloudy Weather* for my companion. The encampment was still in a state of agitation, and seemed, indeed, now to be menaced with new horrors. To the ravages of whiskey, and the cruel wars which they are perpetually, and often causelessly, waging against each other, the Indians may justly ascribe their progressive extinction.

The lake was rough and the weather stormy, and I was always a bad navigator. When we were in the bay which conducts you to the river, a violent wind from the south-east drove us on the opposite bank. We again embarked however, but all our efforts were useless, and we passed there the night of the 13th. On the morning of the 14th, I landed at the establishment of the South-West Company, near the exit of the Leech river, in hopes of replacing in some measure my *Bois-brulé*. But we found only a single person there, left to take care of the place; and it was quite impossible for him to leave it; I was therefore obliged to go on with *Cloudy Weather* only. However, I obtained all the instructions that were necessary to enable me to proceed with information as far as Sandy lake; and I found myself gradually more intelligible to my new Indian associate.

We resumed the navigation of the Mississippi just where I had quitted it. On my return the wild rice was in a state of ripeness, and we were consequently in the midst of abundance. But, owing to a singular circumstance, I was situated like Tantalus, and unable to eat, though my food abounded immediately before me.

When leaving Leech lake, I had parted with my large boiler to my *Bois-brulé*, and kept for myself only a small one, thinking that *his majesty* would be sure to supply the deficiency out of his royal outfit. But he had not, in fact, brought with him even his bark spoon, and the whole of his wardrobe consisted merely of his buffalo's skin. On the second day after our departure, we saw a hut of Indians in a wood, near the river; and my companion, after going to speak to them, returned and took up my kettle. As he had in the morning intimated that it was too small, I supposed that he intended to change it for a larger one, but he came back without any. All my injunctions and all my resentment were of no avail. He had bestowed it on one of his partisans. These Indian kings, in order to ascend or preserve themselves upon the throne, will actually deprive themselves of everything. No being is more destitute and miserable than an Indian chief; indeed, the results of a blind ambition to rule and reign are everywhere similar. I was now therefore reduced to my tin cup; from the luck of the pot I passed to that of the goblet, or what perhaps was about a sufficient allowance for a hungry black-bird. My eccentric companion laughed at seeing me obliged to go through my culinary process three distinct times before I could at all appease my appetite, and enjoyed the sight of my dinner of three acts as much perhaps as he would a comedy. For his own dinner he took the rice without any preparation whatever, and at last I was compelled to do the same myself.

The Mississippi continues to flow almost uninterruptedly over quaking and boggy land, as far as down to the little falls which the Indians call *Kekebican*, about seventy miles from the confluence of Leech river. At about fifty miles we find, on the western side, the *Pakegamanaguen*, or Hook lake; and at sixty, the *Onomonikana-sibi*, or Vermilion river, which enters on the east.

These falls may be subdivided into six divisions. They commence by a great rapid divided by a small island, the first that occurs in going down the river. The vast mass of water then proceeds, in a direction nearly vertical, to dash against some rocks which, by their resistance, work it into a state of foam, the operation of the sun's rays on which produces all the beautiful phenomena of the rainbow. Impetuous and boiling waves next rush over an inclined plane for about fifteen paces, and are then hurled down two more successive falls at a little distance from each other; and a second rapid, still more violent than the first, closes the scene: it comprises the space of about a mile, which we passed by *portage*.

A hill, clothed with mournful cypresses, dark pines, and majestic cedars, overhangs these falls on the west; and a small hillock, verdant with foliage, and luxuriant with shrubs of delightful flower and fragrance, bounds it on the east, while numerous rocks are seen scattered around, rearing their striking forms in the shape of obelisks and pyramids, and the melody of birds of every engaging note and song produces an impressive contrast to the hoarse croakings of the raven. Such a mixture of sublime and romantic attraction imparts to this extraordinary scene of nature something even of the marvellous. And a crash so awful and tremendous in the midst of eternal solitude! I must leave it to yourself to form a just conception of so wonderful a spectacle, and to indulge the exquisite feelings appropriate to it.

About ten miles from these falls, the *Sassicy-Woenne*, or *Thundering Rapids*, presented the spectator with another agreeable variety. At this place a portage is usually made; but my royal Indian chose to distinguish himself and his fellow-traveller from the vulgar crowd, and we passed over them in the canoe. What is new and extraordinary generally affords the mind gratification and delight. This result I experienced on the occasion in question, although the agitation of the waves, the rolling of the canoe, and the rocks that threatened our course, kept us, for the space of half a mile, I may almost say, within two fingers'-breadth of eternity: it was however soon over; we could not be said to navigate, but rather flew.

On the evening of the 17th we arrived at Sandy lake, on the east, *(Lamitonga-aguen)* which is about one hundred and twenty miles from the last-mentioned place, about three hundred from Red lake, and about three hundred also from Leech lake. In the space between the Thundering Rapids, and the exit and discharge of the river out of Sandy lake, the Mississippi receives *Muskotensoi-sibi*, or Prairie river, *Wa-*

haske-sibi, or Roebuck river, *Namago-sibi*, or Trout river, and *Wabazio-sibi*, or Cypress river, all which fall into it on the east. On the western side it receives the *Singonki-sibi*, or Marten river. Three rapids occur also in the above mentioned distance, two of them between Cypress river and *Willow Portage*, (a place so called from a portage which communicates between the Mississippi and Willow river,) and the third lower down.

All the maps, whether of former or recent date, even those constructed conformably to *expeditions*, are exceedingly incorrect with respect to the situation of Sandy lake. They place it at the S. E. of lake Leech, though it is nearly at the east; and this error draws after it others respecting its latitude and longitude. I have observed this mistake by the due application of my compass, the result of which corresponds with the opinions of the Indians on the subject, who, indeed, are very seldom deceived in their geographical statements.

We will now, my dear Countess, rest awhile, for we have far to go before we reach the mouths of the Mississippi, being as yet only four hundred miles from its Julian sources.

LETTER XXI.

Fort St Charles, on the Missouri,
Oct. 24, 1823.

WHENEVER I resume my pen to write to you, my dear Countess, it is under an implied engagement with myself to spare at once your patience and my own, by presenting only a general view of the most remarkable places and incidents that I meet with; but, continuing as I still do, in regions so remote and almost unknown, where nature developes herself under forms so new and diversified, I am irresistibly attracted beyond my designed limits, and my system of rapid and sketchy observation is frequently broken in upon either by the admiration of some novel object presented to my senses, or by the exquisite emotions which, on particular occasions and in particular circumstances, agitate my heart. It is not every one who is gifted as the Turk is, to sit with the most apathetic indifference on the noblest monuments of Egypt and of Greece. Rapidly as I pass over a variety of subjects, I experience more and more the difficulty of being laconic, and at the same time of giving you a narrative of my progress with any tolerable exactness. It is, indeed, nearly impossible to avoid occasional repetitions, either through the necessity of great explicitness to attain desirable perspicuity, or through the deep interest excited by occurring scenes and circumstances, when describing a river, perhaps the most grand and interesting in the world, the chief points of which may be of the highest importance to future generations, and whose charms and wonders would nearly exhaust all the terms which language can supply. But let me return to where I left you in my last letter—to Sandy lake.

This lake is a handsome basin, about ten miles in circumference. Some neighbouring hills, four islands, and a number of small promontories, attach to it abundant and agreeable variety. The river of the same name issues from it on the west, and enters it at E. N. E. By means of a portage it communicates with the river Savannah, which runs into the St Louis, as that does into lake Superior, exactly at the place called the *End of the Lake*, at its most westerly point. This passage, from Sandy lake to lake Superior, may be effected in two days; which is a new proof that Sandy lake is much more to the east of Leech lake than it is marked upon the maps. Through this channel are conveyed all those articles which constitute the staple of commerce with the Indians in these regions; and of which, as has been already mentioned, *Michilimakinac* is one of the South-West Company's two general *entrepôts*. Sandy lake receives on the S. S. E. Wild Oats river, *(Menomeny-sibi,)* which proceeds to a great distance into the interior.

Its banks constitute the rendezvous of a tribe of Indians, amounting to the number of about five hundred, who roam in small and scattered bands, or even single families, and reunite in autumn and in spring to barter with the Company. The Company's establishment is near the spot where Sandy river falls into the Mississippi.

There also, as at Leech lake, we found only one person, a housekeeper or guard of the establishment, a Canadian, possessed of great good-nature and kindness, but who had nothing besides wild rice and potatoes; and who, to console me under my privations, gave me a list of those which he had himself experienced, and indeed was experiencing still; among others, he stated that he had been ten years without once tasting bread: however, he procured for me a kettle, a rug, a little rum, and some ammunition. It is only at this season that the directors of each establishment are at their post, and they were, on my arrival, actually on their route; but I was unable to make any stay. They supply the Indians with everything necessary for their winter hunt, and receive from them in the spring the skins obtained by them in the chace, which they take with them to Michilimakinac, where, in summer, they balance their accounts, and prepare again for what they call their *winter quarters*, employing the whole of the autumn in travelling to them. It was here, as I have already observed, that General Cass left nearly the whole of his expedition, when he went up to Red Cedar lake.

On the 21st of September I quitted the Canadian and the Sandy river. The frost had already set in on the night of the 19th. Being fatigued with rowing, and desirous of giving free indulgence both to my eyes and thoughts, I engaged another Indian. But I found myself again still without an interpreter.

I will, in the first place, describe to you the principal directions of the river as far as Fort St Peter, in order to give you in one continuous view an idea of its course to that point, and to avoid distracting your thoughts, by these details, from what is more interesting to observe, and to admire.

It flows W. S. W. as far as Pines river, a distance of about one hundred and fifty miles. It then turns, and continues in a course S. S. W. as far as Raven's Plume river, about ninety miles; it then proceeds in a southerly course to the falls of the Great Rock, a distance of one hundred miles; beyond that it runs south-easterly as far as Rook's river, one hundred and fifty miles lower; after which, finally, it traverses about sixty in the direction of E. S. E. to Fort St Peter; which is just about nine hundred and fifty miles from the Julian sources, and five hundred and fifty from Sandy lake.

As the Sioux much haunt the banks of the river, chiefly below the mouth of the Raven's Plume, in order to carry on war against the Cypowais, I elevated my umbrella as a standard, or rather a signal by which they might understand that the canoe was navigated by a foreign and neutral power.

Willow river is the first that we meet with below the Sandy river. This is the river to which Pike gave his own name, and by which he first went up to the Leech lake. The Indians call it *Meaogeo-sibi.* It is about forty miles from Sandy lake.

Were I to acquaint you with all the storms that I have experienced, I should be under the necessity of exposing you almost incessantly to peals of thunder and flashes of lightning: but, much as I am inclined to spare you, I cannot help noticing that which occurred on the 29th, because it was a really remarkable one.

We were compelled to seek a landing; not to find shelter—for in such a deluge that was utterly impossible—but because the drops of rain were of so enormous a size as almost instantly to fill the canoe. The surface of the river was struck by them with such violence, that over its whole appearance it exhibited the appearance of a spouting-up fountain.

Peals of thunder succeeded each other with scarcely the slightest intermission; but in this country the electric fluid, although excessively abundant, discharges itself simultaneously by such numerous channels, that the objects on which it lights are struck by it less violently than in Italy. Our canoe was merely grazed by it, and a few trees were stripped of their bark.

The fall of rain was inexpressibly heavy, and must, I imagine, have been equally extensive, as on the morrow the river had risen to the height of eight feet. Even the Indians did not recollect an instance of so great and sudden a rise. We were obliged to lie by the whole of the 23rd, for everything was soaked completely through, and my Indian sovereign was ill. At night, I went with the other Indian to hunt the roebuck, in a manner that was new to me.

The hunter covers the whole of his breast with a coating of oak-bark, and on a shelf or ledge attached to this carries a lighted torch made of pine-wood. The roebuck, dazzled and confounded by his appearance, makes a sudden halt, and the hunter then fires. We were, however, unsuccessful.

At the distance of a hundred miles from Sandy lake, we find the second island that adorns the Mississippi. The Indians call it *Minitik*, or Great Island. Between it and Wild Oats river, the Stamp, (or *Sossabegoma-sibi,)* the Pitchers, (or *Piskociokoako-sibi,)* the Red Cedar, (or *Kamoskoaka-sibi,)* which issues from the second lake of that name, all flow into the great river on the east; and on the west, the Little Willow, or *Sissimonageo-sibi*.

At Pines river, *(Singuoako-sibi,)* which enters also on the right, the chief was disturbed at not finding his son and two of his partisans, whom he had appointed to meet him at that place, which they were to have reached by a course of portages, in order to go down with us as far as St Peter's. With respect to myself, however, I was better pleased as the case was. I had three ferocious brutes less to guard against. These three Indians had distinguished themselves by their savage conduct in that horrid scene which I gave you an account of in my last letter.

As far down as the Pines the river is gentle and even, if we except three small rapids situated above that river, and which are only at a small distance from each other. Its bed is always very deep; its banks wear a constant and funereal gloom, everywhere abounding in pines, cedars, and cypresses. Afterwards the scene changes: a lovely island receives the waters of Pines river, and divides them into two branches. The great river becomes at once more gay and more majestic, and the landscape more varied with hills and prairies, copses, and forests.

At six miles distance from the Pines, five islands form, as it were, a crown for a sixth, which rises magnificently in the midst of them. Nothing but a temple is wanting to give it the appearance of another *Cytherea;* and, as it was not known by any name, I called it by that.

In the evening of the 26th we were joined by a small party of Indians from Sandy lake: they were desirous of accompanying me down to visit Mr Tagliawar. They were fifteen in number, and occupied five canoes. On their arrival, I was employed in eating my allowance of wild rice, which I continued to do without even looking at them, or uttering a single word. I gave my Indian chief to understand that I was determined to keep my fire and my kettle to myself. After finishing my supper, I ordered them to be called; and, distributing among them a little tobacco, I smoked with them the pipe of peace and civility. On the morrow, I gave each of them a glass of rum, but still without any communication by word or gesture. This, my dear Countess, is the proper way to prevent their insolence and command their respect. They behaved like angels during the whole of the voyage, scarcely allowing themselves to laugh when they saw me washing my face; and probably would have completely avoided it, had I been able myself to help laughing when I saw them rubbing over their own with charcoal or kettle black, or with white, red, or yellow clay. They employ much more time in thus completing their toilet opposite a looking-glass, than would be required by the most fashionable of our coquets for her smartest gala preparations. The rain frequently deranged their operations, and it was not a little ludicrous to see how it veined and marbled their faces.

Raven's Plume river is a grand discharge of various lakes which on the west empty their waters into the Mississippi. It is a truly magnificent river, and, at their confluence, is, I think, as large as the Mississippi itself. Its principal source is White Bear lake, where Mr Morse's *American Gazetteer* has placed the sources of the Mississippi. Two delightful islands divide it into three branches, at its mouth, and render it highly majestic and picturesque.

The *Wokco-sibi*, which flows from the east about twenty miles from the last river, is deemed remarkable among the Indians: it was the abode of a Cypowais, who passed for a prophet, and it has inherited his name.

Six miles lower down, the river forms a small lake; and how luxuriant and delicious a view does it afford! Nature has scattered over it twelve islands, which Lenotre himself could not have distributed with finer taste; and has diffused over its banks such delightful scenes as even Catullus has only inadequately described in the picture he gives of his charming residence at the lake of Garda. I have called these islands the *Sirens*.

From Bitch river *(Mosko-sibi,)* which flows also from the west, we pass through a succession of rapids, till we reach that of Great Rock *(Kekebicaugé,)* which is a small fall. Here generally a portage is made, which we however avoided by passing through a narrow channel on the east, behind an island. This fall is formed by a small strait. The river, confined between two rocks, forms a gulph, from which it rushes with a tremendous roaring.

On the evening of the 28th we encamped about twenty miles from this fall, at a place where the river, surrounding a very noble island, of a figure precisely round, suggests to the memory the temples which the ancients consecrated to the sun, and the Druids to their gods. The stately and superb forest which embosoms the basin, corresponds finely with the image here suggested. I have named the island, therefore, the *Island of the Sun*.

Between this place and the Great Rock, the river receives the tributary streams of *Wabizio-sibi*, or *the Swans* (the second of that name,) and *Kanizotygoga*, or the Two Rivers, which flow from the west.

At a little distance lower we find, also on the west, the mouth of the *Zakatagana-sibi*, from the name of a certain species of wood, which is the only kind of tinder that the Indians make use of. It is difficult to find a better match: I have kept a sample of it among my Indian curiosities. The confluence with Pines Tail river *(Bekozino-sibi)* takes place at a very short distance farther on the east.

Here is the commencement of extensive prairies, which spread both to the east and west, but are interrupted by woods and thickets. In winter, buffalos are frequently found here.

Between the *Bikabikao-sibi*, or Shuffle-board, on the east, and the Renards *(Oxaguio-sibi,)* on the west, there is another fine river also on the west. It is perfectly unknown even to the Indians. I would have given it a name; but as it is within only a few days distance from the Fort St Peter, I did not choose to infringe on a right which might be supposed to belong to the officers of that garrison. There are among these gentlemen men of merit, highly capable of serving the government in the plans it seems to entertain of exploring and becoming fully acquainted with this mighty stream, and these interesting regions. A single individual, possessed of practical philosophy and genuine philanthropy, with a moderate knowledge of geography and astronomy, would, in a country beset on every side with obstacles and difficulties, and among tribes of men peculiarly subtle and suspicious, accomplish much more than an expedition fitted out at great expense. For, in proportion to the number of persons attached to the expedition, will be the alarm with which the Indians will be impressed by it, the dangers in which it will be involved, the wants to which it will be exposed; dangers and wants which frequently detain and obstruct it when it would be of the utmost importance that it should proceed, when advances into the interior of the country would be most indispensable to attaining the object of their mission. As I have begun this subject, I feel bound to communicate to you the various reflections I have made upon it.

The advantages which have been hitherto derived from these expeditions have not, I believe, answered the views of the government, or the expectations of the public. They have consisted of a few plants, with which perhaps all but the members of the expedition were acquainted, *and which swell that mass of unintelligible hieroglyphics, that scientific but tasteless and terrifying nomenclature, unfortunately consecrated by a great name, serving merely to overlay the memory and to blot out the lovely picture of nature;* a few gaudy butterflies and other insects, of which we have already too many everywhere; of birds, which can only gratify curiosity and luxury; of stones, suggesting a thousand conjectures of their nature and origin, and which, whether *silicious* or *calcareous*, or designated by any other learned terms, serve as materials for the idle discussions of pretenders to science, but contribute little or nothing to the benefit of the public;—such have been the principal results of these pompous and costly enterprises.

The study of natural history is unquestionably a study by no means to be neglected, particularly so far as it is connected with utility. But it ought not to be made a principal object by an enlightened and liberal government. It is the grand business of such a government to study practically the nature and character of man, and to provide for his real wants; and man, even in his uncivilized and savage state, is not unworthy of its careful attention. By acting on such principles as these, the administrators of the power of states may procure a name dear to humanity and venerated by their dependants.

Let a single officer then, a man deserving of confidence, accompanied merely by clever interpreters, and two good rowers, (Canadians,) be employed to explore the territory of the Indians. Let him attentively observe their manners, their customs, their physical and moral tendencies, and their means of subsistence; let him investigate, on the very scenes which he visits, what must become of these people when their hunts fail to procure them adequate supplies, a period which now cannot be very remote; and what may be the result of such a crisis to civilized nations in their immediate neighbourhood, if, on the one hand, these barbarian hunters emigrate or become extinct, or on the other turn their attention to agriculture and the useful arts. In proportion as his views enlarge, while examining closely all the local peculiarities, let him contemplate the means of facilitating, and turning to the best account, a revolution in the manners of these wandering tribes so eminently important. Let him however begin with secular plans and objects; sacred or spiritual ones will follow naturally and of course. In situations such as this, bread is the best preparative for the gospel. The charity of active beneficence, the grand virtue which the gospel inculcates, is of infinitely more value than that which consists barely in preaching. Before announcing to these untaught men the beatitudes of heaven, they should be instructed in the best means of sustaining life, and of enjoying it on earth. The latter is the natural and unerring guide to the former; for in that merciful Providence to which they will be indebted, under a new system of living, for sustenance, security, and tranquillity, they will readily acknowledge an actual deity, of whom they will soon desire a clearer knowledge, to whom they will soon present their thanksgivings and adorations; and, after they have advanced to this desirable point, then will be the season for pouring spiritual reasonings into their docile minds, and effecting their gospel regeneration.

The work of Mr Morse on this subject is animated by a piety and philanthropy truly exemplary; but it is deficient in that spirit of philosophy, without which every physical or moral system is destitute of value in proportion as it is weak in its foundation. We frequently talk of heaven, but our meditations and affections are ever recurring to earth, as we are every moment experiencing wants which press imperatively and overwhelmingly on our mortal existence. A being therefore so material and unspiritualized as the Indian, must be operated upon and absorbed by such wants still more than ourselves. This subject, my dear Countess, brings to my recollection an Indian chief who, when the interpreter was explaining to him one of Mr Morse's sermons, in doing which it was necessary to make frequent use of the word *bible*, asked eagerly *whether the bible was anything to eat?*

All the French missionaries in Canada, who adopted and acted upon these principles, attained most completely the object of their mission, and made the greatest number of proselytes among the Indians. They were indeed the only ones whom they respected, and their memory is still held by them in veneration.

Below Renard's river, rapids follow one another in quick succession, till we arrive at a place where they are terminated by an *Archipelago*. The river here presents a miniature resemblance of that sea which proved so noble a theatre for the ancient inhabitants of Greece in their struggles against Darius and Xerxes, before Salamis and Artemisia, and which is scarcely less brilliantly distinguished by the present glorious efforts of their descendants against the despotism and oppression of the cruel Ottoman. It is wonderful to observe how this river combines all the features of grandeur and beauty, all that can affect and astonish. It comprises at this spot, within a spacious and enchanting enclosure, fifteen islands, rivalling each other in elegance and charms. Nature seems to repose with pleasure in the view of them, and to be proud of her work, like Michel Angelo surveying his picture of the Last Judgment in the Sistine chapel, when he exclaimed, *How beautiful it is!* Even the Indians stopped, with some indication of emotion, or at least they seemed affected by mine.

I had here a very fine opportunity of perpetuating my name in these Indian territories, by giving it to this enchanting place; and you will perhaps be surprised at my so completely neglecting myself. After my death, my dear Countess, men will dispose of my name, as God will of my soul, according as I shall have well or ill deserved during my life; and I leave to my friends and to those who have had opportunities of becoming acquainted with my heart, the charge of defending my memory, should it ever be attacked by injustice or prejudice. But not to dwell upon this, a strolling excursioner, without commission or pretension, like myself, who writes his letters on his knees in the midst of vast deserts, as Cæsar wrote his Commentaries on the pummel of his saddle and amidst the tumult of a camp, could hardly perhaps place himself upon a level with celebrated travellers and professional authors. Do not, my dear Countess, for a moment imagine that, by recurring to Cæsar for a little analogy, I am weak enough to think myself his rival in glory.

About seven or eight miles from this Archipelago, we again meet with violent rapids. The Indians encounter them with an intrepidity and dexterity truly surprising. They do just whatever they like with their canoes. I frequently discovered new subjects of admiration in our little pasteboard-like flotilla, which, scattered as they were over the surface of the agitated stream, frequently led me by their form and movements to recollections of antiquity.

On the evening of the 27th we stopped at a place where a roebuck, which my Indian chief had fired at from his canoe, had gone to die; a spot of the most delicious sweetness, and to which we were led by the merest chance.

In every situation there are moments when man feels a sort of necessity for abandoning himself entirely to his own thoughts, but never more so than after he has been for some time exclusively in the society of an uncultivated people, and in the midst of forests and deserts. I ascended a slight elevation, commanding the river and the adjoining country, and there I fixed my camp in complete solitude. In the morning, sitting on my bed, which had been made by the hand of nature, inclining my head against a tree whose spreading top constituted my pavilion, and the uncovered part of whose root had been my pillow, I beheld the rising of that beneficent star which returns every day to reanimate the world and rejoice mankind with his all-cheering beams. How lovely did he appear after such a season of storm! I saw the vapours of the dawn soon scattered by his influence, and then beheld, in a new basin formed by the river, a new production of nature, as perfectly fascinating as it was singular. It was an island of a pentagon form, in the middle of the river, presenting a model of the finest work that ever proceeded from the genius and pencil of our celebrated Vanvitelli, the Lazaretto of Ancona. I say the finest work, for on account of the magic art with which he has so admirably and appropriately distributed the offices, both sanitary and commercial, and of the difficulties which he overcame to accomplish this effect; I prefer it even to those wonderful productions, the palace of Caserta and the bridge of Matalone. How exquisitely soothing and delightful was my bed! Even the hours of night itself had unfolded to my solitary vigils objects of high interest and feeling, such as in the bowers of luxurious indolence perhaps never occur. The moon and stars diffused their changeful and fascinating light over pictures of enchanting beauty; and even when the tempestuous weather made my situation unpleasant and painful, I still felt something amidst my sufferings which raised me above them, I might almost say above myself; and my feelings might have been envied by many of those who stagnate under purple and ermine. The Indians call this place *Anikitoucian*, or the Great Echo, which however is considerably inferior to that of Red Cedar lake. It is about twenty-five miles below the Archipelago.

Within a short distance, a considerable river,

also without a name, descends from the west; and afterwards, from the same quarter, the river Clear Water, *(Kawanibio-sibi,)* a name deservedly applicable to it.

The river *Kapitotigaya-sibi,* or river Double, which enters on the east, and which comes from the *Thousand Lakes,* is the termination of the voyage on the Mississippi made by father Hennepin, the first who ever navigated it so high up as this river, to which he gave the name of St Francis, probably from the day on which he discovered it. It is about sixty-five miles from Fort St Peter. An island almost completely blocks up its mouth. It is a river of considerable magnitude, as is also Rook's river, which we reach five miles lower down on the west, and which the Cypowais call *Poanagoan-sibi,* or the Sioux river, for there these hostile nations often meet, and, like Bloody river, it has been often dyed with the blood of battles. I saw here a bear upon a tree; but as my own gun and that of the chief were as usual wet with the rain, he in consequence escaped. At this season, when there are no longer any fruits, the bear returns to his acorns, and climbs up the oaks to find out the softest of them. I should have felt as if I had performed an extraordinary achievement, had I killed a bear perched on a tree like a bird.

On the night of the 29th all around us was winter, and the weather, although so early, terribly cold. But I could scarcely help feeling myself warm, when I looked at my half-naked companions, who had nothing to cover them, by night or by day, but a single rug or skin which, notwithstanding all their dexterity in managing it, frequently escapes from one part while they are endeavouring to cover with it another; and even this, their only garment, is seldom entire; for whenever they want a bit of rag to clean their gun, they resort to this wardrobe, which indeed comprises their whole stock.

In the morning I shot an animal to which naturalists, if I am not mistaken, give the name of *mouffeta*. It deserves a few minutes notice.

It is about the size of a small otter, being nearly as long, but its muzzle is much longer and more pointed, and its legs are somewhat shorter. This prevents its running with sufficient speed to escape the hunter, who takes it the more easily from its not being amphibious, and therefore unable to take refuge in the water. But nature has given it a weapon of mighty power against its assailant, consisting in the intolerable stench of a liquid which it conceals under its tail, (as the serpent conceals its poison under its fangs,) and which it darts on the pursuer with such force, that it reaches him sometimes at the distance of sixty paces. Naturalists pretend that it is the animal's urine; but in this they are in error, as they are in many other of their statements; a circumstance not unlikely to happen to men who study nature only in the seclusion of their closets.

I dissected the animal, and found the fluid to be contained in a bladder completely distinct. I was nearly suffocated by the horrible smell which proceeded from it and infected the air around during the operation. It almost took away my senses and breathing. If it is spilt on any clothes, all the essences and detergents in the world would be insufficient to disinfect and purify them; and it is remarkable that the smell is not impaired, or at least only very slightly so, by time. The Indians have discovered no method of removing it but by burying the apparel, that happens to be thus polluted, for some days in the earth. It is also worthy of notice, that the quantity of this fluid thrown out by the animal is always in proportion to its irritation and danger, as in the case of the negroes, who never so copiously exhale the odour peculiar to them as when they are assaulted or exasperated. The like effervescence or ebullition is also produced by the bilious humour of a splenetic and melancholy man, when he is gnawed by bitter passion and mortification.

After passing the confluence of the *Missay-guani-sibi*, or river Brandy, on the east, and that of another river, which is unknown, on the west, I approached that grand and interesting spectacle which I mentioned to you in my fifteenth letter, the Falls of St Antony. We heard the roar of the enormous mass, which rushes down with such impetuosity that rocks, unable to resist its force, are carried away and broken by its violence. I already saw rising from the foaming waters a dense haze, which concealed the horizon from our view. The strength of the current hurried forward our canoe with alarming rapidity; and at length I discerned between the trees, and in a pleasant back-ground, the roof of a house, indicating of course civilized habitation. This was the mill for the garrison at the fort. On reaching this place, my mind, still dwelling on all the grand and terrible scenes which had occurred to me in the course of three months, while traversing eternal deserts, among barbarous tribes and unknown regions, was agitated with emotions which I could scarcely describe or discriminate.

The sight of this object, which announced my approach to the residence of cultivated man, produced in me a conflict of opposite feelings. I regretted the independence of savage life, while at the same time I experienced a thrill of delight at returning within the sphere of civilized society.

After having cleared the portage, I completed my Indian toilet for the last time; that is, I shaved myself without either soap or glass, and with razors which were much like saws. I took my bath in the river, and dressed myself as well as I was able, in order to appear at the fort as decently as possible. But I was beset on all sides with dirt and squalidness: these perhaps have in fact formed the greatest of my sufferings. My head was covered with the bark of a tree, formed into the shape of a hat and sewed with threads of bark; and shoes, a coat, and pantaloons, such as are used by Canadians in the Indian territories, and formed of *orignal* skins sewed together by thread made of the muscles of that animal, completed the grotesque appearance of my person. I am indebted for my new wardrobe to the fair *Woascita*, who had compassion on the nakedness to which the thorns and brambles of the forest had reduced me. The Indians attach a high value to the skin of the orignal, which is the most beautiful of quadrupeds, the monarch of rein-deer, and only very rarely to be met with. The gift therefore is valuable in itself, and as such I shall preserve it with care, but still more as a memorial of regard and friendship. *Woascita* deserves the appropriation of a few pages to record her merit, nor probably would they by any means be destitute of interest. But the world has been so filled with *Attalas*, that history is no longer deemed worthy of credit. I therefore check my pen. On some future occasion however it is by no means impossible that I may more worthily record her genuine excellence.

My Indians announced their approach in the customary manner, that is, by the discharge of guns loaded with ball, and with shouts and chants accompanied by the sound of their harmonious drums.

Melancholy rumours respecting my safety had been circulated at the fort, and young Snelling, on his return to it, having expressed the apprehensions he felt on my account when we parted at Pembenar, had thus strengthened the belief in them. These gentlemen in fact supposed me to be dead.

On the arrival of the flotilla all the officers hastened down to enquire about me. They were answered by the supposed dead man himself. While replying to their kind questions I divested myself of the skin covering which I had on, in the disguise of an Indian; a character which my countenance and general appearance greatly contributed to my supporting. I saw in the expression of their physiognomies both a movement of surprise, and sentiments of affection and friendship. The excellent Mr Tagliawar embraced me in the most cordial manner, and the colonel, his respectable wife, and his children, received me with demonstrations of the most lively joy. I was much moved, and could not help shedding tears of gratitude and attachment. This was the first time since fate began to steep my existence in anguish that I beheld a gleam of those happy moments which, in Italy, friendship always procured for me whenever I returned from my occasional absences. And during the short time that I remained among them I experienced nothing of the constraint, nothing of the cold and formal politeness which Americans in general are accustomed to affect, particularly towards strangers, and which, like a moral rust, tarnishes their natural benevolence and impairs the value of their hospitality. They were indignant against Major Long for acting towards me in the miserable manner that he did. With respect to myself, I felt towards him a sort of gratitude for having by his disgusting manners only strengthened my determination to leave him, in order to discover the sources of the king of rivers; and it is partly to him that I am indebted for the fortunate success of my enterprise, as the Americans are for the jealousy which that success has excited in them.

My Indians arrived in time. We found there deputations from almost all the distant bands of Sioux, who exhibited a novel spectacle, and indeed a somewhat imposing one, by the pomp and diversified costumes which the respective deputies displayed in the assembly, where they were all met, to present to Mr Tagliawar their homage and complaints, their pretensions and their compliments. They smoked new calumets of peace, and I again became a witness on the occasion. God knows how often this peace may have been violated before the moment in which I am now relating it!

I learnt from these deputations themselves the correctness of the idea which had suddenly struck me, when my two Cypowais were attacked on Bloody river. But they were eager to convince me that it was also out of regard for myself that they had abandoned the field of battle. I pretended to believe them, and with great profession of gratitude thanked them, making them a present of some tobacco. They told me, moreover, that I had acted judiciously in making myself known to them by means of my umbrella signal, as I should otherwise have experienced a shower of balls as well as arrows.

I did not forget to notice and recommend my *Bois-brulé* to Mr Agent Tagliawar. His unhappy family deeply interested me.

That gentleman objected to me in the first place the bad qualities of the man, his aversion to the Americans, his connection with the English. The charge was certainly true; and I did not undertake to justify him. But if we cannot subdue a dangerous enemy, we should, I observed, try to win him over by caresses. This, I remarked, was a maxim with greater politicians than ourselves. I added that this was the policy of Herennius, when the Samnites enquired what they should do with the Romans whom they held blocked up in the Caudine valley, and which the enquirers were so very injudicious as to reject. I even ventured farther to observe that, as long as this man was debarred from tasting American bread, he would be constantly tempted to assuage his misery with that of the English; that, after having in vain offered his services, he would become a declared enemy, as hatred may be sometimes pardoned, but contempt never can be; that he had great influence over the whole of these Indians, in the midst of whom he directed and governed alone; and finally, that he was by far more dangerous from uniting great talent with great guilt. Mr Tagliawar, whose disposition is naturally kind, was convinced of the justness of these observations, and approved the sentiments by which they were dictated; and he accordingly gave me a commission, which I sent off immediately to the *Bois-brulé* by *Cloudy Weather*. Titus complained, with reason, that he had lost a day when its course had been unmarked by some act of beneficence; for those hours, which recall to our recollection benefits performed to humanity, are the most valuable and delightful of our lives. They furnish an inexhaustible source of consolation, which will never quit us on earth but to conduct us to unalloyed enjoyment in heaven.

I did not neglect the opportunity of sending by the above conveyance some memorial of my ardent gratitude to the beautiful *Woascita*, and of my admiration to the young hero of the dreadful tragedy of the 12th. Before I for ever take leave of my Indian king, I must add one word to all that I have already said respecting him, in order to fix your ideas as much as possible on the subject of the sentiments or instinct of these peculiar people.

You have seen from my last letter that I saved his life at the peril of my own, and that I prevented him from completing the murder of his intimate friend. He frequently talked of this, and mentioned it in a very handsome way, but never manifested the slightest degree of gratitude. Even a dog, after such events as these, would have continued to manifest his thankful feelings for a long time by gestures and caresses. I made him several presents to compensate for his services as my pilot; but I gave the kettle which I had bought at Sandy lake to my other guide, with a significant smile, intimating to his majesty that I intended by this to punish him for parting with the first so very unseasonably to one of his partisans. Without entering, however, at all into my raillery, he haughtily turned round to me, saying, "*Thou hast frequently reproached us with being vindictive; but at least we are vindictive for objects of consequence and value, while you Whites are so for the merest trifles.*" My presence had saved these men twice from the ambushes of the Sioux, on Bloody river, and on the Mississippi, near the Raven's Plume, where a party was lying in wait for them, and spared them solely from their observing my signal of the umbrella; yet before they left me, they said, "*Thou art always obliging us to make peace with the Sioux, that they may murder us more securely.*" However, I still think, that the Cypowais, speaking generally, are less barbarous and depraved than the Sioux, and perhaps more brave.

I was very desirous of resuming my project

of passing from Fort St Peter to that of Council Bluff on the Missouri, across the deserts which separate them; but, besides the circumstance of the season being too far advanced in these excessively cold climates, war was raging in the countries through which I must have gone, and would have rendered my plan somewhat hazardous. To satisfy your curiosity on this subject, I will explain my meaning in a few words.

A new American Company, under the denomination of the *Missouri Fur Company*, has just started a new system of speculation on the Indian territory, which is, in fact, a new aggression on the property of these people, and an addition to all the numerous vexations and oppressions to which the rapacity of civilized nations has exposed them ever since the discovery of America. This Company has engaged, and keeps in pay, a number of men to become hunters themselves in those parts where the most valuable animals are most abundant, and consequently to usurp the rights of the Indians, and destroy the only means of subsistence now left to these miserable nations,—to whom Mr Morse would, in exchange, communicate the Bible, thus profaned as it is every moment before their eyes! This newly-raised legion was attacked in June last by the Rikara Indians; and, after sustaining a great loss in killed and wounded, had barely time to make a retreat. Colonel Leavensworth, the commandant of Fort Council Bluff, was called in to their assistance, and he immediately moved up the river with three hundred men; but, on arriving at the camp of the rebel Indians, struck perhaps with the injustice of the cause of the new adventurers, instead of avenging the American blood and name, as was expected, he granted terms of peace: and, at the moment I am writing, the only war that exists is carried on in the newspapers, between him and the agents of the new Company.

I left Fort St Peter on the 3rd of October. Though I have in general the greatest aversion to return the way I came, yet the Mississippi has still developed to me new charms. I could, indeed, never restrain my admiration of it. What a beautiful—what a majestic river!

Our voyage was very favourable, in a decked vessel called a *keel-boat;* and I found excellent company in some gentlemen travelling from the military academy at West Point, near New York, and whom I met with at Prairie du Chien, to which place they had conveyed recruits by the route of the lakes and *Owisconsing*.

These gentlemen are going with the rank of officers to Fort Council Bluff. They are very well informed, as those generally are who come from that establishment, which is the Polytechnic School of the United States. What a pity it seems, that they should be thus doomed to pass their days in such inhospitable wilds, remote from all respectable society, and surrounded by such a corrupt and degenerate race of beings as the Indians in the neighbourhood of these establishments always are! Thus delivered up to their own management and discretion at a season of life susceptible of all kinds of impressions, it is to be feared that they may soon forget the knowledge they have acquired, and that the polished manners, moral principles, and elevated sentiments they now carry with them, may be succeeded, at no distant period, by habits of intemperance and libertinism. The government is, in my opinion, much to blame for not having established a professor of mathematics at Council Bluff, and another at Fort St Peter, in order to keep up the knowledge of the young officers it appoints to them. Besides withdrawing them, by this means, from the danger of idleness, they would be training a number of men to become useful to the Indians, to their own country, to government, and to society; and the expenses attending expeditions from Washington might well be spared. The appointments in these expeditions are often as ill arranged as possible, and prove that favouritism may prevail in a republic as well as in a monarchy.

From St Louis, which I reached on the 20th, I am now arrived at the place of date, for the sake of a milder climate and a little repose.

LETTER XXII, AND LAST.

New Orleans, 13th Dec. 1823.

The day of my arrival at New Orleans was a day of real consolation. I had long been deprived of all correspondence with those whom I most esteem and love. Judge then, my dear Countess, of the delight I experienced on finding at this place two letters from yourself, and others from various relations and friends: it was the day on which I began to contemplate with less regret and frequency than before the independence of savage life.

I wrote my last letter to you from St Charles on the Missouri. The course which I am now going to take, from that place to the mouths of the Mississippi, you are partly acquainted with; I mean that part between St Louis to the mouth of the Ohio. We have now, therefore, only to survey the territory intervening between the Ohio and the Gulph of Mexico, which has been described by geographers and even celebrated by poets. Think not that I mean to follow the example of the latter. I do not mean, as I proceed in my extensive tour, to lull you to sleep, in order to make you dream like them at the expense of truth and common sense; to embellish agreeable fictions, or to adorn with flowers the truly gloomy and monotonous banks of this part of the Mississippi. I have described to you the enchantment which I felt at the sight of the admirable scenery which it presents from its origin to the Ohio. I shall now only call your attention to a few points, in order to render more complete your view of the entire course of this truly great river, and to notice some prevailing geographical errors.

St Charles is a handsome little town, though as young as the Missouri State, of which it is the capital. It is situated on the left bank of this great river, twenty-two miles from St Louis. Opposite to it, on the right bank, there is a small town forming a charming object in the view, and fronting the little capital on the south. Rows of finely tufted trees which line the banks of the Missouri, ornament it on the west and east; and on the north luxuriant meadows furnish a beautiful perspective, closed by the woods which border the Mississippi.

By its situation it would seem destined to become a place of great importance; and its progress would be still more rapid than it is, but for the conspiracy of a few selfish speculators to remove from it the seat of government, in order to fix it at the mouth of the Osage, about three hundred miles farther up; the object of which is to increase the value of considerable grants or acquisitions of land, which they have obtained there at different times by different means.

About four miles to the south of St Charles, there is a small village precisely corresponding in fact to the name it bears, and which is *Florissant*. It lies in the midst of a magnificent plain variegated by wood and prairie, and in which the operations of the plough have been already highly extensive and productive. M. Dubourg (the bishop of St Louis) has already formed an establishment of nuns, well calculated to promote the education of the daughters of the persons residing there; and also another of Jesuits, by whose means he proposes to spread the Catholic religion among the Indians dispersed over the border countries. May they answer the evangelical and philanthropic views of this prelate, if he sincerely entertain such!

But the ultra-jesuitism which he has hitherto promulgated, and is still incessantly promulgating, authorises the belief that he is merely the zealous tool of the junta of Montrouge. Several well-informed persons have assured me that the principle of these gentry is in perfect accordance with the vulgar maxim "to stick by one another."

From St Charles I returned to St Louis across an immense prairie, which conducts, at E.N.E. to the Sioux portage. Small hills or mountains are scattered over the prairie in great profusion, and, on account of their form, are called *Nipples.*

From the tops of these hills the eye is presented with a view of the most delightful and impressive character—the encounter between two rival streams, which, after mingling their waters, are seen for a long distance flowing on with majesty and beauty. Setting out in their course at a considerable distance from each other, although nearly in the same latitude, they traverse an immense extent of territory incessantly drawing nearer to each other, down to the moment when the more impetuous Missouri rushes on the Mississippi, and darkens its stream by mixing with it waters less clear but more salubrious. From the summits of these hills we look down upon a country the most variegated and enchanting, at the sight of which even the most material and sensual of human beings can scarcely help becoming spiritualised and meditative. Herds of cattle and flocks of sheep, intermingled frequently with the does and roebucks, with pelicans, cranes, swans, and golden plovers, which feed without collision or jealousy over the vast expanse with which they are surrounded, form delightful varieties in this magnificent display of nature. These hills, moreover, seemed to constitute one grand Indian cenotaph, which naturally furnishes a strong presumption in support of the opinion, that these people were formerly extremely numerous.

The highest pyramid of Egypt would, I conceive, be compelled to lower the standard of its pretensions before the *Nipples* of the prairie of St Charles ; for unquestionably it does not command the prospect of two such superb rivers, such verdant plains, such fragrant groves, or so many interesting tribes of animal life as serve to diversify this astonishing spectacle.

From this spot, my dear Countess, I again beheld the chain of perpendicular rocks resembling the substructions of the palaces of Pompey and Domitian, which I mentioned to you in my Fourteenth Letter. The illusion is complete. And as I viewed these rocks rising above the thatch-roofed village of the Sioux Portage, I fancied that I beheld the palace of Armida looking down from its haughty eminence on the humble cabin of Baucis and Philemon.

The Sioux Portage is so called, because formerly the Sioux extended their territorial pretensions to this point, and made a portage here for the sake of a short pass from the Mississippi to the Missouri, over the tongue of land extending between these rivers to the point of their confluence. It exhibits a collection of about thirty huts, inhabited by a people who have descended from Indians, and who may be considered as demi-Indians.

These poor creatures, on hearing that I was an Italian, pressed around me—men, women, and children—with a warmth of feeling absolutely filial, enquiring for intelligence of their common father. "Do you know him? (they asked.) Oh, what a deal of good he has done us! what love he has shewn for us! what sufferings he has gone through for us! We shall never have another father like him! We have perhaps lost him for ever!" Affected by such a scene of tenderness, I enquired who it was that they so much regretted. They then named M. Acquaroni, an Italian priest. This ecclesiastic, during a residence of three or four years among this worthy people, had become their idol, by the piety and charity which had distinguished his ministry. To give all he had to feed the poor; to collect for them; to cultivate the ground with his own hands, in order to obtain a subsistence for them as well as himself; to rest from bodily labour merely for the purpose of engaging in spiritual; such was the life of this excellent missionary. I have had the pleasure here of being introduced to him, and I embraced him with sentiments of attachment which true virtue only can inspire. He is vicar of this cathedral, coadjutor of the abbé Moni, who is himself eminent for his meekness and christian virtues. When I meet with a good priest, or a good king, it is a day of happiness and triumph to me, as I deem nothing on earth more truly venerable. That I have so seldom opportunities of exercising this veneration must be ascribed to kings and priests themselves. To find those who are truly worthy of it, is nearly as difficult as the search after the philosopher's stone.

I departed from St Louis on the 9th of last month, with arms and baggage; by the latter of which I particularly mean my Indian curiosities, and my faithful companion the celebrated canoe of Bloody river, for which I also engaged a passage in the Dolphin steam-boat.

Human infirmity will ever be discovering and exposing itself. I must acknowledge it to you, that I am as yet inconsolable for the loss of my highly valued canoe, and I am convinced I shall still be so for a long time to come. The captain was a man of an austere and unkind nature, and, indeed, wholly destitute of politeness. Without the slightest attention to my remonstrances, he seemed resolved to place it without care or caution in contact with the outside of the steam-boat; which, happening to get a-ground about seven or eight miles from St Louis, the violence of the shock broke my poor canoe to shivers. How can I possibly help lamenting my much-loved little skiff, which had conveyed me in safety amidst a thousand rocks and over a space of more than two thousand miles! We had sustained together such a number of vicissitudes—we had by turns carried each other—we might be supposed to cherish mutual hopes of recalling in old age the embarrassing and difficult regions we had traversed, the labours we had endured, and the dangers we had defied. Alas! a single instant destroys our illusions, and has reduced to annihilation the object of my sincere attachment! My mind, long ruminating on mournful ideas, accustomed to reflect even on the slightest incidents of life, beholds in everything around me the destiny that overwhelms me, and the melancholy impress of human fragility—the situation of one who has the misfortune to survive that which he held most dear. I owed a tribute of gratitude to my departed vessel, and have written the following epitaph on it.

Quod petis infandum, Dilecta Liburnica, fatum!
Vesuvioque procul Stabia * dira tibi est.
Vidisti jam tanta ubicumque pericula victrix;
Teque triumphantem cœdit iniqua manus.
Indomitas sprevisti mecum, sævasque catervas;
Sed solus repetam, te pereunte, Lares.
Nunc eris in superis index Mortalibus alter.
Exultant fletu sidera cuncta meo.

You may recollect, my dear Countess, that wooden house which I have already mentioned as apparently rising out of the water at the confluence of the Ohio and the Mississippi. On repassing the spot at this time I could not perceive it; though my eyes searched for it with the utmost eagerness I could see nothing. I imagined that it had been swallowed up: it was however at length pointed out to me at a great distance from the bank, to the E.N.E., of the confluence. This phenomenon, which would be highly curious on our petty rivers, is far from being so here, where it is renewed every year. The periodical rising (which is sometimes truly extraordinary) of these two large rivers, had placed it in the middle of the waters, and these on withdrawing within their regular channel, had left it as it now stood, on dry land.

* It was in his *liburnica,* or little boat, and near ancient Stabia, in the gulf or crater of Naples, that Pliny was destroyed by the ashes of Vesuvius, in the eruption of 79, in the reign of Titus.

The steam-boat having stopped for a supply of wood, I had the curiosity to take a nearer view of it, and found it to be really the same I had first noticed. It was erected on piles fifteen feet in height, which, when I saw it first, were entirely concealed by the water. To enable you to estimate the astonishing increase of these two rivers in spring, it is as well for me to mention that the house in question is at present as it were upon a hill more than fifty feet above the level of the waters. The Naiads had deserted the place, to avoid the insalubrity of its air in summer.

The river below the mouth of the Ohio is very wide, and comprises within its bed large islands: that known by the name of Wolf island is the largest that it meets with or has formed in its course, being five miles long and two wide. It is at this part also that the river is widest, it being estimated to be here six miles broad. This place is about eighteen miles from the Ohio. The Mississippi, from the Ohio to its several mouths, with scarcely an exception, passes through a country remarkably flat.

New Madrid, forty-four miles from Wolf island, is in fact neither new nor old. It is now nothing. An earthquake in 1812, and another in 1819, destroyed or swallowed up the houses which composed it, and which indeed were but few and mean. Its situation however is well adapted to become an *entrepôt* of commerce between civilized nations and the Indian tribes in the rear of it, and this might have rendered it a place of considerable consequence. The land on which it stood, and that around it, has sunk considerably, and is now unfit for any purpose whatever. The Mississippi, like all great rivers, has its periodical overflows, generally in May or June, when its inundation spreads often to the extent of a hundred miles. It then constitutes what may be almost called a sea.

Forty-three miles lower, the river has opened a new passage for itself across a peninsula, which is now become an island. This extraordinary event happened no longer ago than two years, and is as yet unknown to geographers. This new pass saves more than twelve miles of circuitous navigation. Some have supposed that this channel has been effected by the force or momentum of the enormous volume of water, but the depth of it and its unequal form induced me to consider it as the result of an earthquake. This passage is about three quarters of a mile in length, and is called the *New Cut*.

About forty miles lower we find a considerable hill, called *Chikasaw Bluff*, and three others in succession, under the same denomination, in the space of between fifty and sixty miles: they are all on the eastern bank, in the state of

Tennessee, which on the river is contiguous to that of Kentucky on the north, and on the south to that of Mississippi. They belonged, as well as all the surrounding territories, to the Indians of that name. But the Americans are always afraid that they shall be in want of land; though, as I have already mentioned, they do not cultivate a nineteenth part in twenty of what they already possess. They have likewise driven them away on the west of the Mississippi, at the Arkansaws, White river, &c. There is indeed reason to apprehend that the Americans, in consequence of thus hunting and driving the savages before them, may at length become savages themselves. I have met with some of that people in the forests and deserts, who were to be distinguished from Indians only by their language and the characteristic cleanliness of their persons and dress. These three Bluffs are as it were insulated points, which admirably interrupt and diversify the tiresome extent of flat territory.

Between the mouth of Wolf river and the last of these Bluffs, there is pointed out to you a place called the city of Memphis. But there is nothing of the ancient, nor the progress of the modern. The place is an inconsiderable village, which the annual inundations threaten to destroy. It has however encreased twice its former size since it has belonged to the United States.

You will naturally ask, as I did myself, why do they not erect the village on the Bluff? When the inundation ceases, the exhalation of miasma is absolutely mortal on the Bluff, whilst farther down it is only slightly injurious.

About fifty-six miles lower we reach the mouth of the river St Francis, on the west. I am told that it is navigable for more than three hundred miles, that it ascends nearly in a parallel line with the Mississippi on the N.N.W., and that its sources are near those of the Merrimac, which discharges it, as we have already noticed, near St Louis. An iron mine has just been discovered between the sources of these two rivers, the ore of which is abundant and so excellent that it is malleable after the first fusion: it must certainly in this case be invaluable. Near the mouth of the St Francis, also, there is a bluff, the only one existing (and a remarkable circumstance it is) on the right bank of the Mississippi, from Cape Girardeau to its mouths, a course of about thirteen hundred miles.

You will recollect, that we have already met with a river St Francis, above the Falls of St Peter. I imagine that M. la Salle, who was descending the Mississippi as Father Hannepin was ascending it, discovered this very river on the same day that the latter discovered that higher up, and that this circumstance led to the application of the same name to both. The mouth of this river, and the lower part of its course, are in the territory of the Arkansaws, which is bounded on the north by the Missouri state, on the south by that of Louisiana, on the west by the mountains of New Mexico, and on the east by the Mississippi.

Eighty miles, or somewhat more, below the St Francis, White river enters the Mississippi, on the same side. This river is an apple of discord among the American geographers. Some of them generously bestow on it a navigable course of twelve hundred miles, while others limit the whole extent of its flow within three hundred. Some maps fix its principal sources in the direction of N.N.W. near its tributary, Black river, and others in that of W.S.W.: in short, it is mentioned by some with a tone of perfect knowledge and confidence, though they know if possible still less of it than myself, who acknowledge my perfect ignorance on the subject. I have, however, seen the mouth of it. One thing that may be depended upon as certain is, that about twenty-five or thirty miles above its confluence with the Mississippi, it communicates with the Arkansaws by means of a *Bayou*, a term applied to express all the channels which nature has formed, of communication or discharge, in the Lower Mississippi.

Twenty miles from White river, the Arkansaws pours its tributary stream into the great river.

This river (the Arkansaws,) next to the Missouri, the Ohio, and the Red river, (which we shall meet with lower down,) seems to be the largest that flows into the Mississippi. Opinions are much divided respecting its sources and the length of its course. Hence, you will easily conclude that nothing on these subjects is positively known, yet all these regions have been traversed by grand expeditions. The amiable Major Long also made one, but his expedition, as I have been led to understand, was equally fruitless with the others, though he has contrived to spin out two volumes upon the subject. But whether the river descends from the Black Mountains, or Rocky Mountains, or Cypowais Mountains; whether it is navigable for a space of *one thousand nine hundred and eighty*, or *two thousand miles*, or its whole course is limited within *fifteen hundred*, it still is incontestable that its sources are in the direction of New Mexico, and that it is a very large river. It must be admitted, that this is rather a loose and vague account of its geography; but, having seen merely the mouth of it, I can tell you nothing more on the subject, unless indeed, like others, I were to substitute invention for facts, and betray your confidence.

Twenty or thirty miles lower we stopped in the evening at a small cabin which was inhabited by a happy family, consisting of a father and mother and two children. They cultivate a little maize, and have a stock of cattle; and the father calculates that, *before his children become of age, and can properly quit their paternal mansion, they will have earned him at least fifteen hundred piastres each,* by cutting wood for the steam-boats, transporting it to New Orleans in flats, (a species of covered rafts,) and by other speculations which that grand mart has laid open to the various and vast regions of the interior. He added, that then, as far as he could judge, he should have no farther need of their services, and they might leave him and go in peace, to form, like the beavers, a colony of their own. These people are *Yankees.*

The next day we stopped at another small hut, consisting also of Yankees. An American gentleman, who had formerly been acquainted with them at another place two or three thousand miles distant, enquired what adventure had induced them to abandon their first establishment. The head of the family replied, that it was to get out of the way of neighbours; and that he was going also to leave his present situation, as a family had just come and settled in his *neighbourhood,* about sixty miles off. The gentleman asked him where his wife was; she was gone, he said, to see a neighbour, one of her relations, about *eighty miles* from home. You see therefore, that the space which in Italy can supply us with half a dozen sovereigns, is too confined in the New World even for a single family of Americans. It seems as if the spirit of association had, in that quarter, scarcely any natural operation, or that the collisions of interest impel to separation. Colonel Boon, who was one of the first that penetrated into the vast deserts of Kentucky, to attack and hunt down the Indians and wild beasts by which it was infested, had so complete an antipathy to *neighbourhoods*, that for forty years he continued retreating farther and farther still into the interior in order to avoid them; having proceeded from the eastern boundaries of Kentucky, by a series of removes and stations, till at last he reached the river Osages, a distance of thirteen hundred miles. A family with which I am acquainted, having settled a hundred miles in his rear, was just rousing him to one remove more, when death rendered him finally stationary. It is supposed, that had his life been spared but a short time longer, his eagerness to fly from approaching *neighbours* would have hurried him to the Pacific Ocean, whence probably some new neighbourhood would soon have driven him to the region of New Holland.

The Yazoo river flows from the east and separates the Tennessee and the Mississippi states. It traverses a large part of Western Georgia and the whole space of territory between the limits of that state and the Mississippi river. All the countries through which it passes were also a short time since the property of Indians. It is about one hundred and seventy miles from the river Arkansaws.

Twelve miles farther down is a beautiful hill, called Walnut hill, which pleasantly interrupts the monotony of these eternal marshes.

We next, arrive at Natchez, the first place after St Louis which presents traces of an advanced civilization. We must halt here for a moment, and this it is the more necessary to do so as, before we go any farther, it will be proper to take a general survey of what these countries have been, in order duly to appreciate what they at present are. I can however only shew you what they have been in reality and what they are. If you desire to see them in a microcosm and with a microscope, read the *Natchez* and *Attala*.

The town of Natchez is built upon a hill which commands the eastern bank of the Mississippi. It is about eight hundred and fifty miles from St Louis; six hundred and seventy-one from the mouth of the Ohio; two hundred and eighty-five from that of the Arkansaws, and one hundred from that of Yazoo, on the north. On the south it is about three hundred miles from New Orleans; one hundred and seventy-five from *Baton Rouge*, and seventy-three from the mouth of the Red river.

I mentioned in a former letter, that the French were the first discoverers of the territory called Upper Louisiana. We are now in Lower Louisiana, the discovery of which was also made by the French.

M. la Salle, a man of firmness and enterprise, was not discouraged by the ill success of his discoveries on the Illinois. His constancy was not only unabated, but even increased by his failure, and he proceeded with new attempts. After fixing an establishment at Kaskaskia, which he also confided to his faithful Achates the Chevalier Tonti, he, in 1678, went down the Mississippi as far as Natchez. He returned to Canada without exciting any suspicion of his secret, and thence sailed to France, where, after communicating to the court his recent discoveries and his plans, he obtained a squadron, men, and all the necessary means, for a transatlantic expedition, and the formation of new colonies.

He arrived in the gulf of Mexico about the year 1684, and passed in front of the mouths of the Mississippi, which he was actually in quest of; but, whether through obstinacy or presumption, he refused to attend to the opinion of those who pointed them out to him. When off St Bernard's bay, he became convinced of his mistake. He was then desirous of going back, and getting into the proper course; but the commander of the squadron turned a deaf ear to all his representations, and carried his cruelty so far as to land him on that inhospitable shore, where this intrepid man, worthy of a better fate, was murdered by the adventurers who had followed him. Such is the history of the first expedition.

The mania for discoveries prevailed at that time among the French as well as among various other nations of Europe. Monarchs, instead of attending to the happiness of their subjects, in hopes of finding new means of gratifying their love of pomp and profligacy, ruined the Old World in order to ransack the regions of the New. M. d'Iberville went out next to La Salle, and landed, in 1699, in the bay of Mobile, where he raised an ill-constructed fort, which he called Fort Dauphin, or *Massacre* island, so named from the number of human skeletons which he found there.

He again reached the Mississippi, by an overland passage, with a detachment of his men, and ascended the river as far as the place now called Natchez, which perhaps had been pointed out by M. la Salle; and here he erected a fort, which he called Fort Rosalie. Natchez was the name of the Indians who inhabited these territories, and who received the French with hospitality.

The same M. d'Iberville established another small colony at the mouth of the Perdido, which he named Biloxi; but the unhealthiness of these places, and the distance of the establishments from each other, prevented their flourishing; and in the following year he returned to France.

He was succeeded by M. Crosat, as farmer-general of the whole colony for ten years; but, before the expiration of that time, he resigned, and succeeded in extricating himself from a privilege that had already swallowed up his private fortune, though a very considerable one.

The new settlers were totally averse to agriculture, without which no colony can prosper. The petty commerce with the Indians could only supply them with a few furs, but furnished no bread; and while they were hunting after mines of gold and silver, which they never found, they lost the few resources they had possessed, and incurred diseases by which they were destroyed. Such are the causes of the little success with which all their enterprizes were attended.

In the year 1718, the famous Company of Law, or the Indies, took possession of Lower Louisiana. But, though M. Bienville was a able and enlightened governor, the vexatious and harassing conduct of the company to the industrious colonists, who had at length devoted their exertions to agriculture, the taxes with which they were loaded, and the monopolies which cut down the profits of their industry, the influx into the colony from the mother country of all the dregs of its population, and lastly, the hostilities of the Indians, whom the injustice and rapacity of officers appointed without judgment or feeling had unappeasably exasperated; all these circumstances combined to render still more wretched the establishments of Lower Louisiana, and compelled the government, in 1731, to recall the privileges it had granted to a company which was ruining both France and its colonies, and was also one of the remote causes of the revolution which that delightful country has recently experienced.

The colony was not more prosperous from 1731 to 1763, at which epoch France ceded Lower Louisiana to Spain, with all the territory she possessed to the west of the Mississippi, giving up at the same time to England all that she held on the east of it, Canada included. Spain used it only to enrich a few favourites and governors; and Natchez and New Orleans, with all the dependent territory, began to flourish only when, in 1803, the United States obtained them from Napoleon.

The Americans do not perhaps individually possess more merit than the French or Spaniards, nor should I wish to indulge in those odious comparisons which are too often made both between nations and individuals; but I will assert and repeat, with the utmost publicity and confidence, that a liberal government is alike advantageous to the people and to the monarch, and that a despotic government is essentially and universally a bad one. In the first, the sovereign is assisted by the best of his subjects, who, having a common interest with himself, and, having no apprehensions from addressing him in the language of truth, impart their advice to him with judgment and freedom. Whereas, in the other case, his will has no check, and he becomes always a mark and victim of the intrigues of favourites stimulated by their insatiable rapacity, and of ministers who end by making him their slave.

I would by no means however assert that the government of the United States is without faults. Human nature does not admit of perfection. But I do not hesitate to say, that I do not think there is another government in the world that has so few, not even the republic of St Marino itself, which consists simply of the little town from which it derives its name, and the whole territory of which may be surveyed from its church-clock.

I have mentioned, my dear Countess, the wars to which these Indians were provoked by the conduct of a few Frenchmen: it may not perhaps be injudicious or unentertaining for a few moments to direct your attention to them.

The Natchez being those who had felt with most severity the vexations and oppressions inflicted on them by the commander of Fort Rosalie, and some other officers as unprincipled and unfeeling as himself, resolved to execute upon them summary vengeance. Too weak to act openly, they conspired with all the other Indian nations to effect a general massacre of their oppressors. As they had no almanack by which to fix upon the important day, they decided that each tribe should set up in its encampment fifteen stakes on the very day on which their solemn determination was agreed to, and that one of these should be removed every day, the last that remained being to be considered as the signal for massacre. In consequence of this arrangement, on the appointed day, and almost at the same hour, a considerable number of Frenchmen were massacred at Fort Rosalie, on the Yazoo, and in other places. But, those who survived avenged the destruction of their countrymen by the almost total destruction of the Natchez tribe; and the town of Natchez has been erected, and now flourishes, on the very spot where these Indians once had their principal encampment, and where the French afterwards built Fort Rosalie; and the woods, where that unfortunate tribe hunted the doe and the roebuck, are now plains and hills abounding in the growth of cotton.

The town is a really beautiful one, and its environs contain a great number of handsome country-seats, where the planters for many years made and enjoyed ample fortunes, though, by the depreciation of cotton, they are now in a state of rapid impoverishment.

In the present year the yellow fever has committed dreadful ravages. Nearly four hundred persons have died, and the emaciated and pallid faces that met my eye in every street, plainly indicated that numbers of the living had narrowly escaped. Among the dead were four physicians.

Large three-masted vessels come up to this place, although at more than four hundred miles distance from the sea, and would ascend still higher were they certain of obtaining cargoes. It is in the state of Mississippi; and its population, previously to the late ravages of the fever, amounted to about five thousand.

The farther we proceed downward, the houses on the river's banks become more numerous: cotton and maize are the principal articles of cultivation there.

The mouth of Red river, as I have already mentioned, is seventy-three miles below Natchez. It presents a noble view on the west. This river flows through a country exceedingly rich in cotton, the fineness and length of whose fibre render it nearly equal to that of Georgia.

The first establishment formed there by the French, was under the government of M. d'Iberville, in the Natchitoches. This colony was the most flourishing of the whole, on account of its superior government. It was under the direction of M. St Denis; an officer possessing at once courage and wisdom, who by his prudent management completely conciliated the affections of the Indians, and was thereby enabled to extend its commerce into New Mexico, notwithstanding the vigilant jealousy of the Spaniards. But all the establishments of Red river, since the country has come into the possession of the Americans, have made astonishing advances. The town of Owachitta has already a population of almost three thousand; Natchitoches of more than eight thousand; Alexandria, or the Rapids, of about seven thousand. These towns are all comprised within the state of Louisiana, the capital of which, as I before stated, is New Orleans. Steam-boats pass up to all these establishments without the slightest obstacle.

This river is a very considerable one, and its course of great extent, but its sources are entirely unknown. The persons composing a certain *expedition*, however, thought they had discovered them. When descending some river, they rather prematurely settled the latitudes and longitudes of Red river, the general direction of its course, and its various windings; they described the beauties of its banks, and even saw some *red sand* at the bottom of its bed. At its mouth, the gentlemen of the expedition conceived themselves to be of course on the Mississippi, whilst they were in fact in the Arkansaws; and the river which they had just descended was the Canadian, which flows from the south-west to the north-east, whereas Red river runs from north-west to south east. I was informed of this blunder by an officer who was with Major Long in the same expedition, and who accompanied us in the steam-boat: he gave the account very circumstantially and confidently, and his statement was confirmed by the captain of the steam-boat and several passengers, who appeared well acquainted with all the particulars.

Red river is the last tributary stream to the Mississippi, as Heron river, near the Julian sources, (agreeably to what I mentioned in a former letter,) is the first.

Below Red river, the Mississippi may be said to become tributary itself, for all the issues found along its banks, and which are called *Bayoux*, are, properly speaking, only vents or passes, which it has formed for itself, to carry off its waters, in periods of overflow, into the sea. Thus, on the right, across the low lands which were formerly inhabited by tribes of Indians, and which still retain the names of Opeloussas, Attakapas, Alchafalaya, it discharges itself into a succession of lakes communicating with the sea on the side of St Bernard's bay, and some of the mouths of the Sabine. On the left it flows through lakes Pontchartrain, Maurepas, and Borgne, towards Beloxi and Mobile.

The river Sabine separates Louisiana from Texas, on the west, the territory disputed between Mexico and the United States, and where the colony, or expedition, under the direction of General Lallemand met with such misfortunes. This province ought to belong to the United States, for the Rio del Norte, which bounds it on the west, seems to have been appointed by nature as the limit on that side to New Mexico. We now return to the *Bayoux*.

The Louisianians in these *Bayoux* ought particularly to admire the order of Providence; for, without the expedient it has thus brought into operation, the two banks of the river, from Red river even below New Orleans, would be constantly inundated, or, more accurately speaking, would no longer exist, and New Orleans itself would be annihilated. All the immense regions which extend from Natchez, as high up as New Madrid, are flooded almost every year by the Mississippi, which sometimes rises fifty feet above its usual level, while at New Orleans it rarely rises beyond thirteen, and that city is never inundated. Such is the effect of these tutelary *Bayoux*.

The articles cultivated in these plantations are sugar, cotton, maize, and rice. Indigo completely degenerated there, and is no longer grown: the land is too moist and too hot for corn.

After making these general observations, we shall now return to our regular course.

Baton Rouge is a pleasant little town, situated on a small eminence, which is the last to be found on the Mississippi. It commands the river, and affords an extensive and admirable view of both sides of it.

The government of the United States is erecting in this place extensive barracks; for the purpose perhaps of making it a depôt for troops destined to repel any attacks that may be made on a place so important as New Orleans.

Fourteen miles lower down, the *Manchac Bayou* presents a fine situation for opening, by means of a canal of no great length, a convenient and very useful navigation from the Missouri to lake Pontchartrain, and thus communicating with the Mobile, Pensacola, &c.

I pointed out to you the first island of the Mississippi, in the midst of the *Little Falls* above Sandy lake; I must now notice its last. It is thirty miles below the *Bayou Manchac*, and might with great propriety have been called by the distinguished name of d'Iberville, who was the first European that ascended this part of the Mississippi. Eleven miles from this island is Donaldson, a small town situated on the *Bayou la Fourche*, which leads to the Attakapas, Opeloussas, and various other regions. It is seventy-five miles from New Orleans. The space between these two places may be considered as one continued town, consisting of the habitations of planters. While passing over the distance, I was reminded of the Persian prince, who, when accompanying the emperor Constantius towards Rome, thought he was entering that city while yet fifty miles without its walls, at the Augustan bridge near Fescennia. I saw in it likewise some resemblance to those delicious tracts on the banks of the Brenta, between Padua and Venice, which the wealth and good taste of the Venetians have formed into an earthly paradise.

When Law's Company of the Indies took possession of Louisiana, the seat of government was still at Fort Dauphine; but, a dreadful tempest having blocked up Mobile bay with sand, it was transferred by governor Bienville to the place where New Orleans now stands; a name bestowed upon it to remind posterity of the regency and the *wisdom* of Philip of Orleans. I consider the date of this city, therefore, to be 1718 or 19. The establishment of Biloxi, also, was afterwards transferred to it; that place being both barren and unhealthy; but this accession had no effect in promoting the prosperity of the new city. It continued to languish while under the Spanish domination; and it is only owing to its being placed under the government of a nation whose rulers, instead of being the people's tyrants, are merely the depositaries of their will—it is only owing to its freedom from all vexatious restrictions on its industry, commerce, and prosperity, from capricious abuses of power, profligate monopolies, and selfish corporations,—that this city has risen to the astonishing prosperity which distinguishes it at the present moment.

It is built on the left bank of the river, in the form of a crescent, in an island about one hundred and fifty miles in circumference, formed by the Mississippi, *Bayou Manchac,* and lakes Maurepas and Pontchartrain.

The new buildings, which are nearly all of brick, present a striking contrast to the old ones, which were built of wood. It is inhabited in a great measure by foreigners, and Creoles of French extraction, as well as Americans who are attracted thither by its facilities for commerce, and of course for acquiring wealth. It is more brilliant than any other American city that I have seen. It contains about forty-five thousand inhabitants; a prodigious population for a place which may be said to have just emerged from a swamp, and where the yellow fever and the natural insalubrity of the climate every year effect deplorable ravages.

A stranger who entered it by night would imagine himself arrived at some grand capital; for the streets are well lighted with reflecting lamps, and the busy agitation and rapid movement of carriages, in connection with that circumstance, easily lead to such a conclusion.

It is astonishing that a place which may be said to be only just stepping out of its infancy, should already exhibit, in the department of amusements, a number of those attractions which are displayed in the capitals of Europe. Horse-races, dramatic representations, concerts, balls, and gaming *academies* of every description, are here to be met with. Within its comparatively small compass there are not fewer than six public gaming houses,—more in fact than exist in Paris. I acknowledge that I did not expect to find this passion in such intense operation among a commercial, active, and republican people; I supposed it confined to courts, dissipation, and idleness. The Lacedemonians looked upon gaming with such horror, that Chilon, when sent to conclude a treaty of alliance with the Corinthians, was so indignant at finding them absorbed by this practice, that he almost immediately left them, with the rebuke, "that it would tarnish the glory of Lacedemon to ally itself with a nation of gamblers." So much has been written on the fatal consequences of this habit, that nothing new is to be advanced on the subject; and we can only repeat what the greatest men have said before us both in ancient and modern times. Tacitus remarks, that such is the dominion of this passion over a man completely addicted to it, that the Germans often finished by staking themselves, that is, by gambling away their freedom and their persons.

It is difficult to explain this attachment to so dangerous a diversion in a place abounding with so many other means of dissipation.

Besides the attractions of private societies, public amusements are extremely frequent.

Two theatres furnish high gratification both to the eye and ear, and the actors who perform there would not be despised even in Europe: I must add that, during my repeated attendances, I have observed nothing of those dirty buffooneries and obscene equivoques which, among nations pretending to greater refinement, frequently put decency and modesty to the blush.

The American theatre, though smaller, is more regular in its form than the French; and both are very convenient, and most judiciously adapted, though the architects never perhaps studied Vitruvius or Bramante.

The French theatre has accessory rooms and offices, such as are probably not to be met with in any provincial theatre in Europe; particularly a large room, where subscription, dress, and masked balls are given, which would rival those exhibited in our capitals; where the beautiful Creoles fascinate and dazzle under the forms of the Graces, and where luxury and decorum are in happy combination. Louisiana is indebted for this elegant establishment to Mr Davis, who has sacrificed to it a great part of his fortune. There is also a Spanish theatre—which is, indeed, in every sense Spanish.

The French theatre, to the precision and fascination of the machinery introduced upon the stage, adds decorations of the most superb description and almost marvellous effect. M. Fogliardi, who is the painter, has obtained a well-merited reputation, and is thoroughly acquainted with the true theory of perspective. This excellent artist would need nothing but to have been the pupil of a Gonzaga or a Cagliari, to acquire celebrity even in Europe. He distributes objects with such discrimination, brings them out with such distinctness and breadth displays such admirable adaptation of light and shade, that the scene, small as it is in itself, by a sort of magic power becomes extended and spacious, and the eye and imagination of the spectator see almost with the conviction of reality the very spot where the action of the piece is supposed to pass.

Though a great admirer of the ancients, I avail myself of every opportunity, consistently with my reverence for our all-staunch antiquaries, of expressing my just admiration of the moderns. Though the ancients were our masters in almost all the arts, they could not possibly contest with the moderns the glory of having carried to perfection the science of perspective.

Albert Durer and Pietro del Borgo may be considered as its inventors. Titian, Dominichino, and Balthazar Peruzzi, were eminent masters, who left successors still more eminent than themselves, particularly in the French and Flemish schools; and at present, Granet, Bassi, Werstapen, and various others, do honour to the age by their skill in this delightful and almost miraculous art, which on the stage has been carried nearly to perfection. We must, however, while circumscribing the merits of the ancient painters, beware of adopting the opinion of Perault, in denying them any knowledge of perspective whatever. The discovery of the ruins of Pompeii and Herculaneum must, I imagine, have contributed to render his presumptuous assertions on this subject still more ridiculous than they were before.

To superior talents for what may be called *scenography*, M. Fogliardi unites those of design; of that art, the benefits and wonders of which cannot be too highly eulogized, and which ought to be pursued by our youth with almost idolatrous attachment.

Man is only the interpreter of nature; but the mere hand of nature, powerful, indefatigable, and plastic as it is, is sufficient only for a few effects. A servile imitation of the external appearances of nature never produces grand results. It is only by the aid of that genius with which she inspires her favoured votaries, that genius which is her most precious gift, and by those rules which she has permitted it to invent for its guidance, that she may be said to re-produce herself under the aspect of a nature still more beautiful and sublime; and the exercise of this genius and of these rules is the offspring of the great art of design. Nature creates forms, design perfects them, and, like a Prometheus, animates them with a spirit which makes them appear to the most ignorant and stupid observer possessed of all the vigour and truth of reality. Without the aid of the genius of design, nature could not have produced the supreme and almost divine beauty of the virgins of Raphael and Sasseferrato, and of the angels of Corregio and Guido Reni; the voluptuous attractions in the works of Albano, or the speaking expression of the figures of Giotto and Cimabue.

It is design which introduces us to the mysteries *delle tre Arti Sorelle*, of the three sisters so important and indispensable to the wants of luxury which man has created for himself—architecture, sculpture, and painting; and it is by these three arts that civilized man may be considered as distinguished from the savage. They are the most enduring depositaries both of his virtues and infirmities. History herself derives from this source her most correct and her most impressive lessons. I have seen her myself in Latium, in Magna Grecia, and elsewhere, resorting to the venerable monuments of antiquity to find out what had previously escaped all her researches, or to correct errors which she had been led into by the conjectures of the learned. In short, to the art of design, the three kingdoms of nature owe their highest advances.

M. Fogliardi, who was the first to open an academy in this place for the promotion of these objects, deserves both eulogium and encouragement, and I doubt not that he will obtain them. For, how insignificant and worthless among an enlightened people must that man appear, who makes no effort and feels no wish to co-operate in the means which revive the image of a beloved friend, or transmit to posterity the memory of transcendant minds and beneficent citizens? The government, to whom the nation confides the charge of superintending the progress of its civilization, and who are able justly to appreciate the virtuous efforts which produced this institution, will unquestionably give it their highest support.

I have visited, with great pleasure, the establishment of this distinguished artist and most excellent man; but I have seen, what is to be seen also in many of our own countrymen—I have observed the young people who attend him too eager to free themselves from the restraint of rules founded on experience, and from long received theories. A house is never begun to be built at the roof; but always at the foundation. It is impossible ever to paint or sculpture an entire human figure without previously becoming acquainted with the particular parts. It is impossible to represent a landscape in due perspective without knowing the forms which ought to be given to trees, and the place appropriate to them in the picture: without being acquainted with the peculiar motion, shape, and character of animals, intended to constitute figures in it; and without attending to the principles which regulate distribution and grouping. No painter or sculptor will ever be able to adjust the drapery to a figure before he has studied it in its naked state; as an architect will never be able to complete a Corinthian column without being well acquainted with the rules of the Doric and Ionic; for, otherwise, the results would be absolute monsters, like the edifices proceeding from the extravagant pencil of our countryman Borromini; who, in consequence of endeavouring to innovate on architecture, became its Attila, completely barbarising it.

But, for the present, let us leave New Orleans, and follow the course of the river to its mouths.

Between five and six miles lower down, I must stop to show you the scene on which the Americans triumphed over the English in the celebrated battle, called the Battle of New Orleans. It is on the left bank of the Mississippi, and between the plantations of Rodriguez and Welcome.

The Americans have, no doubt, talked about it a great deal, but it certainly appears that they were well justified in doing so; for, though they were nearly all militia, not more than four or five thousand strong, and collected in haste, yet, for fifteen days successively, they repulsed, and on the sixteenth completely beat and drove back, a force of about twelve thousand, commanded by one of Wellington's celebrated generals, General Pakenham, who seemed to despise the enemy he came to fight, but who paid for his audacity with his life.

This battle procured a well-merited fame for General Jackson. He displayed in the critical conjuncture in which he was placed, courage, skill, and firmness, which enabled him to overcome, in the first place, obstacles which appeared to be wantonly thrown in his way to thwart and irritate him, and afterwards the enemy in the field. He rescued Louisiana from the English yoke.

The gratitude of his fellow-citizens was manifested to the triumphant commander in a thousand different ways. He was carried in triumph through the public streets, and crowned in the theatre amidst the applauses of a crowded audience absolutely intoxicated with joy and victory. It is a remarkable circumstance that, at the very time when he was thus hailed by the people as their liberator, one of the judges sentenced him to a fine of a thousand piastres for a breach of the laws; and what adds to his glory is, that he paid it, like a citizen who bent in due submission to the tribunals of his country when its safety was no longer in danger, and no longer, therefore, required the application of martial law, which he had considered it necessary to enforce with vigour, in circumstances so highly critical, that half-measures could have only tended to produce greater anarchy.

The firmness of the zealous magistrate who condemned the victorious general would probably have excited more admiration, if by so doing he had not in fact been avenging an insult committed against his own person and authority. It is a serious fault, which can never long continue under a wise and liberal constitution, to permit a magistrate to be at once party and judge, and more particularly when the object in view is to avenge with the arm of the *impassible* law a personal offence or insult, which stimulates our passions more powerfully even than interest, strong as it is universally admitted to be. It is one of those cases which are included in the judicious maxim of the ancients, "*Judicis incompetentis factum, pro iniquo et nullo habèndum est.*" General Jackson, in the course of events and transactions which preceded the battle, had committed this judge to prison, for having granted a Habeas Corpus to a member of the legislature who had opposed some of his measures, from an idea that they were arbitrary.

The valour of the general was admirably seconded by that of the troops, who consisted principally of the inhabitants of Tennessee and Louisiana.

The ladies of New Orleans on this occasion distinguished themselves by their humanity as much as their brothers and husbands did by their valour. I cannot help thinking that these amiable Creoles contributed not a little to the victory; for the idea of being enabled, like another Medorus, to become the object of the attentions and compassion of some lovely Angelica, might add greatly to the patriotism and bravery of the combatants.

People may say what they please, my dear Countess, but women constitute the grand spring by which men are influenced. You may perceive it in my own case. I write long letters to you, though I never before wrote any but short ones; and the pleasure I find in it arises from the impulse to display before you, to the best of my ability, whatever incidents or views deeply impressed my own senses, affections, or imagination. Were I merely to attempt to write to beings of the hard and rocky nature of that sex in whom I never found anything but malignity—who have already inflicted on me so much misery, and who, as you well know, are still inflicting it, and that purely from the pleasure of giving pain and doing harm—both my mind and pen would recoil with disgust. Let us return, however, to our subject from this digression.

For the period of more than a year before this battle, General Jackson had proceeded on in a steady course of victory. He had completely defeated the *Creeks,* whom the English, assisted by the Spaniards of the Floridas, had excited against the Americans from the beginning of the war. They are a nation of Indians, of great ferocity, and were at that time very numerous, residing in the territory which separates the states of Tennessee, Georgia, and Mississippi, from the Floridas. They are now almost entirely destroyed—the natural fate of those who suffer themselves, like despicable satellites, to be basely worked upon by venality and intrigues. The Spaniards themselves soon began to repent their having promoted the projects of the English, as they thus furnished the Americans with a plausible pretext for taking possession of the Floridas, which they have since obtained by a treaty concluded between the United States and the Cortes.

A little lower than the field of battle commences the Lazaretto, which has nothing in common with the sanitary establishments of Europe but the name. The chief object of this pretended Lazaretto is to prevent the introduction of the yellow fever, which was supposed to have been imported to New Orleans from the island of Cuba. The Spaniards of that island made reprisals, and obliged the vessels that arrived from New Orleans to perform quarantine. I conclude from these circumstances that the yellow fever is indigenous to both countries.

Twelve miles farther, where the Mississippi makes a considerable bend, is the place they called *English Turn;* a name applied to it from the circumstance of the English, on arriving in the beginning of the last century at this spot with a view to ascend and examine the Mississippi, turning back, on finding that they had been anticipated by the French.

At Plaquemine bay, on the left, is Fort St Philip, which serves to protect that pass to the sea. Only small vessels however are capable of navigating it. It is seventy miles from New Orleans.

Eighteen miles farther, on the right, there is another grand passage to the sea, which is called *South-west Pass*, and another, three miles farther, called *South Pass;* six miles beyond is the great pass, also on the right, called *South-east Pass* and *Main Pass;* and, almost immediately beyond, two others, one of which, called *Otter Pass*, is on the north-east; the other, to the north-west, has no name. These are all the different passages which constitute the mouths of the great river Mississippi, the sources of which you have seen close to lake Julia, and the navigation of which we have now completed through its whole course of about three thousand and two hundred miles.

I observed to you, my dear Countess, that the Mississippi was perhaps the first river in the world: now, however, there is no *perhaps* in the case. I declare, and will maintain it to be so, without fear of contradiction. In order to convince you of this, it is necessary that we should now return to its sources. Do not, however, be alarmed.

You will find that our voyage up will be much shorter than that we have just finished downward.

You have seen that the Mississippi, by its various *bayoux* or passes on both sides, communicates with all the lands of Louisiana, with an infinite number of lakes, and with the sea.

By Red river, it communicates with New Mexico.

By the Yazoo, it traverses all those regions which are found on the limits of the Tennessee and Mississippi states; and, as the Yazoo is navigable up to its sources, in Georgia, it may communicate, by means of some portage, with rivers that fall into the Atlantic Ocean. The sources of Tombecbee are also near those of the Yazoo, and consequently an easy communication may be effected with the Alabama and the lands surrounding the bay of the Mobile, into which the Tombecbee discharges itself.

By means of the Arkansaws, it serves as an inlet to the establishments formed in the west territory of that name; and, as it is presumed that the sources of the Arkansaws are almost contiguous to those of the Colorado, it follows that, by means of a portage, the Mississippi could communicate with the gulph of California.

By White river and the St Francis, it penetrates a great way into regions highly fertile and rich in mines.

You have seen, with what immense countries, with what numerous states, it communicates by means of the Ohio, which is the life and soul of the western states, Illinois, Indiana, Ohio, Kentucky, Tennessee, of western Pennsylvania and Virginia. But, should the canals which are projected be completed, other communications would result far more important. The Monongahela would join the Potowmac which flows through Chesapeak bay into the Atlantic. The Alleghany would join lake Erie, and consequently, by the new canal of Buffalo, it would communicate with New York, and by the St Lawrence with the whole of Canada and the Northern Atlantic; with all the lakes, or the Canadian sea formed by the lakes St Clair, Huron, Michigan, Superior, and others. These projects would also tend to join the Muskingum, the Miami, and the Wabash, to lake Erie. We now resume our course.

By means of the river Kaskaskia, it penetrates far into the lands known by the name of the American Bottom, which are considered as the most fertile in America, and through which some pretend that the Mississippi formerly flowed.

The Marimak conveys down to it the lead and iron supplied by its mines.

The Missouri, by its southern and western sources, would establish the communication of the Mississippi with the rivers Lewis and Clark, which run into the Columbia, and of course with the Pacific Ocean.

The Illinois would enable it to communicate, by means of a small canal (which is in contemplation,) with the river Cikago, which discharges itself into lake Michigan.

You have seen the rivers Le Moine, Yawoha, Rocky, Fever, Turkey, &c. bearing large boats on their streams far into the interior.

The Owiskonsing, another tributary to the Mississippi, communicates also with lake Michigan through a portage at the Foxes river.

The river Cypowais, near lake Pepin, communicates by means of a portage with the Menomeni, and consequently with lake Superior.

The St Croix also communicates with it, by a short portage from its sources to the river *Bois-brulé*.

You have already seen the direction of the course of the St Peter.

The rivers Brandy and St Francis, communicate, by means of the *Thousand Lakes* whence they issue, with other rivers which also pour themselves into lake Superior.

The Raven's plume, by means of Leaf river, which flows into it near its sources, communicates with Otter Tail lake, from which issues the river of that name, which the English have named also Red river and which falls into Hudson's bay.

You recollect, that Sandy river, which falls into the Mississippi, communicates likewise by a short portage, and by the rivers Savannah and St Louis, with the end of lake Superior, and that by means of Pines, Willow, and Bloody rivers, the Mississippi communicates with immense regions inhabited by Indians.

At the end of the second lake Winipeg, on the north of it, it communicates by a short portage with Oak river, which falls into Rainy river, by which we may descend both to Hudson's bay, by lake Wood, and to the Atlantic Ocean by Rainy lake, lake Superior, &c.

You have seen that, from Red Cedar lake, these Indian territories may be traversed on the west as far as Bitch lake.

Also, that the Julian sources are almost contiguous to those of Bloody river, and that consequently the Gulf of Mexico communicates at three different points with the Frozen Sea, across the immense space of about four thousand five hundred miles; that is, by means of the Raven's plume, lake Winipeg, and the Julian sources.

You recollect that a canoe can ascend as far as the sources of the river, and a large boat within three miles of them.

That a river, of such immense extent, presents no other obstacles to its navigation than three short portages at the falls of St Antony, the great rapids, and the little falls.

That a steam-boat has gone up as far as Fort St Peter, and that it might pass up the river St Peter as high as about sixty miles.

You have seen that the steam-boats run over, in every sense, the whole valley of the Ohio, and penetrate even into the interior of the states watered by that river; that they traverse the Arkansaws territory, Red river, the *bayoux*, &c.

That large three-masted vessels may ascend this great river more than four hundred miles from its mouths.

We have traversed together on its stream one of the most extensive and beautiful vallies, and perhaps also the most fertile, in the world, and we have noticed innumerable tributary rivers flowing into it as into a common centre prepared for them by nature.

You have seen that, by facilitating commerce, that inexhaustible source of wealth, it imparts occupation and life to a world.

Finally, you have admired with me its beauty, its opulent mines, its almost always smooth and tranquil course, and the wisdom of nature in its *bayoux* or passes.

Judge now whether another such river can be

found on the globe which thus communicates with every sea and at various points, which combines so many wonders with such great utility, which surveys more than one hundred steam-boats gliding over its waters, with an infinite number of other vessels freighted with the productions and manufacture of both worlds, and to which futurity promises such brilliant destinies. Judge whether the Mississippi be not the first river in the world!

The Amazon, and the la Plata, may exceed the Mississippi in the volume of their waters; but in all other respects, far more important, they cannot be compared with it; and what confers on the latter a decided superiority is, that along the whole extent of its banks man can breath the air of liberty, and industry meets with no restriction.

I cannot, and indeed ought not, to quit New Orleans without mentioning to you Father Anthony. He is a venerable Spanish capuchin, who for eight and forty years has devoted his life to imparting the consolations of faith to this population, with simplicity, and without either fanaticism or intolerance. As he could never bring himself to say that it was midnight at midday, or midday at midnight, he has not been made a bishop; but he is not, on that account, less regarded as the patriarch, the father of the

Catholic religion in this city, and the founder of all its churches; and he is, by the inhabitants in general, highly esteemed and beloved. Monseigneur Dubourg is the bishop of New Orleans.

You have seen, my dear Countess, with me the cradle of the Mississippi, and the deep tomb which swallows it up on its closing its long and brilliant course. Madame Deshouillière, in a charming idyl, compares the life of man to the agitated course of a river. This interesting image is justly applicable to ordinary men; but nothing, in my opinion, resembles so nearly the course of this great river as the career of that extraordinary *man* who, originating in obscurity, exhibited a brilliant course of glory, and was at length entombed in the ocean of his own triumphs.

The hand of Providence has brought me to the conclusion of an enterprise which, solitary, and in all possible ways thwarted as I was, I scarcely dared to consider practicable, and the recollection of which brings back to my mind privations and dangers which make me shudder.* I cannot however help surveying this mighty river, the scene of all these sufferings, with satisfaction and pride. Though it appears here in

* I escaped death, I imagine, only because those barbarous people thought they saw in that *temerarious solitary man* some extraordinary supernatural being.

all its majesty, it seems towards me to display a carriage of less hauteur, a demeanour less overwhelming. I have obtained over it a sort of empire. I alone penetrated into the seclusion of his sanctuary, where the deity of the stream had concealed himself from mortal eyes. I saw him in the first struggle of his birth, apprehensive, cautious, and starting from the touch even of a bark canoe; and while announcing and upholding his sovereign dominion, I may be considered to have impaired the honours of his divinity by developing to the world all the secrets of his prodigies, and incidents of his course.

I have discovered the place of his origin in space, but who can disclose to us his origin in point of time? Did the first beams of the sun constitute also the first of his days? Does he belong to incalculable antiquity or to modern ages? Here are questions of "height and depth," the discussion and solution of which I leave to those who are fond of plunging in the ocean of immensity. For my own part, I require repose and breathing-time to prepare myself for new labours and travels. I am going to proceed to Mexico, and perhaps to countries still farther distant.

You perceive, my dear Countess, that I am almost always in motion and in divertion of mind......But there are voids which nothing can fill up; there are impressions which neither time nor travel can wear away!....I am not a little inclined to think with Æsop, that Prometheus moistened with tears the clay from which he formed man; and to exclaim with the sage—

O curas hominum! O quantum est in rebus inane!

No other consolations are now left me than the recollection and veneration of those extraordinary virtues which we cherished with common feelings, and the friendship of those whom I sincerely esteem. May you, my dear Countess, never withdraw from me yours!

THE END.

REFERENCE

TO THE

PLATES OF INDIAN ORNAMENTS, &c.

PLATE I.

1 A Medicine Sack, made of the coat of an animal.
2 A Pouch (Sioux).
3 A Knife-sheath (Cypowais).
4 A Woman's Apron-pouch.

[All these ornaments are embroidered with porcupine quills].

PLATE II.

1 A War Pipe (Sioux).
2 A Scalp of a Sioux,, given to M. Beltrami by the Great Eagle Chief of the Cypowais.
3 A Necklace made of the claws of the White Eagle.
4 A Pipe-bowl (Saukis).
5 A Knife-sheath (Sioux).

[The ornaments 1 and 5 are embroidered with porcupine quills].

PLATE III.

1 A Mocassin (Sioux).
2 ———— (Cypowais).
3 ———— (Ditto female.)
4 A Basket made of bark, and embroidered with coloured grass.
5 A Wooden Idol (Cypowais).
6 A Pewter Pipe-bowl (Ditto).

[The ornaments 1, 2, and 3, are embroidered with porcupine quills].

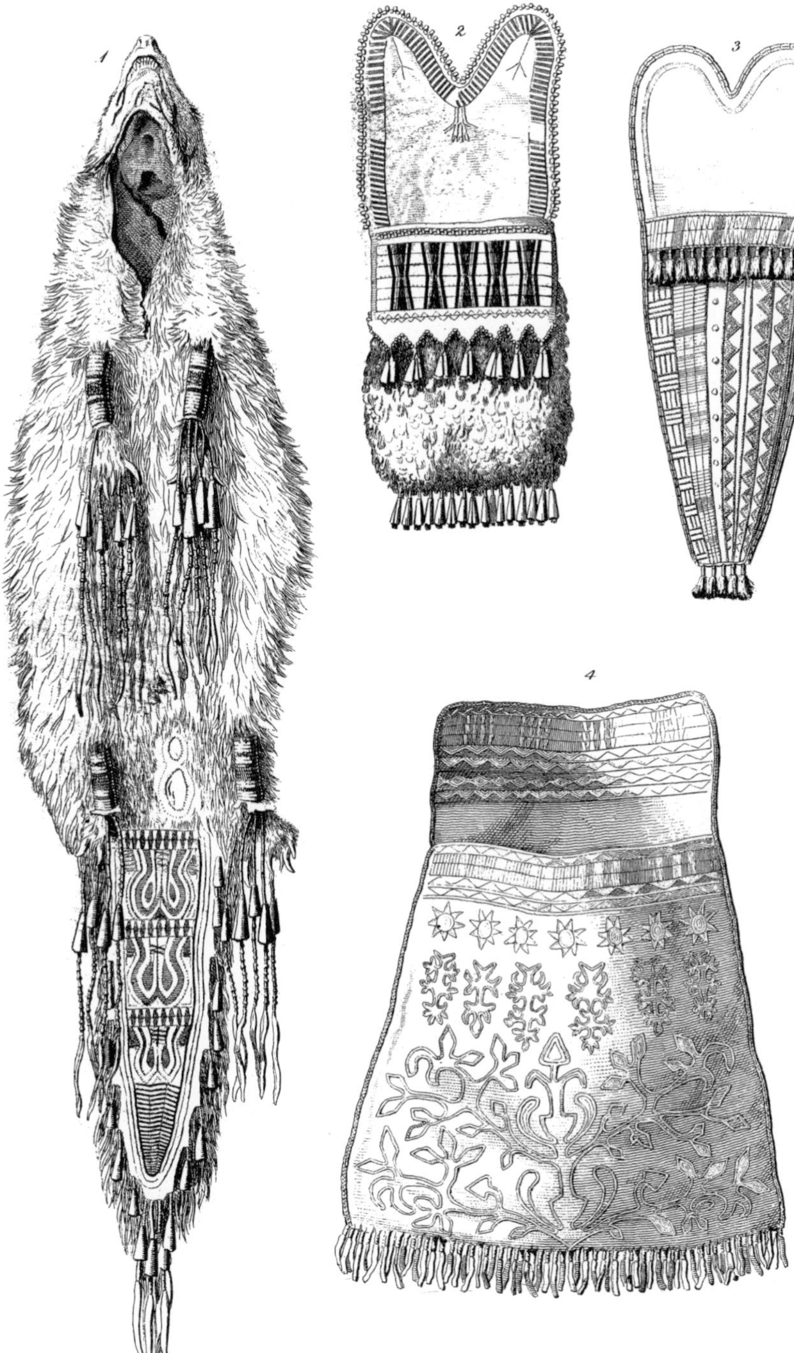

Etched by T.B.

London: Published Dec. 1827, by Hunt & Clarke, York Street.

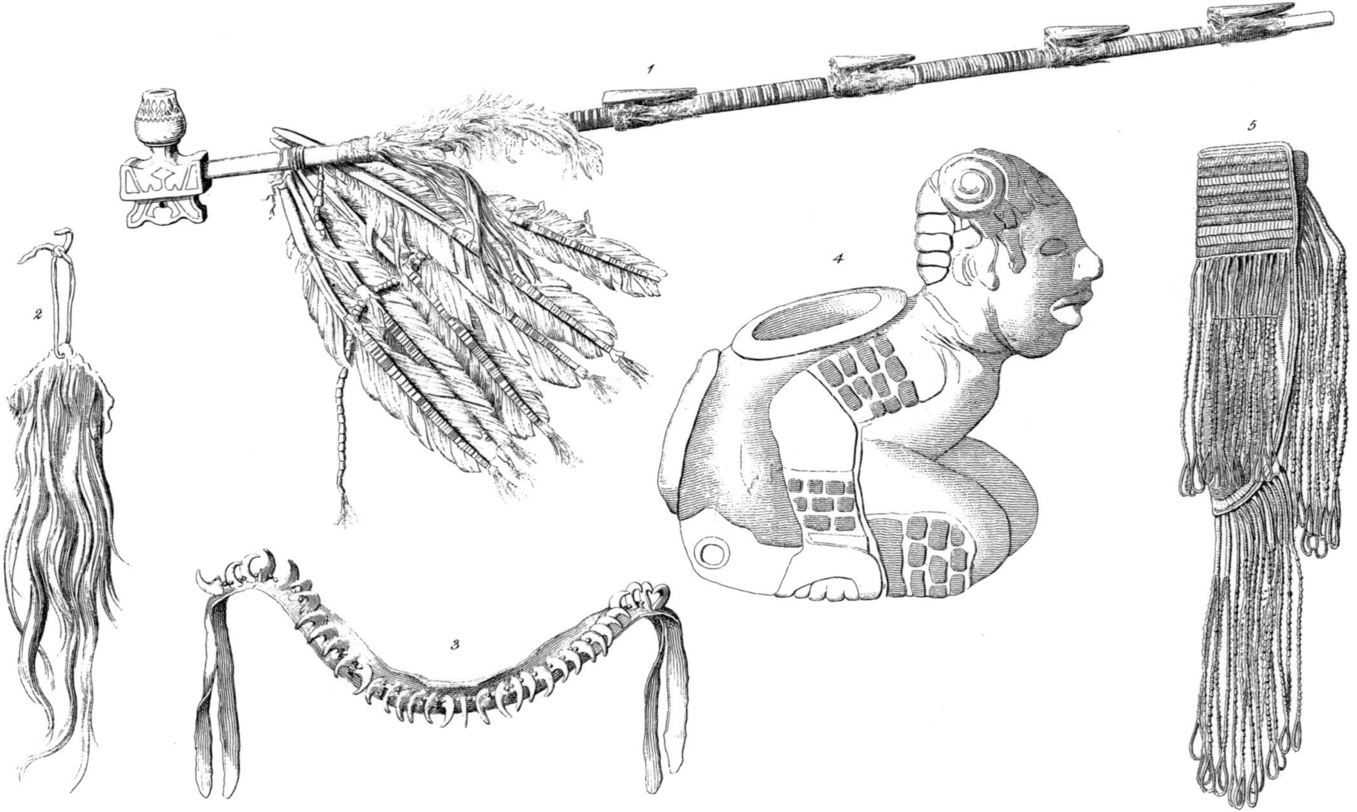

Etched by T.B.

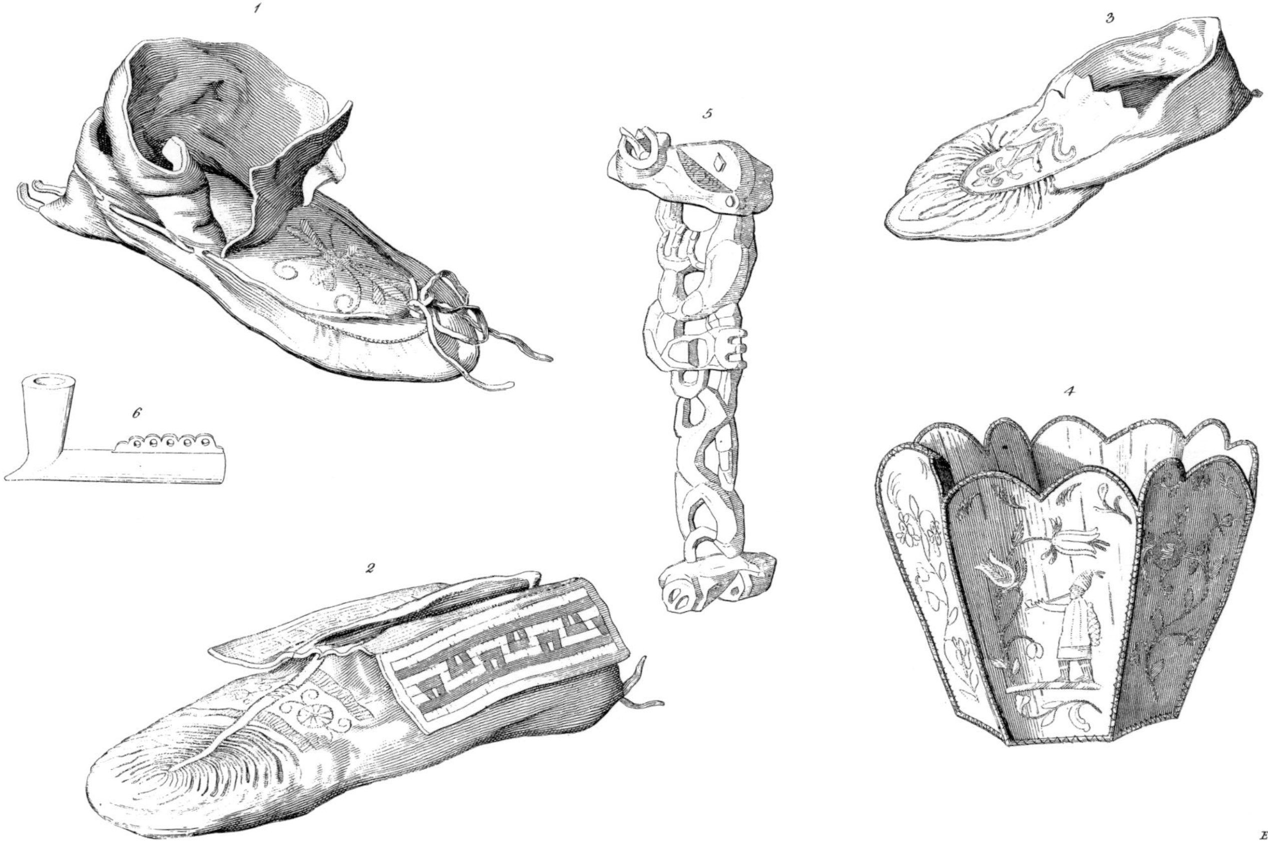

Etched by T.B.

London: Published Dec. 1827, by Hunt & Clarke, York Street.